John Ball

Dolomite Alps

John Ball
Dolomite Alps
ISBN/EAN: 9783743435421
Printed in Europe, USA, Canada, Australia, Japan
Cover: Foto ©Andreas Hilbeck / pixelio.de

John Ball

Dolomite Alps

Ball's Alpine Guides

SOUTH TYROL

AND

VENETIAN OR DOLOMITE ALPS

BY

JOHN BALL, F.R.S., M.R.I.A., F.L.S., &c.

LATE PRESIDENT OF THE ALPINE CLUB

LONDON
LONGMANS, GREEN, AND CO.
1873

LIST OF MAPS.

Key Map . . . . *To be pasted inside the cover at the beginning*
The Eastern Alps—General Map . . *To face title-page*
The Dolomite Alps of South Tyrol . . . *To face page* 471

ABBREVIATIONS AND EXPLANATIONS.

The following are the chief abbreviations used in this work:—

hrs., m.—for hours and minutes. When used as a measure of distance, one hour is meant to indicate the distance which a tolerably good walker will traverse in an hour, clear of halts, and having regard to the difficulty of the ground. In cases where there is a considerable difference of height, the measure given is intended as a mean between the time employed in ascending and descending, being greater in the one case and less in the other.

ft., yds.—for feet and yards. The heights of mountains, &c., are given in English feet above the level of the sea, and are generally indicated in the manner usual in scientific books, by the figures being enclosed in brackets, with a short stroke.

m.—for mile. Unless otherwise expressed, distances are given in English statute miles.

rt., l.—for right and left. The right side of a valley, stream, or glacier, is that lying on the right hand of a person following the downward course of the stream.

The points of the compass are indicated in the usual way.

Names of places are referred in the Index to the pages where some useful information respecting them is to be found.

Throughout this work the reader is frequently referred for further information to the Section and Route where this is to be found. When the reference is made to a passage occurring in the same Section, the Route alone is mentioned.

CHAPTER XVI.

SOUTH TYROL AND VENETIAN ALPS.

Section 57.

LOWER VALLEY OF THE ADIGE.

Route A—Botzen to Verona, by the Valley of the Adige	402
Route B—Trent to Riva, on the Lake of Garda	408
Route C—Roveredo to Riva, by Mori	410
Route D—Riva to Desenzano, by the W. shore of the Lake of Garda	412
Route E—Riva to Peschiera, by the E. shore of the Lake of Garda	414
Route F—Roveredo to Garda, by the Monte Baldo	416

Section 58.

RECOARO DISTRICT.

Route A—Roveredo to Vicenza, by Val Arsa and Schio	420
Route B—Vicenza to Recoaro. Excursions from Recoaro	422
Route C—Recoaro to Roveredo	425
Route D—Schio to Recoaro	426
Route E—Montebello to Recoaro, by Arzignano and Crespadoro	427
Route F—Caldiero to Ala, or Recoaro, by the Val d'Illasi	429
Route G—Verona to Ala, by the Monte Lessini	430
Route H—Schio to Trent, by the Valley of the Astico	430
Route I—Vicenza to Bassano, by Asiago. The Sette Comuni	432
Route K—Asiago to Trent	434
Route L—Vicenza to Bassano, by Marostica	437

Section 59.

VALLEY OF THE BRENTA.

Route A—Trent to Bassano, by Val Sugana	439
Route B—Roveredo to Levico	447
Route C—Bassano to Feltre, by Possagno	448
Route D—Bassano to Feltre, by Monte Grappa	450
Route E—Bassano to Primiero, by Primolano and Fonzaso	450
Route F—Primiero to Predazzo in Fiemme, by San Martino di Castrozza	458
Route G—Borgo di Sal Sugana to Primiero, by Canale di San Bovo	461
Route H—San Martino di Castrozza to Borgo di Val Sugana. Ascent of the Cima d' Asta	463
Route I—Borgo di Val Sugana to Cavalese in Val di Fiemme	467
Route K—Agordo to Primiero by the Passo della Cereda	468
Route L—San Martino di Castrozza to Cencenighe	469

Section 60.

FASSA DISTRICT.

Route A—Trent to Caprile, by the Valley of the Avisio	473
Route B—Lavis to Cavalese, by Val Cembra	479
Route C—Botzen to Vigo, by the Seisser Alp. Ascent of the Schleren	480
Route D—Vigo to Botzen, by the Caressa Pass	485
Route E—Predazzo to Cencenighe, by Paneveggio, or San Pelegrino	487
Route F—Caprile to Vigo, by the Forcella di Ombretta	489
Route G—Botzen to Bruneck, by the Grödnerthal and Gaderthal	491
Route H—Bruneck to Cortina d'Ampezzo, by passes at the head of the Gaderthal	496
Route I—St. Ulrich in Gröden to Pieve di Andraz	500

Section 61.

CADORE DISTRICT.

Route A—Bruneck to Conegliano, by Cortina d' Ampezzo	503
Route B—Cortina d' Ampezzo to Schluderbach, by the Monte Cristallo	509
Route C—Cortina d' Ampezzo to Belluno, by Agordo	511
Route D—Feltre to Forno Avoltri, in Friuli	516
Route E—San Stefano to Cortina d'Ampezzo, by Auronzo. The Croda Malcora	518
Route F—San Vito to Pieve di Cadore. Monte Antelao	522
Route G—San Vito to Longarone, by Val di Zoldo. Monte Pelmo. Monte Civetta	523
Route H—San Stefano to Innichen, by the Sextenthal	527
Route I—Welsberg to Cortina d'Ampezzo, by Prags	529

IN the preceding chapters of this volume the northern and the central ranges of the Eastern Alps have been described. There still remains an extensive mountain region bounded to the W. by the Adige and the Lake of Garda and extending eastward into Carniola and Lower Styria. The limit between this region and the central chain is sharply defined by the valley of the Eisack and that of the Drave. Within the bounds here indicated two distinct tendencies are exhibited in the general aspect and configuration of the surface. In the eastern portion the chief masses are arranged in continuous ranges after the fashion usual elsewhere in mountain regions, but in the western portion, lying between the Adige and the head waters of the Piave, there is an absence of any approach to regularity in the disposition of the mountains. High peaks rise abruptly without any apparent mutual relation, and are almost isolated by valleys that are often contracted to deep clefts. In the principal valleys there is, indeed, a marked tendency to assume a common direction from NE. to SW., which can scarcely be explained by mere accident.

Although dolomite limestone exists in many parts of the Alpine chain, and some idea of its characteristic scenery may be formed in the east of Switzerland, and elsewhere in the Eastern Alps, dolomite rocks are nowhere developed on so great a scale as in the region lying between the Adige, the Eisack, and the Piave which is included in the present chapter. The larger part of this region, though mainly inhabited by people of Italian origin, and speaking an Italian dialect, belongs to Tyrol, but some considerable mountain masses lie within the ancient territory of the Venetian republic now united to Italy. The line of frontier, which may yet afford subject for dispute between the neighbouring states, seems to have been traced in defiance of all intelligible principles, as though dictated by mere accident or caprice. In default of any single appropriate designation the writer is forced to entitle the region here described as South Tyrol and Venetian Alps; but it is right to add that technically the term South Tyrol includes the district of Giudicaria, lying W. of the Lake of Garda, and described in § 40; while the Carnic chain, noticed in the following chapter, may be considered as forming part of the Venetian Alps, inasmuch as it was included in the territory of the republic. The limits of the region here included are marked by the Lake of Garda, and the road from Riva by Trent to Botzen, on the W.; by the road through the valleys of the Eisack and Rienz from Botzen to Innichen on the N.; by the track through the Sextenthal to San Stefano on the Piave, and the high road thence to Conegliano on the E.; and to the S. by the plain of Venetia. Some portions of this district, more especially the valley of Fassa, have long been known to men of science, for scarcely any other district in the Alps has offered so many objects of interest to the geologist and the naturalist; but for a knowledge of its extraordinary attractions, even to the unscientific traveller, the English public is chiefly indebted to a well-known volume by Messrs. Gilbert and Churchill, entitled 'The Dolomite Alps.' Further information, especially of a kind interesting to the mountaineer, has still more recently been given in the annual volumes of the Austrian Alpine Club; and the consequence has been to attract an annually increasing number of visitors to places which till very lately were unheard of beyond their own immediate neighbourhood. The writer fears lest his personal predilection for this region should lead him into exaggeration; but it is certainly not too much to say that a traveller who has visited all the other mountain regions of Europe, and remains ignorant of the scenery of the Dolomite Alps, has yet to make acquaintance with Nature in one of her loveliest and most fascinating aspects.

SECTION 57.

LOWER VALLEY OF THE ADIGE.

REFERENCE has been frequently made in preceding portions of this work to the great breach in the continuity of the Alpine chain which is marked by the valley of the Adige. The importance of this feature in the physical geography of Northern Italy is forced upon the attention of the ethnologist, the historian, and the politician by its effects on the migration of races and the limits of empires; but there is some reason to believe that the boundary marked by this great valley between the Lombard and Venetian Alps has in some form subsisted throughout a cycle of ages in which that of the human race is but the latest and the shortest. Many facts seem to show that the geological history of the districts on either side of this boundary has been essentially different, and there are not wanting indications of such an alternation of elevation and subsidence, that the one region may have formed dry land, while sedimentary deposits were being accumulated over the area corresponding to the other.

In speaking of the valley of the Adige, we include the broad basin filled by the Lake of Garda, which orographically represents the southern portion of that valley, although it is separated from the actual bed of the river by the long narrow ridge of Monte Baldo. It is for those who believe that the actual configuration of the surface is altogether due to meteorological agency to account for the formation of the narrow trench through which the river flows from Roveredo to Volargne by the side of the vastly broader and easier outlet afforded by the basin of the lake.

The great importance of this line of valley, and its slight relations to the districts on either side, have induced the writer to devote a separate section of this work to the course of the Adige and the basin of the Lake of Garda, including of course the range of Monte Baldo and the Monte Bondone which separate them.

Although we here describe a line of valley that has been marked by nature as the main highway from the North of Europe into Italy, it is but slightly known to the majority of travellers. For several years the line of railway from Botzen to Verona has been open for traffic, and this having been extended across the Brenner Pass to Innsbruck, it is now linked to the railway system of central Europe. Travellers pass through it in increasing numbers, but, beyond passing glimpses from the railway carriage, few have any conception of the beauty and grandeur of its scenery. The absolute height of the mountains is not great, for but few points exceed the limit of 7,000 ft., but they rise steeply from a valley that is but little above the level of the sea, and it is not easy to point to any other of the greater valleys of the Alps that surpasses it in attractions for the artist and the lover of nature.

The Lake of Garda is far from having attained the celebrity of its two Lombard rivals, Maggiore and Como; yet some lovers of nature give the preference to the stately and stern grandeur of this vaster basin.

The traveller must bear in mind that although peace has been restored between the contending governments of Italy and Austria, a jealous feeling still survives among subordinate officials, which makes some caution advisable in regard to excursions close to the line of frontier, and somewhat hampers the freedom of navigation on the lake. He will do well to have his passport at hand in case of difficulty.

§ 57. LOWER VALLEY OF THE ADIGE.

ROUTE A.

BOTZEN TO VERONA, BY THE VALLEY OF THE ADIGE.

	Kilo-mètres	English miles
Branzoll	10	6¼
Auer	6	3¾
Neumarkt	6	3¾
Salurn	10	6¼
S. Michele	7	4¼
Lavis	7	4¼
Trient	11	6¾
Matarello	8	5
Calliano	8	5
Roveredo	7	4¼
Mori	4	2½
Ala	13	8
Avio	5	3
Peri	10	6¼
Ceraino	11	6¾
Verona (Porta Nuova)	26	16¼
	149	92¼

Some small stations near Verona are omitted. Railway trains three times daily each way. Travellers bound for Verona, and intending to halt there, should take their tickets for Porta Nuova; but if going on towards Venice should ask for tickets for the Porta Vescovo station, on the opposite side of the city.

The least interesting portion of the valley of the Adige is that which lies before the traveller who leaves Botzen to follow southward the high-road, or the rly. which now absorbs most of the traffic. After crossing the Eisack, the peaks of the Rosengarten, so conspicuous in all the views from Botzen, are lost to sight. On the E. side the valley is bounded by a range of porphyritic rocks of moderate height, whose rounded edges speak of the prolonged action of the elements, and the passage of one of the greatest of the ancient glaciers of the Alps. On the W. side the background is formed by the ridge of the Mendel, or Mendola, which, though composed of dolomite, shows little of the characteristic forms of that rock. Between the river and the base of the Mendel rises the undulating plateau of Eppan, along whose eastern base lies the present bed of the stream.

The junction of the Eisack with the Adige lies nearly 2 m. W. of the rly.;

and from that point the united stream, now grown nearly to its full proportions, creeps onward, a stately but sluggish river, with a fall of but two or three ft. per m., bordered on its l. bank by a broad belt of marshy land, partly cultivated with maize, but in great part producing merely reeds, sedges, and intermittent fevers. Where the soil is tolerably dry the mulberry predominates, while vines are grown on the warm slopes at the foot of the mountains. At

Branzoll, rly. and post-station, flat-bottomed barges, usually laden with timber, are launched upon the Adige, which here becomes navigable. The next station on the rly. is

Auer—Ital. *Ora*. Here the porphyry formation is left behind, and thenceforward the mountains on both sides of the valley are composed of pale grey or nearly white limestone, that readily receives the varying and delicate tints of a southern atmosphere. The new road to Cavalese (§ 60, Rte. A) may be joined close to Auer, but there is a better prospect of obtaining a vehicle at the next station,

Neumarkt — Ital. *Egna.* — (Inns: Krone; Engel). In this part of the valley the remains of old castles, some of them dating from a very remote age, become frequent, especially on the slopes of the comparatively low ridge that separates the Adige from the Val di Cembra. Besides the new road leading to Cavalese, there are several paths across the same ridge which are noticed in § 60, Rte. A. The rly. is carried, chiefly along the rt. bank, through a swampy tract, almost uninhabitable in summer from heat and flies, from the Neumarkt to the

Salurn station (Ital. *Salorno*). The village of that name, standing at some distance on the l. bank of the river, is the last German place in the main valley. It has two very fair inns (Adler; Cavallo Bianco). The valley here bends to the SW., and the scenery becomes more interesting. Precipitous limestone mountains rise abruptly on either side, and the valley is wide enough to allow of a full view of their bare faces from top to bottom. On the rt. bank, at the very base of the sunbeaten cliffs, nestles *Aichholz*, producing a wine of local repute. Through a ravine that opens above the latter village a track leading to Val di Non mounts steeply, and crosses the range which is the southern extension of Mendola. A little farther the Adige bends again nearly due S., and presently the opening of the narrow defile of Rocchetta, through which the Nos descends from Val di Sole and Val di Non to join the Adige, comes fully into view. On the slope above the l. bank of the Nos is seen the village of *Mezzo Tedesco* or *Deutschmetz* (Inn: Mezza Corona), while on the opposite bank of the same stream, whose destructive torrent is confined by a massive embankment, stands *Mezzo Lombardo*, or *Welschmetz*, which also has a tolerable inn (Corona). These names, which date from the time of the Lombard kings, show that the junction of the Nos has continued for many centuries to form the boundary between the German and Italian populations in the valley of the Adige; and those who desire permanent peace and friendly relations between Austria and Italy must wish for a final adjustment of the political boundary between those States, which shall at once satisfy the feelings of the people and afford a sufficiently defensible frontier to each of them.

Opposite the opening of the Rocchetta defile the rly. crosses to the l. bank of the Adige, near the station of *San Michele* (Germ. *Welsch Michael*). This part of the valley abounds in memorials of warfare. The hamlet of Grumo marks the site of a bloody engagement between the Lombards and the Franks; and in more recent times this has always been held to be one of the most defensible positions in the valley. The scenery constantly increases in interest, and the traveller arriving from the North is struck by the peculiar tints of the southern landscape, undefinable and evanescent, yet never to be forgotten by those who have been familiar with them.

To the l., on slightly rising ground, is seen *Lavis*, a market town standing close to the junction of the *Avisio*, the last considerable affluent of the Adige before it escapes into the plain of Venetia. Its course, extending from hence to the base of the Marmolata, is described in § 60, Rte. A. From this point the view is extremely grand. The broad valley of the Adige stretches due S. for about 14 miles, bright with frequent villages, and richly cultivated with maize, mulberries, vines and fruit trees. In the background rise the limestone cliffs of the Monte Scanupia (7,027′) to the l., and those of the Orto d'Abram (7,193′) to the rt. Set in the midst of this gorgeous frame stands the capital of the Italian Tyrol, whose towers and belfries come into view as the traveller approaches

Trent (Ital. *Trento*—Germ. *Trient*). This important and interesting town contains numerous inns which are sometimes all crowded. First in rank is the Europa, good, but foul smells, rather dear; Corona, or Krone, frequented by Austrian officers; H. de la Ville, formerly Chiave d'Oro, new and good; Rebecchino, newly fitted up, tolerably good and reasonable. The aspect of the city is thoroughly Italian, and the massive houses, or *palazzi*, of several of the principal families may vie with those of Milan or Verona. Cafés abound in the principal streets, and there are fairly good shops. The prosperity of the silk trade, and the circumstance that the adjoining districts almost completely escaped the vine disease which has been peculiarly destructive in the Venetian provinces, have made this city and Roveredo amongst the most thriving places on the S. side of the Alps; but that circumstance has in no degree tended to make the population satisfied with their enforced connexion with the German Tyrol.

The city contains several objects that deserve the stranger's notice. Of its 16 churches the most remarkable is the Duomo, or cathedral, commenced in the 11th century, and not yet completed. The romanesque architecture will interest the ecclesiastical antiquary. Amongst other monuments is one to Sanseverino, slain at Calliano when commanding the Venetian forces, which were there defeated by the Trentines in 1487. The church of Santa Maria Maggiore has not much of interest to the sightseer beyond the fact that it was the place wherein was assembled the famous Council of Trent. It contains a fine organ ornamented with curious carving. The Castello del Buon Consiglio, once the residence of the Prince Bishops, is a vast and curious building now converted into a fortified barrack. Some of the rooms contain curious fresco paintings of considerable merit. Another ancient castle stands outside the town. An interesting collection of works of art and antiquity bequeathed by Count Giovanelli is preserved in the public library of the city. Within the last few years a new channel has been excavated for the bed of the Adige which formed a great loop just outside the town, and the ancient bed is now nearly dry. This important work, which is partly seen from the rly. carriage, has facilitated the drainage of some land above Trent, but is said to have increased the danger from floods in the lower part of the valley. Trent is only 626 ft. above the sea-level, and in the next 17 miles the Adige falls but 90 ft.

After suffering from the varying fortunes or misfortunes of war during the invasions of the Goths, Franks, and Lombards, with intervals of prosperity under Theodoric and Charlemagne, Trent enjoyed for several centuries almost unbroken quiet and independence under the virtual sovereignty of Bishops who held the city and the adjoining valleys as an immediate fief of the Empire. The title of Prince Bishops has survived to the present time, although the temporal jurisdiction was finally lost in 1802. Besides the main road through the valley of the Adige, two important roads meet at Trent. That leading to Riva is described in Rte. B, and the road to Padua by Val Sugana and Bassano in § 59, Rte. A. Omnibuses for Riva and Borgo di Val Sugana start twice a day, from the Rebecchino.

In the centre of the valley, close to the city, rises a remarkable rock, known as *Dos Trento*, and also called La Verruca, formerly frequented for the sake of the beautiful view which it commands. Since 1857 it has been strongly fortified, and permission to ascend to the summit is not easily obtained.

The neighbourhood of Trent affords excellent opportunities for the study of most of the sedimentary rocks of the Eastern Alps, which is facilitated by the cuttings made in constructing the new roads to Riva and Val Sugana, and by the numerous quarries worked near the city. To the N. and NE., in the neighbourhood of Gardolo most of the subdivisions of the Trias may be identified, culminating in dolomite. The series of jurassic and cretaceous rocks may be best studied on the E. side of the city, following the new road to Val Sugana. Fossils are abundant at many points. Nummulitic rocks also appear in the same direction, but they are more extensively developed near Sardagna, S. of the road to Riva. A man named Ferraresi is recommended as a guide to geologists in this neighbourhood. He usually has a supply of fossils for sale.

The botanist not already familiar with this region may reap a rich harvest in the neighbourhood of Trent. On the E. side *Farsetia clypeata*, and *Tragus racemosus* are abundant. On the rocks of Dos Trento grow *Capsella pauciflora* and *Ephedra distachya*, but these cannot now be reached without a special permission.

The most interesting mountain excursion is that to the *Monte Bondone* (7,412'), or the *Orto d'Abram* (7,193'). These are the two highest summits of the range SW. of Trent, which may be considered a northern prolongation of that of Monte Baldo, though separated by the deep trench through which runs the road from Mori to Torbole (Rte. C).

Starting from the low level of the city the ascent is somewhat laborious, and it is well to be off some time before daylight, to avoid heat and gain a better view. The botanist will find in this excursion many of the characteristic plants of Monte Baldo. See Rte. F.

Below Trent the high-road and, save for a short distance, the rly. also, keep to the l. bank of the Adige, till it issues into the plain near Verona. The first considerable village is

Matarello (647′), standing at the opening of *Val Sorda*, through which narrow glen a country road is carried to Levico in Val Sugana. Three or four miles below Matarello the main valley is contracted between the bases of the Monte Scanupia and Orto d'Abram, forming a defile, which commences at the hamlet of Aquaviva, and extends to Calliano. From Aquaviva, to the point where the river issues from the mountains below La Chiusa, the valley of the Adige is locally called *Val Lagarina* (Germ. *Lägerthal*). For a long period Val Lagarina formed a nearly independent state, under the jurisdiction of the powerful family of Castelbarco, whose descendants still have large possessions here. The castle from which they take the family name may be seen on the rt., about 4 m. N. of Roveredo. After passing the village and station of

Calliano, where a picture in the parish church recalls the bloody victory gained by the people of Trent over the Venetians under Sanseverino, the rly. leaves on the l. the opening of Val Folguria, a favourite summer resort of the people of Roveredo. For a notice of the pleasant path leading that way to Val Sugana see § 59, Rte. B. The main valley now bends to the W., but after passing *Volano* the Adige soon resumes its southerly direction, and before long the traveller reaches the town of

Roveredo (Inns: Corona; Cavaletto; both very fair). The increasing population, now approaching to 9,000 in number, owes its prosperity to the silk trade, which rose to importance after this part of the Val Lagarina passed from the Lordship of the Castelbarco family under Venetian rule, in the 15th century. The first spinning-mill is said to have been erected by a Venetian in 1548. There are now a number of large *Filande*, where the cocoons are unwound, and of *Filatoje*, where the raw silk is spun into thread. In these establishments nearly the entire population found remunerative occupation until the disease in the silkworm seriously diminished the supply of raw material within the last few years. The people of Roveredo maintain a high character for intelligence, activity, and probity, and their undisguised sympathy with the national movement in Italy is doubtless increased by traditions of former prosperity under Venetian rule.

The church of San Marco, and the adjoining piazza, deserve a visit; but the general aspect of the town is not nearly equal to that of Trent.

Close to Roveredo the stream of the Leno, used to work a large paper-mill and other establishments, issues from *Val Arsa*, through which runs the interesting road to Vicenza described in § 58, Rte. A. Through an eastern branch of the same valley (called *Val di Terragnolo*) a track crosses the steep range that encloses the head waters of the Astico.

Below Roveredo the Adige runs SW. for about 4 m. Numerous castles are perched upon the slopes on either hand, some of which date from the time of the Romans. That of *Lizzana*, on the l. of the rly., is remembered as having been the halting place of the Emperor Henry II. on his return to Germany, and still more for the visit which Dante here made to one of the lords of Castelbarco. On the rt. bank of the stream, opposite Lizzana, is *Iscra* producing a wine of ancient fame, said to be the best in S. Tyrol. About 4 m. from Roveredo is the station of

Mori, close to a bridge over the Adige. The village near at hand, on the rt. bank, is Ravazzone, that of Mori being more than a mile distant. Omnibuses start twice daily from this station for Riva, which is reached in about 3 hrs. by a very interesting road. See Rte. C.

The Mori station stands on the verge of a vast mass of débris, that stretches across from the mountain on the E. side of the valley to the banks of the Adige. This is locally known as *Slavini di San Marco*, from the adjoining village of San Marco. Huge blocks of stone, mingled with smaller masses, lie piled up in wild confusion, and cover a space of nearly a square mile. A little close examination would have saved an able French geologist from describing this as a moraine left during the retirement of the ancient glacier of the Adige. The blocks are all of the same material as the adjoining mountain, and they are not accompanied by the quantity of finer matter, including glacial mud, that always characterises a true moraine. The pile of ruin is undoubtedly caused by a bergfall or great landslip, from the slope of the mountain on the l. side of the valley. With great probability this has been identified with an event of that nature recorded in A.D. 883, whereby the bed of the Adige at Verona was left dry for several days. Nearly 3 m. below the Mori station is

Serravalle, standing, as the name expresses, at the entrance of a defile in the main valley. Like most of the strongholds in Val Lagarina, the ruined castle once belonged to the Castelbarco family. For some miles the valley is contracted, but it opens out somewhat before reaching

Ala (Inns; Vapore, tolerable; Cervo), a small town, once famous for its velvet fabrics. It stands at the opening of a narrow lateral glen called *Val di Ronchi*, through which lies a path to the Revelto pass, leading either to Recoaro, or to Badia in the Monti Lessini (§ 58, Rte. C). The easiest and shortest way to the Pieve di Val Arsa does not lie through Val di Ronchi, as stated by Schaubach. The true path leaves the valley of the Adige near the church of San Valentino, about 1½ m. N. of Ala. The next station is that of

Avio (447′). The village, connected with the station by a ferry, stands on the rt. bank, at the opening of *Val Aviana*, one of the glens that runs deepest into the range of Monte Baldo. The church contains a good picture of St. Anthony, by Guercino. The last Tyrolese village is *Borghetto*; a short distance beyond it the traveller passes the Italian frontier, and soon reaches the station of

Peri. Here the traveller bound for La Madonna della Corona crosses the ferry over the Adige (Rte. F). That remarkable sanctuary may be descried by the passing traveller on the face of a perpendicular precipice in a deep recess of the Monte Baldo. On the E. side of the main valley a path mounts from Peri SE., through an opening in the range which on that side hems in the course of the Adige, and leads by *Sta. Anna* to Val Pantena, noticed in § 58, Rte. G. This depression separates the plateau of the Monti Lessini from the *Monte Pastello*. This name is given collectively to the ridge which extends for about 9 m. SW. of Peri parallel to that of Monte Baldo. Both mountains exhibit the same geological structure; with this difference, that the strata of Monte Baldo dip at a considerable angle to the W., while those of Monte Pastello are inclined in the opposite direction. Hence the rocks on either side present very steep fractured faces to the valley of the Adige, while the opposite slopes are comparatively uniform and of moderate steepness. It is difficult to resist the conviction that the valley of the Adige, in this part of its course at least, owes its origin to a fracture which ran along the line of anticlinal flexure, and this belief is confirmed by the absence of rolled pebbles or glacial drift from the terraces on either side of the valley. Had it owed its origin to erosion these witnesses could scarcely have disappeared. The range of Monte Pastello scarcely exceeds 3,700 ft. in height, nevertheless some subalpine species of plants inhabit the ridge, while several other interesting species are found on its warm slopes. Among the former the most interesting is *Astragalus Pastellianus*, probably a variety of *A. vesicarius*, confined to a very small area not far from the summit. Besides this may be found *Cytisus purpureus, Campanula Alpini, Pæderota Bonarota, Allium ochroleucum*, &c. Of the plants growing on the middle and lower slopes *Cytisus argenteus, Leontodon incanus, Echinops sphærocephalus, Hyssopus officinalis*, and *Erythronum dens canis*, deserve notice. The northern botanist will see with interest many southern bushes, such as *Pistacia Terebinthus, Cercis Siliquastrum*, and *Quercus Ilex*.

Below Peri the mountains on both sides begin to subside towards the plain, but the scenery continues to be extremely bold, worthy of the historic interest attaching to this entrance into Italy. As the traveller advances southward the nearly vertical cliffs that rise on either hand seem to close together, and in the famous defile of *La Chiusa* the space required for the high road and the rly. has been obtained only by blasting the rock. At the narrowest part the cleft through which the Adige pours its copious waters becomes very tortuous, and the rly. engineers have been forced to adopt curves of small radius in order to follow its windings. The traveller will not forget that above the precipices on the rt. bank of the river extends the famous plateau of Rivoli, where contending armies have so often fought for the key of Verona, a city whose unique position makes its possessors the masters of Northern Italy. The strong forts erected by the Austrians during the preceding 18 years for the purpose of commanding the defile and the plateau of Rivoli, had not their efficiency tested during the campaign of 1866, and it may be hoped that their present occupants will have no occasion to defend the position against new aggressors. At *Volargne* (420′) the traveller finally issues from the defile, and presently gains the first view of the line of low hills extending westward from Verona, that fill so large a space in military history. Near at hand, just beyond the Adige, is *Pastrengo*; farther south, *Somma Campagna*; beyond that, *Custozza*; and, in the far distance, the tower of *Solferino*.

For several miles the rly. runs SE., parallel with the high road, having on the l. hand the slopes which produce the excellent wine of Val Policella; but for strategic reasons it was not carried directly to the walls of Verona. About 4 m. from the city the rly. turns abruptly to the S., and joins the main line from Milan at Santa Lucia. This slight detour is scarcely a matter of complaint to the traveller, who gains beautiful and varied views before he finally reaches the gates of

Verona (Inns: Due Torri, good, dear; Torre di Londra, good; several other second-rate houses, of which the best is probably the Czara di Moscovia). A description of this city, whose attractions are scarcely exaggerated in the glowing pages of Ruskin, does not fall within the scope of this work.

It may be well to remind the traveller who should contemplate excursions in the valley of the Adige that the bridges over that impetuous stream are few in number. Ferries, most of them of high antiquity, are established at fixed points, at intervals of 2 or 3 m., and in regard to these local information should be obtained.

Route B.

TRENT TO RIVA, ON THE LAKE OF GARDA.

	Italian geog. miles	English miles
Vezzano	6	7
Drò	10	11½
Riva	5½	6¼
	21½	24¾

Carriage-road, traversed by omnibus twice daily each way, in 4½ or 5 hrs.

Though not quite equal in picturesque beauty to the way from Roveredo, described in the next Rte., this is an extremely interesting road to the ordinary tourist, and especially to the geologist. Something of the scenery may be seen from the *coupé* of the omnibus, but a more agreeable course is to engage a small open carriage at Trent or Riva, or, in cool weather, to go on foot.

Passing close under the rock of Dos Trento, the carriage-road ascends westward from Trent to a narrow cleft in the steep limestone range that encloses the valley of the Adige. The pedestrian traveller may make a slight detour from the road to visit the pretty *Waterfall of Sardagna*. To reach the summit of the pass, which is guarded by two forts, involves an ascent of nearly 1,000 ft. from the city, and the traveller, emerging from the cleft through which the road is carried, finds himself on a rather bare limestone plateau, near the hamlet of *Cadine* (1,614'). To the rt. lies *Terlago* (1,487'), with a small lake scarcely seen from the road. Descending westward over undulating rocky slopes the road leads the traveller to

Vezzano (1,250'), a rather large village with a poor but tolerable inn in the main street. From hence several interesting excursions may be made. A glance at a good map will show that the adjoining mountains are disposed in parallel ridges, with minor undulations all running from NNE. to SSW., of which general type Monte Baldo is the best known specimen. The range immediately W. of Vezzano is the *Monte Gazza* (6,518'), whose uppermost portion forms a broad plateau, extending southward to the opening of the Sarca defile, and northward to the opening of Val di Non. The traveller who makes the ascent will be well rewarded for his trouble, if he extend his walk far enough to reach the verge of the steep slope overlooking the blue waters of the Lake of Molveno, backed by the noble pinnacles of the Brenta Alta. He may then turn southward, and descend by Ranzo to Castel Toblino. See § 40, Rte. H. A guide is scarcely needed for this walk. Another excursion may be made to *Cavedine* (1,734'), a village lying in a small lateral glen (a fold in the limestone strata), parallel to the valley of the Sarca. It is close to the foot of the Orto d'Abram which may be more easily ascended from hence than from Trent. About half-way between Vezzano and Cavedine the ruined castle of *Madruzzo* (1,797') crowns a projecting rock. It was once the seat of a powerful and wealthy family, and one of the finest castles in S. Tyrol. It is said that the present owner, a Genoese nobleman, has not only allowed it to fall to ruin, but actually sold the carved stones remaining in the building. The pedestrian, bound to Riva from the upper part of the Adige valley, may avoid Trent, and reach Vezzano by a path that mounts from Mezzo Lombardo to *Zambana*, a village overlooking the Adige opposite to Lavis (Rte. A). Thence the track, passing some very small lakes, keeps to the W. of Terlago, and descends to Vezzano. This walk would be of interest to the geologist as he passes over the course which (as is now believed) was once followed by one branch of the great glacier of the Adige. From Vezzano the road descends rapidly to the *Lake of Toblino*. This is an extremely picturesque little sheet of water, 786 ft. above the sea-level, with an ancient castle (*Castel Toblino*) now one of the numerous possessions of Count Wolkenstein. The castle stands on a little rocky island united to the shore by a causeway. A strong, but rather sweet, white wine of good flavour is made in this neighbourhood from grapes that are let to hang on the vine till mid-winter. It costs on the spot about 1 florin a bottle. Close to the castle mounts the path to Ranzo, by which the traveller may reach the beautiful Lake of Molveno (§ 40, Rte., H). Very soon after leaving the S. end of the lake the road from Trent joins the very remarkable road issuing from the defile of the Sarca, which is described in § 40, Rte. D. The group of houses with a very poor *osteria*, about 200 yds. from the junction of the two roads, is called Le Sarche. Here passes the country diligence which plies daily to Tione in Giudicaria. Although it is only at this point that the valley is traversed by a considerable stream, it is clear that the road from Vezzano to Le Sarche, and thence to Riva, as well as the above-mentioned path from Zambano to Vezzano, lie in what is orographically the southern prolongation of the valley of the Adige; as the Monte Gazza, and the mountain W. of Drò, are the prolongation of the range of the Mendola.

For some miles below Le Sarche the valley presents an alternation of rich cultivation with scenes of barren ruin. Several considerable bergfalls, one of them on the grandest scale, appear to have occurred in this valley; but the present position of some huge blocks may perhaps be better accounted for by glacial agency. For a distance of several miles the stream uniting the Lake of Toblino with another small lake in the main valley is divided from the Sarca by a low rocky ridge parallel to the stream. The ridge on the rt. presents a curious appearance as the strata are tilted at a high angle, with a steep uniform slope towards the Sarca. At one point the seemingly impracticable slope is surmounted by a goat track. After passing *Drò* (403′), a large village with no decent inn, the valley, though still narrow, is more richly cultivated, and the olive, so rarely grown with success in the north of Italy, becomes a prevailing tree. Passing under the precipitous castle-rock, the road, which has constantly kept to the rt. bank of the Sarca, reaches

Arco, a small town, only 301 ft. above the sea, nestling at the foot of an extremely bold promontory that once rose above the head of the lake of Garda before the space (about 3 m. in length) extending hence to the present shore was filled up by the deposits of the Sarca. The rock, which rises 600 ft. above the plain, is crowned by the towers of the *Castello di Arco*, the original seat of a powerful family that, throughout the contests between the Emperors and the Venetian Republic, always took the side of Germany, and whose modern representatives have large possessions in Austria and Bavaria.

The level tract extending hence to the shore of the lake is famous for its extraordinary fertility, and the mildness of its climate. In few places north of the Apennines is the olive cultivated to so much advantage, and many other plants that do not bear the climate of the plain here flourish luxuriantly. The only scourge of the agriculturist here is one unfortunately too common along the southern base of the Alpine chain. Hailstorms of short duration, but extreme violence, are not unfrequent during the summer months, and often effect an incredible amount of damage in the course of a few minutes. With reference to recent controversies as to the origin of Alpine lakes, the geologist will not fail to note the position of the *Monte Brione* (1,225′), a detached rocky hill of nummulitic limestone, rising in the middle of the broad valley close to the present shore of the lake. The Sarca flows into the lake through a broad opening on the E. side of this eminence; while the Varrone, and two minor streams from the mountains N. of Riva, reach the lake on the opposite side. As the maximum force of the advancing glacier which once filled the basin of the lake must have been exerted against this obstacle, it may be asked how the glacier failed to remove it altogether. if it be true that we owe to this agent the excavation of the entire lake-basin.

At the E. foot of the Monte Oro, whose grand crags of limestone, rising tier over tier, defend it from the afternoon sun, stands the town of

Riva (Inns; Sole, good and beautifully situated; Giardino, much improved, comfortable and reasonable), without question one of the most attractive of the many beautiful places to be found on the Italian lakes. Too hot for most Englishmen in the height of summer, it is a delightful stopping-place in spring and autumn, and a milder winter residence than most of those frequented by foreigners in Italy. In the writer's opinion the position is superior to that of Como, Lecco, or Locarno; and, as a centre for interesting excursions, it is at least equal to any of those places. Most of these have been described in § 40 (see Alpine Guide, vol. ii), and it will be sufficient to say here that no traveller should omit to visit the charming Lake of Ledro, returning, if possible, by moonlight—see § 40, Rte. E. A longer excursion, also practicable in a light carriage, is to go to Tione by the valley of the Sarca, and return by Condino, Storo, and Val di Ledro.

It may be necessary to repeat the caution given in a preceding volume against the overcharges of the postmaster at Riva. Carriages may usually be hired from other persons in the town. The botanist may gather near the town many southern species, rarely seen so near the high Alps. Amongst those may be named *Reseda phyteuma, Cytisus argenteus, Ononis Columnæ, Convolvulus cantabrica, Piptatherum multiflorum*, and especially the evergreen oak —*Quercus Ilex*—which extends as a stunted bush as far north as the slopes above Castel Toblino. *Vallisneria spiralis* is seen in the waters of the lake near the town; and among other local species may be named *Moehringia Ponæ* and *Euphorbia nicæensis*.

ROUTE C.

ROVEREDO TO RIVA, BY MORI.

Railway to Mori. Carriage-road thence to Riva—about 14 English miles.

The traveller wishing to take advantage of the omnibus, which plies twice a day in connection with the rly. trains, should take a ticket from Roveredo to the Mori station, rather more than 3 m. distant from the town; but, unless he can secure a place in the coupé, he will see little of the beautiful scenery. It is a securer course to engage a small carriage at Roveredo, which will convey him in about 3 hrs. to Riva. This road traverses a deep cut in the range that extends along the W. side of the Adige from near Lavis to the plateau of Rivoli, the summit of the pass being only about 300 ft. above the bridge over the Adige near the rly. station of Mori. After crossing this bridge, the road leaves *Ravazzone* to the rt., and ascends very slightly to the larger village of *Mori* (658'). Here opens the comparatively wide valley that separates the Monte Baldo on the l. from the range to the rt. that culminates in the Orto d'Abram. Unlike most passes of the same character, this is not a cleft between steep impending rocks. Comparatively gentle slopes, covered with the richest verdure, with just enough of crag to add picturesque effect to the scenery, rise on either hand; and the road is carried, nearly at a dead level, through a succession of gardens and fields, where the mulberry, vine, and maize are the prevailing crops. The pedestrian who would wander from the direct road will find paths leading to numerous villages, nestling in sheltered recesses of the mountains on the rt. hand, and extending upwards to more than 3,000 ft. above the sea. On the opposite side a track leads to Brentonico (Rte. F).

Following the carriage-road the traveller before long reaches the charming little *Lake of Loppio*, in a glen of miniature dimensions, but exquisite in all its details. The road passes along its southern shore, fringed with reeds, sedges, and *Cladium Mariscus*, and mounts the low ridge that encloses it on the W. side, when the summit level is reached about 200 ft. ('77 ft.' Schaubach—but there must be some error) above the level of the lake of Loppio. The view towards the valley of the Sarca and the lake of Garda is not at once gained in its full beauty. To enjoy these to perfection the traveller must pass the village of *Nago*, and reach the verge of the slope immediately overhanging the valley. At this point the pass is guarded by an Austrian fort, and the road is made to pass through one of its outworks. With surprise, the traveller, who has forgotten that the level of the Adige is fully 300 ft. above that of the Sarca, finds himself at a relatively great height above the latter stream, overlooking the point where it is lost in the blue waters of the lake of Garda. The road turns sharply to the l., and descends diagonally the steep face of the rocky slope, whose bare strata dip at a high angle towards the lake and the valley of the Sarca. At the foot of the descent is *Torbole*, a poor fishing village, surrounded by olive trees, and commanding a beautiful view. Additional interest is given to the road leading from the Adige to this spot when we recollect the extraordinary feat achieved in 1439 by the Venetian engineers, who, in three weeks, conveyed a flotilla, including 5 large galleys, and 25 smaller vessels, from the Adige to the Lake of Garda, across this pass, to contest the mastery of the lake with the Milanese under Filippo Maria Visconti. Along a causeway constructed for the occasion, the galleys were drawn to the lake of Loppio, then floated to its farther end, and dragged up the steep incline to the summit of the pass by harnessing from 200 to 300 oxen to each galley. Not less difficult was the descent to Torbole; but all obstacles were overcome, and the flotilla was launched upon the lake, only to be almost completely destroyed in the following November by the superior daring of the Milanese commander. The Venetians then learned, however, the strategic importance of the possession of the Lake of Garda, which seems to have been forgotten by the Italians in their recent campaigns. They constructed a new flotilla at Torbole, and in the following spring gained a decisive victory over their Milanese antagonists, which secured the control of the lake during the remainder of the war.

The road from Riva to Torbole runs close to the lake shore, passing under the Monte Brione, where the Austrians have built a fort armed with heavy guns that defend the approach to Riva from the side of the lake. After crossing the stream of the Varrone the road reaches that town. See last Rte.

ROUTE D.

RIVA TO DESENZANO, BY THE W. SHORE
OF THE LAKE OF GARDA.

	Kilomètres	English miles
Limone (by water)	8	5
Tremosine	7	4¼
Tignale	6	3¾
Gargnano	6	3¾
Maderno	9	5½
Salò	7	4¼
Desenzano	12	7¼
	55	34¼

These distances are mere approximations, the lake shore being too irregular to allow of accurate measurements.

The unfriendly condition of the political relations between Austria and Italy has been a chief cause of the deficiency in means of communication between the N. end of the Lake of Garda, belonging to Tyrol, and the southern shores, belonging partly to Lombardy, partly to Venetia. When not altogether interrupted, the intercourse by steamer has been inconveniently arranged. The hours of sailing of the steamers are fixed to suit the markets in the towns and villages on the shore, and vary from one day to another. It may however be expected that better provision for travellers will now be made. To travel by land, especially along the western side of the lake, is possible only for an active pedestrian, and would be a slow course, owing to the roughness of the ground, though doubtless an interesting walk.

The lake of Garda is the most considerable of the Italian, and one of the largest of the Alpine lakes, ranking in extent next after those of Constance and Geneva. The northern portion, about 23 m. in length, is a deep trough parallel to all the main valleys of this region, lying between the range of Monte Baldo and that of the Brescian Alps. It widens gradually from a breadth of 3 m. at its head to nearly 6 m. opposite the point of S. Vigilio, which forms the southernmost prolongation of the range of Monte Baldo. South of that point the lake expands into a nearly circular basin, about 12 m. in diameter, which is partly divided by the long low promontory of Sermione, extending from the S. shore between Peschiera and Desenzano. This southern portion of the lake is not confined within barriers of rock as are most Alpine lakes. The comparatively low hills that circle round its margin, and extend for many miles beyond it, are formed of disintegrated materials transported from the interior valleys of the neighbouring Alps. There can be no doubt but that they are the remains of the vast moraines of a glacier that once filled the bed of the lake, possibly modified by the action of the sea during a period of subsequent submergence.

The scenery of the lake of Garda has not attained nearly so much celebrity as that of its rivals (Como and Maggiore). This has arisen quite as much from the fact that it lies out of the beaten track of travellers as from any real inferiority; and according to the disposition and passing mood of the traveller, he may be inclined to award the palm to one or the other.

If he should miss here the ceaseless variety of exquisite pictures that he has found on the Como lake, and should prefer some of those familiar, yet ever fresh, scenes that endear the Lago Maggiore to his memory, he cannot fail to be impressed with the more stately grandeur of this vaster basin. The contrast of the rich vegetation of the southern and western shores with the stern, and almost menacing, aspect of the grey ridge of Monte Baldo, is perhaps more impressive than any similar effect on any of the Alpine lakes. On none of them does he find in such delicate gradations the pale grey and brown tints so characteristic of the scenery of the South.

The mean height of the lake above the sea-level is but 201 ft., while its depth at some points exceeds 900 ft., and these, as well as other local conditions, have combined to produce the mildest climate to be found anywhere near the base of the Alpine chain. This remark applies especially to the western shore, which, as it faces SE., receives the full force of the mid-day sun. Reference was made in Rte. B to the presence of several species of wild plants near Riva, that properly belong to the Flora of central Italy, but the most significant fact in regard to vegetation is the cultivation of lemons and citrons on a large scale. This had already grown to importance at the end of the sixteenth century, and still supplies a local trade of some extent. It is true that the cultivation requires special precautions. The trees are grown in narrow plots of ground, each of which is enclosed by a high stone wall, except on the S. side. With the help of marble pillars, standing at intervals, the whole space is covered over during three or four winter months with a light covering of matted reeds; and in case of severe frost, which is of rare occurrence, fires are lighted to protect the plants.

In the present route we proceed to notice the chief places on the W. shore of the lake.

Until the completion of the very remarkable road from Riva to Val di Ledro, mentioned in § 40, Rte E, the precipitous shore of the lake between that town and the waterfall of Ponal was absolutely impassable; and visitors to the waterfall could approach it only by boat. South of Ponal the mountains still rise very steeply above the lake, but there are several practicable paths leading across the frontier between Italy and Tyrol. The more frequented of these is by *Pregasena*, a village near to which, as the writer is informed, there is a considerable deposit of erratic blocks, probably consisting of the peculiar granite of the Adamello group. The first considerable village on the Lombard shore is

Limone, which derives its name from the extensive cultivation of lemons, here first seen on a large scale by the traveller arriving from the N. As the steamer coasts along the shore, many a village and scattered villa is seen on the steep slopes, adding life and variety to the scenery. The village of

Tremosine stands conspicuous on a shelf of rock, whence a steep path descends to the beach. After passing the mouth of the Campione torrent, which has borne a pile of débris into the lake, the shore becomes less steep, and a tolerable path is carried along, at no great distance from the lake, as far as

Gargnano, a village which suffered rather severely from the fire of the Austrian steamers during the last campaign. The track extending hence to Salò, being the warmest and most sheltered portion of the lake-shore, is locally known as *La Riviera*. It is one continuous garden, in which lemons and citrons give place at intervals to figs, grapes, mulberries, olives, pomegranates, and laurel trees, and to the gardens and pleasure-grounds that surround the villas of proprietors. A level and tolerably good road extends along this part of the shore. One of the finest villas, seen some way S. of Gargnano, belongs to Count Bettoni. A low promontory is now seen to stretch out into the lake. This is a considerable delta formed by the Toscolano torrent which drains Val Vestino, Val Toscolano, and some tributary glens. On the NE. side of the delta is the considerable village of

Toscolano, with a poor but bearable inn. This is a place of great antiquity, whose former importance as a mart for the neighbouring district is attested by many Roman remains. It possesses a considerable paper-mill, which has been worked for at least two centuries and a half, besides some other industrial establishments. On the opposite or SW. side of the delta, about 1 m. from Toscolano, is

Maderno, at one time considered the chief place on the lake. It still contains many stately houses. Passing *Gardone*, not to be confounded with the place so named in Val Trompia (§ 39, Rte. I), the traveller reaches

Salò (Inn: Gambaro, very fair), a beautifully situated town, which will doubtless be frequented when better known to travellers. It lies at the W. end of a deep bay, surrounded with gardens and plantations of oranges and lemons, and there are probably few spots in the N. of Italy that enjoy so mild a winter climate. The town is screened from the northern winds by a comparatively high mountain mass, of which the chief summit is the *Monte Pizzocolo*, so conspicuous in all distant views of the lake, and even from the neighbourhood of Verona. It is more easily accessible from this side than from Toscolano. A carriage-road leads from Salò in little more than two miles to the valley of the Chiese, through which runs the road mentioned in § 40, Rte. A, leading in one direction to Brescia, and in the other to the Lake of Idro, and to the chief scenes of Garibaldi's late unsuccessful campaign.

On quitting Salò, the steamer is steered due E. to round a promontory that terminates in the rocky islet known as *Isola dei Frate*. South of this headland it passes the opening of a second bay, and leaves to the rt. the *Isola di San Biagio*. The S. and SW. shores of the lake abound in memorials of the past. Pagan temples, Christian churches, and modern villas, have in succession occupied the most attractive sites. On the last-named islet once stood a temple to Jupiter; and another, dedicated to Minerva, adorned the neighbouring headland that has preserved the name *Manerbe*. Steering a little W. of S., the traveller now enters the broad basin that forms the southern division of the lake. It is a nearly circular sheet of water, partially divided by the long low promontory of *Sermione*. Few spots in the neighbourhood of the Alps are richer in historical associations. Sermione, already in Roman times a favourite resort, was visited by Julius Cæsar, and was the chosen residence of Catullus; some remains of Roman buildings being still, with little or no warrant, called the poet's villa. A castle was erected here in the time of Charlemagne; and Ansa,

the wife of King Desiderius, built a monastery, and the church of San Salvatore, part of which still exists. Early in the fourteenth century arose the church of San Pietro, said to contain interesting frescoes, and about the same time one of the Scaligers erected what is still known as the Castello Nuovo, and dug a trench, whereby to convert the point of the peninsula into an island.

At the SW. corner of the lake the traveller lands at

Desenzano (Inns: Vittoria; Albergo Mayer; both on the lake, and commanding a fine view; Aquila), a small town whereat travellers often stopped when the frontier between Austria and Italy lay between this and Peschiera. From the railway station, on the main line between Milan and Venice, a wider view of the lake is gained than from the town itself.

ROUTE E.

RIVA TO PESCHIERA, BY THE E. SHORE OF THE LAKE OF GARDA.

	Kilomètres	English miles
Malcesine (by water)	12	7½
Castelletto	10	6¼
Torri	10	6¼
Garda	8	5
Bardolino	4	2½
Lasize	5	3
Peschiera	8	5
	57	35¼

It is impossible to conceive a more marked contrast than that afforded by the opposite shores of the Lake of

Garda throughout the distance of about 23 m. from Riva to the point of San Vigilio. On the one side nothing can be more varied than the form of the ground; and the union of rich cultivation with a luxuriant growth of wild flowers and shrubs gives softness to the scenery. On the E. shore the peculiar structure of the range of Monte Baldo produces the effect of stern monotony. As seen from a distance this is somewhat dreary and uninteresting; but a nearer view, such as may be gained from the steamer following this shore, rewards the traveller by its quite peculiar characteristics. The mountain range may be described as mainly formed of enormous superposed flags of limestone which have been tilted up at a high angle, with little or no lateral disturbance. In many places the strata, lying in unbroken beds, dip down from a height of several thousand feet to the water's edge without visible break or interruption. Making allowance for the slight irregularities of the topmost ridge, the mountain may be likened to a long range of mediæval roofing covered with slates or flags, each of which measures a quarter, or even half the height of the roof. On these bare surfaces little or no vegetable soil has been able to cling, and it is only at intervals, where some torrent has cut a ravine, and borne down some detritus to the shore, that a little ground available for cultivation has been obtained.

For several miles no habitations are seen on these stern slopes, and but one small hamlet is passed until the traveller reaches

Malcesine, a rather large village built on soil brought down by one of the most considerable torrents that drain this face of Monte Baldo. It was long the head-quarters of the Venetians, and has a high square tower erected for the defence of its little harbour. Several small villages, each surrounded by an oasis of rich vegetation contrasting with the barren rock around, are seen at intervals of two or three miles, and the rocky islet of *Tremelone* is passed before the steamer touches *Castelletto*. Here the range begins to subside towards the south. The slopes are less steep, and vegetation begins to assert its predominance over the barren rock. The traveller intending an excursion in the Baldo range, who has shunned the long and steep ascent from Malcesine, may land at

Torri, whence it is an easy walk to Caprino, and the Madonna della Corona. (See next Rte.). About 3 m. S. of Torri the rocks forming the farthest prolongation of the Baldo range subside into the lake at the point of *San Vigilio*. The view from hence is justly celebrated as one of the finest on the lake, commanding the entire southern basin, and a great part of the northern and more Alpine portion of its shores. A stately villa and several gardens nestle on the sheltered side of the promontory. Here, as well as at some other points of the shore, the Oleander (*Nerium Oleander*) has become wild upon the rocks and steep slopes. After rounding the point, the steamer follows the shore due E. to *Garda*, a small village, though it has given its name to the lake. It rivals Salò for the warmth of its climate, and the luxuriance of the gardens that, at frequent intervals, are seen along the shore. The ancient towers and battlements that surround the rather larger village of *Bardolino* give it an air of importance to which the interior scarcely corresponds. Still more picturesque is the aspect of *Lasize*. Its castle, erected by one of the later Scaligers, is still in tolerable preservation, and the *campanile* of the principal church is a good specimen of Italian Gothic. Near to this village have been gathered *Anemone coronaria* and *Drypis spinosa*, two species of southern plants not seen elsewhere in the neighbourhood of the Alps. Many villas of the Veronese aristocracy are seen along this part of the lake shore. One of the largest is that of Colà, some way from the lake to the S. of Lasize, belonging to Count Miniscalchi, well known as an Arabic scholar, and as a distinguished member of the

Italian Senate. From Lasize the steamer runs direct to *Peschiera* (no good inn, but a tolerable restaurant near the landing place), a small town, at the extreme S. end of the lake, where the Mincio commences its sluggish course through the plain that extends hence to the banks of the Po. Before 1849 this was the smallest and weakest of the fortresses of the famous quadrilateral; but since that date all the surrounding eminences were crowned by detached forts built at a heavy cost by the Austrian government. The botanist who has a few minutes to spare before proceeding to the railway station may gather *Naias major, Senecio paludosus*, and some other interesting plants close to the landing place of the steamers.

Route F.

ROVEREDO TO GARDA, BY THE MONTE BALDO.

The name *Monte Baldo* is applied collectively to the mountainous range that divides the Lake of Garda from the valley of the Adige. This fitly receives a common appellation, for although the higher summits lie in a ridge about 12 m. in length, they are not separated by any considerable depression, and the entire mass shows remarkable uniformity of structure. The four most conspicuous summits reckoning from N. to S. are the *Altissimo di Nago* (6.815'), *Cima delle Finestre* (6,866'), *Monte Maggiore*, also called *la Colma* (7,212'), and *Costabella* (about 7,000'). The second and third of these summits may be scaled directly from the lake shore at Malcesine; but the finest views are gained from the Altissimo di Nago, which is most conveniently reached from Brentonico, or from Costabella, best visited from Spiazzi. The ordinary tourist may well be satisfied with one of these excursions, but the naturalist will do well to devote at least two or three days to making a fuller acquaintance with this famous mountain.

It has long been celebrated as a sort of natural botanic garden, where may be found many of the rarest plants of the Eastern Alps; and since Pona published in 1617 his 'Monte Baldo Descritto,' successive generations of botanists have resorted hither. It appears, however, that within the present century several of the rarer species have been nearly extirpated, in consequence of the increase of sheep and goats, but the traveller who visits the mountain in the early summer is still sure of an abundant harvest. The following list, including only the rarer species, may interest the botanical traveller. *Ranunculus rutæfolius* and *R. Thora, Isopyrum thalictroides, Delphinium elatum, Pæonia officinalis, Papaver pyrenaicum, Arabis saxatilis* and *A. pumila, Petrocallis pyrenaica, Alsine austriaca, Moehringia Ponæ, Linum viscosum* and *L. Narbonense. Geranium argenteum, Acer monspessulanum, Cytisus radiatus* and *C. purpureus, Vicia oroboides, Potentilla nitida, Aremonia agrimonioides, Saxifraga elatior, S. sedoides* and *S. petræa, Ptychotis heterophylla, Athamanta Matthioli* (?), *Ligusticum Seguieri, Heracleum pollinianum, Molopospermum cicutarium, Homogyne discolor, Ptarmica Clarenæ* and *Pt. oxyloba, Doronicum austriacum, Serratu'a Rhaponticum, Phyteuma comosum, Campanula alpina* and *C. petræa (Madonna della Corona), Pæderota Bonarota, Pedicularis fasciculata, P. acaulis* and *P.*

ROUTE F.—MONTE BALDO.

comosa, Horminum pyrenaicum, Lamium Orvala, Primula spectabilis, Plantago Victorialis, Euphorbia carniolica and *E. nicæensis, Salix Pontederana, Limodorum abortivum, Erythronium Dens canis, Veratrum nigrum, Carex baldensis* and *C. gynobasis, Avena sempervirens,* and *Asplenium Halleri.*

The geologist will also find ample occupation in examining the structure of this mountain. Reference has been made in the last Rte. to the remarkable regularity with which the strata on the W. side dip towards the Lake of Garda. The opposite side of the range, facing the valley of the Adige, presents a remarkable contrast. The upturned edges of the strata on this side have been carved into the most varied forms by erosive agency, and perpendicular faces of rock alternate with richly wooded slopes or green pasture. Speaking generally, the outer range of heights that rises immediately above the rt. bank of the Adige is separated from the main ridge by an undulating broken plateau. The waters of the plateau, and the surrounding heights, flow at first in depressions parallel to the general direction of the ridge, and finally make their way to the Adige through deep ravines at rt. angles to that direction. At several points on the E. side igneous rocks (basalt?) are seen to protrude through the overlying strata. A deposit of lignite is found at the N. end of the ridge near the hamlet of Sorna.

A visit to the chief objects of interest on the mountain may easily be made by a traveller, bound from Roveredo to Verona or Brescia, or *vice versa*, but the traveller who does not follow the course here suggested may visit the Madonna della Corona from the Peri station on the rly. between Botzen and Verona (Rte. A), or ascend one or other of the highest summits from Malcesine on the Lake of Garda (Rte. E). Probably the most interesting route for approaching the mountain, at least in point of scenery, is to ascend from Avio (Rte. A) along the Aviana torrent, but the tra-

veller taking that course must prepare to pass the night in a châlet.

The most convenient way for the traveller willing to devote two or three days to the mountain is to leave the rly. at the *Mori* station, a short way S. of Roveredo, and quit the carriage-road at the village of that name. A slight ascent leads to

Turno (793′), whence a mule path mounts to

Brentonico (2,261′). A village picturesquely placed on a spur of the mountain, reached in 2 hrs. from Mori. Accommodation for the night (very poor?) and guides may be found here; and if weather be favourable, the traveller will do well to ascend on the same day the northernmost summit of the mountain —*Altissimo di Nago* (6,815′). The view is of a very high order, though it does not overlook so large a part of the lake as Costabella, the southernmost peak. From the summit the frontier between Italy and Tyrol runs down to the lake, crosses to the west shore, and thence extends westward to the Monte Tremalzo. In the opposite direction it is carried along the topmost ridge of Monte Baldo as far as the summit of Monte Maggiore, leaving the W. slope to Italy, and the E. slope to Tyrol. From Monte Maggiore it again turns eastward, and descends to the Adige with no apparent regard to the conformation of the ground. From the peak of the Altissimo it is quite practicable to follow the watershed, and on the same day reach the summit of the *Cima delle Finestre* (6,866′). From the latter a steep goat-path leads down to Malcesine. Most travellers will prefer to return from the Altissimo to Brentonico, and on the following day ascend the *Monte Maggiore* (7,212′), or else follow a track that coasts along the higher ridge of the mountain, and will lead him by *Ferrara* to the Madonna della Corona and Spiazzi. The writer has ascended only one of the higher peaks—Costabella—but has retained a strong impression that besides the four summits here named, there is a fifth which approaches very near the height of the Monte Maggiore. Whatever course the traveller may take, he should not omit a visit to the sanctuary of the *Madonna della Corona* (2,547′), one of the most famous and most curious of its kind. It is, however, best seen by those who ascend from *Brentino*, a small village on the rt. bank of the Adige, a little below Peri. Here a torrent descends into the main valley from a deep hollow in the mountain. According to the legend, immediately after the taking of Rhodes by the Turks in 1522, a bright light was repeatedly seen by night on the face of the perpendicular wall of rock that rises on the W. side of this hollow. When the spot was at length reached by shepherds, who, by ropes, were let down the face of the precipice, a miraculous image of the Madonna, previously preserved in a church at Rhodes, was found on an inaccessible ledge of rock. After being more than once removed to a neighbouring church, it as often disappeared, and was again found at the same spot. Yielding to the intimation thus plainly given, the people hewed a hollow opening in the face of the precipice, which was consecrated as a chapel; and constructed a pathway partly cut into the rock, partly supported on props, which has ever since been the frequent resort of pilgrims, especially on the 15th August, and on other anniversaries. The pathway is carried by 676 steps hewn in the rock to the summit of the precipice above the sanctuary, and on reaching the top, the traveller sets foot on the plateau of Monte Baldo, where it begins to slope downwards towards the plain country. At this spot, called *Spiazzi*, are a few houses, of which the largest is an inn, where the traveller finds very tolerable quarters, except at times when it is overcrowded with pilgrims. He enjoys a striking scene when, on opening his eyes with the earliest light of day, he sees the blue outline of the Apennine, at least 90 m. distant, rising beyond the vast expanse of the valley of the Po. On the face of the rocks near the sanctuary, the botanist will not fail to remark a very singular species of Campanula (*C. petræa*), for which this was long the only known habitat. It has since been detected in two or three stations of the same character, in the neighbouring valleys N. of Verona, and in the Basses Alpes near Draguignan.

A road, recently much improved, descends from Spiazzi to *Caprino* (883′), —several inns, best is Colomba d'Oro— whence it is easy to reach *Garda* or *Torri*. See last Rte. On certain fixed days the lake-steamer touches at both places, but if bound for the W. shore the traveller may best hire a boat at Torri to convey him to Toscolano, Maderno, or Salò. If bound for Verona, the most interesting course is to go from Spiazzi to the plateau of Rivoli, and thence descend to the rly. station at *Ceraino* (Rte. A). The complete semicircle of low hills that surrounds the plateau of Rivoli is formed by the moraines of the former glacier of the Adige, which did not extend nearly so far southward as that of the Lake of Garda, but rose to a greater height on the E. flank of Monte Baldo than did the greater ice-stream on the opposite slope of the same mountain.

SECTION 58.

RECOARO DISTRICT.

In the last section the reader has followed the course of the Adige from its junction with the Eisack at Botzen to its entrance into the plain of Venetia near Verona. With slight irregularities its course is parallel to that of the Monte Baldo, the Lake of Garda, and the main valleys of Lombardy. To the E. of the Adige no such parallelism is to be found; and whether the traveller follow the course of the chief rivers— such as the Brenta, Piave, Tagliamento, and Isonzo—or of the minor streams that descend into the plain, he finds little if any trace of the relation between the direction of the main valleys and that of the mountain ranges which is elsewhere traceable in the Alps. It will be seen, for instance, that the lakes which form the principal sources of the Brenta lie very near to the city of Trent; but as the course of the stream is at first eastward, gradually turning towards the S., and after some considerable zigzags finally entering the plain at Bassano, an extensive tract of mountain country is included between the Brenta and the Adige. It is this tract which is to be described in the present section. A few short valleys carry inconsiderable torrents to join the Adige and the Brenta, and the larger portion of the drainage of the district flows into the plain of Venetia through the Astico, the Timonchio, and the Agno, with other less important torrents. Nothing can be more irregular than the disposition of the mountain masses and the direction of the valleys, and in regard to the views of those geologists who are inclined to refer the modelling of mountain countries almost exclusively to erosive action, it is instructive to compare a region like this, where such influences have been predominant, with the more common condition where comparative order prevails in the arrangement of ridge and valley.

Although the mountains do not rise to a great height (Cima delle Dodici (7,651'), Monte Pasubio (7,326'), Cima di Posta (7,547')), their forms are usually very bold, and the scenery of most of the valleys offers great beauty and variety. Some of the latter are very deep, but there is a marked tendency to the plateau formation throughout this district, and this is exhibited on a large scale in the singular tract known as the Sette Comuni. The district is most easily approached from the N., by the carriage-road from Roveredo to Vicenza, which divides it into two nearly equal portions; but the other paths leading this way from S. Tyrol into Italy are rough, and for the most part fit only for pedestrians. The natural centre of this district for tourists is found at Recoaro, a watering-place that requires only to be more generally known, and rather better accommodation, to become a favourite resort for strangers, as it now is for the upper classes in the adjoining provinces. Fair accommodation is also to be found at Asiago, and bearable, though rough, quarters may be had at Pieve di Val Arsa, Val dei Signori, and other villages where the naturalist may be tempted to halt. The road from Trent to Bassano through Val Sugana, and the passes leading from the head of that valley to the Adige, are not described here, being more conveniently reserved for the next section.

Few portions of the Alps offer so many objects of interest to the geologist as are to be found in this district. In many places the triassic and overlying secondary strata abound in fossils, while the eocene deposits of Monte Bolca have supplied the richest and most various materials for fossil ichthyology. To other deposits of the same age may be referred the magnificent vegetable remains described by the late Prof. Massolengo, and by Prof. R. de Visiani of the University of Padua. The entire district is remarkable for the intrusion of igneous rocks in the form of lava, porphyry, and columnar basalt, the latter being especially developed in the neighbourhood of Monte Bolca. The important memoir by Sir R. Murchison, 'On the Geological Structure of the Alps, the Apennines, and the Carpathians,' already referred to in the introduction to this work, is not so easily procured, as the Italian version also mentioned. The reader will there find much valuable information respecting the structure of the Vicentine Alps, with instructive sections, some of which were originally published by the same eminent geologist in 1829. A more detailed account of the district is found in a work by Maraschini, entitled 'Saggio sulla Formazione delle Roccie Vicentine,' Padova, 1824; and the traveller will find more complete and more recent information on the neighbourhood of Recoaro in a memoir by Herr Schauroth, the title of which is given in the Introduction. The region is classic ground to the geologist, having been illustrated in the last century by the writings of Arduini, Fortis, and Strange, and in more modern times by the writers already cited, and by Marzari Pencati, Massalongo, and Lodovico Pasini. The last-named eminent geologist may probably give to the world a more complete account of this interesting region than any which has yet appeared. The scientific traveller is further referred to Count Caspar v. Sternberg's 'Reise durch Tyrol in die Oesterreichischen Provinzen Italiens.' Regensburg, 1806, a work containing much curious information.

The continued search for fossils by resident geologists, and the visits of eminent foreigners, have developed the habit of observing such objects among natives of humbler position, and there are several men in this district whose minute acquaintance with the spots where fossils are most easily found is of much value to a geological visitor. One of these guides, by name Giovanni Meneguzzi, is far superior to his colleagues, and from frequent association with eminent geologists, has acquired a considerable acquaintance with the geology of his native province. He lives at Montecchio Maggiore, near Vicenza, and keeps collections of minerals and fossils for sale. An older man, named Catalan, lives at Schio; he has less education, and his local knowledge does not seem to extend far from that place.

Route A.

ROVEREDO TO VICENZA, BY VAL ARSA AND SCHIO.

	Italian geo. miles	Eng. miles
Pieve di Val Arsa	10	11½
Val dei Signori	7	8
Schio	5	5¾
Vicenza	16	16½
	38	43¾

Carriage-road fit for light vehicles. An omnibus plies in summer as far as La Pieve di Val Arsa.

The stream of the Leno, which falls into the Adige close to Roveredo, is formed by the union of two torrents that meet about 1½ m. above the town. The road ascends above the rt. bank of the main stream, overlooking some extensive paper-mills and other factories, crosses the *Leno di Terragnolo* (as the torrent is called that issues from the eastern branch of the valley), and then turns nearly due S. along the rt. bank of the *Leno di Val Arsa.*

The scenery of *Val Arsa*, which is traversed in all its length by a road completed by the Austrians about 1823, is very pleasing, especially towards the upper end, where it is enclosed between some of the highest summits of the Vicentine Alps. The road being rough and rather steep, it is necessary to allow 3 hours from Roveredo to reach the principal village—*Pieve di Val Arsa* (2,653′)—often called in the valley merely La Chiesa. There is here a rough but tolerable inn, where mules may be had by travellers bound for Recoaro (Rte. C). From hence the mountaineer may ascend the *Cima di Posta* (7,547′), the highest summit in the range dividing Val Arsa from Val di Ronchi. In the opposite direction, NE. of the village, rises the *Monte Pasubio* (7,326′), which is accessible by a very steep goat-track, but much more easily from the side of Terragnolo. It is well to observe that the name Pasubio is locally given to a projecting point of rock, conspicuous from the neighbourhood of Vicenza, which is attainable by a steep scramble along the ridge dividing Val Arsa from Val dei Signori; but the true summit of the mountain, higher by some 200 ft., lies some way to NNW., and is here called *Covelalto*, sometimes also L' Incudine. All the surrounding heights are rich in rare plants. *Androsace Hausmanniana* has been found on the Cima di Posta; *Malabaila Hacquetii* and *Cirsium Carniolicum* on Monte Campogrosso, not far from the track to Recoaro; *Silene Alpestris* and *Primula spectabilis* on Monte Pasubio.

The road to Vicenza avoids Campo Silvano (Rte. C), the highest village in the valley, and passes on the N. side of a bold peak, called *Cengio Alto* to reach a comparatively low col—the *Piano delle Fugazze* (4,117′)—which here marks the boundary between Tyrol and Italy, and between the waters of the Leno and those of the Timonchio.

The bare limestone peaks that surround the head of Val dei Signori have a very wild aspect; but the scenery rapidly assumes a milder character as the traveller descends into the valley. On the L hand, a short way below the summit of the pass, is seen the opening of *Val di Canale*, a short glen of the wildest character, enclosed between bare limestone rocks, above which towers the bold projecting point to which the name Monte Pasubio is specially applied by the inhabitants. Along the face of the very steep rocks forming the head of Val di Canale the traveller may sometimes descry moving objects, and will ascertain with surprise that laden mules and horses are driven that way from Posina (Rte. H). After reaching the upper plateau of the Monte Pasubio, they descend towards NW. by a tolerably easy track along the ridge of the mountain called *Col Santo* (6,927′), finally attaining the village of Trembeleno, lying in the fork between the two branches of the Leno.

Through very agreeable scenery the road descends from the head of *Val dei Signori* to the principal village, which bears the same name. It has a tolerable inn. The traveller bound for Recoaro, who wishes to reach that place by a still easier walk than that from Pieve di Val Arsa over the pass of Campo Grosso, may follow the frequented mule-path that leads in 2 hrs. to that gay watering-place from the village of Val dei Signori.

Following the road along the torrent, here called *Leogra*, which, after uniting with the lesser stream called Timonchiello, assumes the name *Timonchio*, the traveller reaches

Schio (Inns: Stella, very fair; and several of less note), a town 685 ft. above the sea-level, whose neat appearance indicates the presence of an industrious and thriving population. The large factory of cloth and other woollen fabrics belonging to Signor Rossi is one of the most important in Italy. Signor Lodovico Pasini, an eminent member of the Italian Senate, best known abroad as a geologist, resides here, and his valuable collection of minerals and fossils, chiefly from the Alps of this district, well deserves the attention of the scientific traveller. NE. of the town rises the Monte Sumano (about 4,300′), known to naturalists as a locality for rare plants and insects. It forms the SE. extremity of the range diverging from the Monte Pasubio which divides Val dei Signori from the valley of the Astico. The traveller intending to visit the Sette Comuni may ascend the Monte Sumano from this side, and then, after descending to Piovene (Rte. H), reach Asiago by the new carriage-road.

The road from Schio to Vicenza crosses the torrent from Val dei Signori, which here receives the name *Timonchio*, and is carried over a richly cultivated plain country to *Malo* (Rte. D), and thence along the base of the hills to

Vicenza (Inns: Albergo Torresani, near the gate leading to the rly. station, an old house with a few large and handsome rooms, the rest very indifferent; Stella, of less pretensions and cheaper; several others of less repute). A city of the second order in point of size and wealth, whose buildings may challenge comparison with those of the greatest towns of Europe north of the Alps. Whether the traveller regards the ancient palaces in the Venetian style, or the more modern, but equally stately, buildings with which Palladio adorned this, his native city, he cannot but feel admiration for a people that has left such memorials of the epoch of its former prosperity. Omnibuses run twice a day from Vicenza to Schio, and also to Bassano; and once daily to Tiene.

Route B.

VICENZA TO RECOARO. EXCURSIONS FROM RECOARO.

Nature has done much to make Recoaro one of the most attractive watering-places in the Alps; and the concourse of visitors from Venice, Verona, and other cities of Northern Italy, affords to the stranger a glimpse of native society, widely differing in its easy simplicity and slight regard for conventional forms, from that of the upper classes in England or France. The drawbacks on these advantages, of which the most serious is the insufficiency of accommodation during the crowded season, may probably be gradually removed, but meantime the place well deserves at least a passing visit, and will afford interesting occupation to the geologist who may be tempted to a longer stay.

The valley of the Agno, at the head of which stands Recoaro, is accessible by carriage-road from three stations on the railway from Verona to Venice— *Vicenza, Tavernelle,* and *Montebello.*

The last is most convenient for travellers arriving from Verona; but it is not always provided with carriages, and the road from the Tavernelle station is somewhat shorter. The distance from Tavernelle is about 23 English m.—from Montebello or Vicenza about 26 m.

Diligences ply to and fro, twice a day in summer, from Vicenza and Tavernelle to Recoaro, but a party travelling together do better to engage a carriage. The tariff, probably not altered since the union of Venetia with Italy, was as follows, in Austrian florins—equal to 2½ francs.

For 2-horse carriages.

	fl.
Tavernelle to Recoaro	7
Montebello or Vicenza to Recoaro	8
Recoaro to Tavernelle	5½
Recoaro to Montebello or Vicenza	6

For 1-horse carriages.

Tavernelle to Recoaro	4½
Montebello or Vicenza to Recoaro	5
Recoaro to Tavernelle	3½
Recoaro to Montebello or Vicenza	4

For these charges the travellers are entitled to the entire vehicle, and the driver is not allowed to claim the *buonamano* which he usually receives.

The roads leading from the three places already mentioned unite a short way below *Castel Gomberto*, where the hills begin to close together on either side of the Agno. Numerous large villas belonging to the Vicentine aristocracy are seen on the heights on either hand, and about 6 m. farther the traveller reaches

Valdagno (885'), a small town, the chief place in the valley of the Agno, with a very fair inn. The chapel of Sta. Maria in Panisacco, standing on an eminence about 1 m. from the town, commands a fine view, but the path is rather rough and steep for ladies. Lignite of fair quality is worked at a spot called *La Cava dei Pulli*, about 2 m. from Valdagno, and petroleum is extracted from the overlying strata of bituminous slate.

Above Valdagno the valley begins to assume a more Alpine character, as the stream of the Agno is contracted between the bases of the mountains on either hand. The old rough road, constructed in 1817, on the line of the ancient mule-track, has been improved, and is now good. About half-way to Recoaro is a spot called *Nogara*, a favourite resort of idle visitors, who find means for whiling away the afternoon at two neat inns, where coffee and other refreshments are served in green arbours. The valley now turns nearly due W., and about 6 m. above Valdagno the road crosses to the l. bank of the stream, and presently enters the village of *Recoaro*.

This is built in straggling fashion, along the northern slope of the valley, there being scarcely any houses on the opposite bank, but the chief mineral spring issues from the mountain at a considerable height on the S. side of the stream, and the group of hotels and other buildings round it is scarcely seen from the village. Hence visitors to Recoaro have to choose between the hotels in the village and those at the mineral spring, or *Fonte Lelia*.

Owing to the shape of the ground, space in both places is restricted, the rooms in all the hotels are small, and lodging comparatively dear. The hotel most frequented by the upper class of visitors is the Vecchio Albergo Giorgetti, close to the Fonte Lelia. Its deficiencies are numerous, especially as regards attendance; but it is generally full throughout the season, and the evening is passed agreeably in a large saloon, where the guests are often amused by music and dancing. The Nuovo Albergo Giorgetti serves to accommodate guests who do not find room in the older house. The Casino Gotico, kept by F. Marzotto, is also close to the Fonte Lelia. It is a small house, but perhaps offers better accommodation and attendance than its rivals. Of the hotels in the village the best are Europa, Due Mori, Trettenero, and La Posta. Visitors who intend drinking the waters usually prefer to lodge near the spring, while those who resort hither as a centre for excursions will find it more convenient to remain in the village. It must be remembered that the place is very full during the months of July and August, when it is prudent to order rooms in advance.

The height of the parish church is 1,502 ft. above the sea, and that of the Fonte Lelia 1,678 ft. After crossing the bridge near the Europa hotel the carriage-road and several footpaths begin to ascend the well-planted slope, which leads to the principal source which has made the fortune of Recoaro. Donkeys are constantly standing in the village for the benefit of those too delicate or too indolent to make the ascent on foot, as well as for the longer excursions which form the afternoon occupation of visitors. The charges for hire are regulated by tariff. Besides the Fonte Lelia there are several other mineral springs in the immediate neighbourhood of Recoaro. The most notable of these are the Fonte Amara, which is close to the first, and the Fonte del Capitello, and Fonte del Franco, both on the slope of the valley above the l. bank of the Ango. All are chalybeate springs, containing carbonate of iron and free carbonic acid. In some cases the waters of Fonte Lelia, which contain a relatively large proportion of the sulphates of lime and magnesia, are less suitable than those of the Capitello or Franco. The number of water-drinkers at Recoaro has been constantly increasing, and of late years has sometimes exceeded 7,000. The beauty of the scenery, the agreeable climate, cooler by 6° or 7° Fahr. than that of the towns in the plain, and the many pleasant excursions to be made in the neighbourhood, combine to make this a pleasant summer retreat; but English visitors will be apt to complain of the accommodation, and especially of the arrangements as to meals. Breakfast is almost unknown, being reduced to a cup of black coffee, or a bowl of light broth; a heavy dinner is eaten at 2 p.m., and a supper at 9 p.m. An English family, wishing to remain some time here, would do well to engage lodgings in a private house, of which there are many available, and arrange meals to suit their own taste. Of many excursions, the only one practicable in a carriage is by the road already described to Nogara and Valdagno. About ½ hr. distant from La Nogara is a deep cleft in the mountain, called La Spaccata, often visited by strangers: numerous paths lead in various directions from the village, and the donkeys of the place are used to carry strangers up and down the steepest hills. Of the shorter excursions, that to the sanctuary of Santa Giuliana, returning by the mineral spring of the same name, and the paths leading westward along the Agno towards the head of the valley, are most to be recommended. A somewhat longer promenade is that to the village of Val dei Signori (Rte. A), also called *Le Valli*, about 2 hrs. distant.

A very agreeable walk, especially interesting to the geologist, is that to the Fonte Catulliana, passing the village of *Rovegliana*. This village stands on the ridge that divides the valley of the Agno from that of the Timonchio (Rte. A). An unauthenticated tradition affirms the former existence of a temple of Diana on the site of the present parish church. A tolerable path, frequented by donkeys and their riders, leads to the top of the ridge (about 2,300'?), whence the traveller overlooks both valleys. To the E. rises a summit called *Monte Civillina*. Hereabouts fossils of triassic age are very abundant, and in tolerably good condition. The path to the *Fonte Catulliana* (2,316') lies eastward, along the flank of the Monte Civillina, at first descending, then remounting to a point on the N. side of the mountain, where a spring, strongly impregnated with sulphate of iron and other vitriolic salts, is received in a reservoir, preparatory to being bottled and sent to a distance. A very few drops suffice for most visitors, the taste being nearly intolerable. From a point near at hand there is a fine view of Schio, Tiene, and the plain extending eastward to the city of the lagoons. 3 hrs. suffice for this excursion, going and returning, exclusive of halts. (See Rte. D.)

The visitors to Recoaro usually limit their efforts in mountaineering to the ascent of a projecting point in the ridge on the S. side of the village called *Monte Spitz*. The ascent (about 1,000 ft.) usually occupies 1 hr. After admiring the view, most visitors descend by Fongara, and thence follow a path that leads in ½ hr. to the Spaccata. The high-road from Valdagno to Recoaro is rejoined at Nogara.

The mountaineer who may be led to spend a few days at this pleasant watering-place will necessarily be attracted by the range of grey craggy peaks that close the head of the valley of the Agno, and form the most striking object in all the views near Recoaro. The highest summit—Cima di Posta (7,547')—is not (?) visible from this side, and is far more conveniently accessible from Val Arsa (Rte. A) than from Recoaro. Ladies who can ride should not fail to make the excursion to Campo Grosso (next Rte.). The beauty of the vegetation in the early summer season will amply reward the effort. The botanist will enjoy a pleasant excursion by effecting a rather steep and rough ascent to the ridge immediately N. of the precipitous crags conspicuous from Recoaro. There is here an unfrequented pass leading to Val Arsa—called *Passo delle Buse Scure*. The more frequented way is noticed in the next Rte., where there is also a notice of the Passo di Lora, which affords the most direct course to the traveller who would ascend the Cima di Posta from Recoaro.

the head of the Valley of the Agno. The traveller intending to put up in the village should follow the track on the l. bank of the stream; but if bound for the hotels near the Fonte Lelia, he should choose the path on the rt. bank and follow a new track leading to his destination by an easy and gradual ascent. The pedestrian having time to spare may diverge from the ridge towards the Passo delle Buse Scure, mentioned among the excursions from Recoaro, and reach his destination by a much steeper path.

2. *By the Passo della Lora.* 7 hrs. to Ala—Railway thence to Roveredo.

Viewing from Recoaro the high dolomite crags that close the head of the valley of the Agno, the traveller will observe, a little to the l. of the higher summits, where the ridge subsides in height by fully 1,000 ft., a long slope of limestone debris extending from top to bottom of the mountain, and will be surprised to learn that this uninviting slope is traversed by a frequented path, and is even used at times by beasts of burden. Though steep, it is less so than it appears to be from a distance; and a well-worn track is carried in zigzags up the declivity. It is less disagreeable to the feet than might be expected, but an early start is advisable, as the heat of the sun beating on the stony surface is oppressive, and trying to the eyes. The summit of the pass is 5,720 ft. in height, according to M.'H. Wolff. Having attained this point, the traveller supposes that he is about to descend into one of the tributary valleys of the Adige, but if he were unwarily to take the path to the l. that leads downwards into the head of the valley below him, he would be carried due S. along the Illasi torrent, through the district described in Rte. F. The way to Roveredo keeps to the rt. along the flank of the mountain, descending slightly to reach a poor mountain osteria, and then reascends by a short but steep climb to the *Passo di Revelto* that separates the head of Val d'Illasi from that of *Val di Ronchi*. Through this latter

Route C.

RECOARO TO ROVEREDO.

1. *By Campo Grosso.* About 19 m. Of the many visitors who come from Tyrol to drink the Recoaro waters, nearly all arrive by way of Val Arsa. Having reached the village of La Pieve (Rte. A), they commonly engage mules or donkeys for the remainder of the way. This is an easy and agreeable walk of about 3 hrs. over the ridge of Campo Grosso. The ascent on the Val Arsa side is gradual—passing *Campo Silvano*, with a tolerable country inn, the highest village in that valley—and there would be little difficulty in carrying a road to the summit of the ridge (about 4,500′?); but the descent towards Recoaro is comparatively steep, offering at the same time fine views of

valley lies the way to Ala on the Adige. The village of *Ronchi* (2,275') lies on the slope high above the rt. bank of the torrent, but the shortest way to Ala is by the opposite bank. A very steep stony track, extremely trying to beasts of burden, leads down to the head of this picturesque glen, and thenceforward follows the l. bank of the torrent, partly through forest, partly over stony ground overgrown by straggling bushes. This way is very little frequented, but is on the whole more interesting to the pedestrian than that by Val Arsa.

On the way between the Passo della Lora and that of Revelto, the traveller leaves on the rt. a sort of gap in the mass of dolomitic crags, whose highest summit is the Cima di Posta. If the writer was not misinformed, this affords the most direct way of attaining that summit from Recoaro; but it is difficult to rely on the information given at that place as to the higher peaks, which fail to attract the attention of visitors or of the inhabitants.

1. *Carriage-road by Malo and Valdagno.* 22 m. The traveller arriving from the N., and wishing to reach Recoaro by carriage-road, may best take the way from Roveredo to Schio, described in Rte. A, and there hire another vehicle for Recoaro. The road to Vicenza is followed as far as *Malo*. A fairly good country road there turns SW., and ascends gently between the hills. The direct way to Valdagno lies about due W., but the road following the sinuosities of the ground winds nearly due S. till it approaches near to *Castel Gomberto*, when it again turns westward, and joins the post-road to Recoaro, described in Rte. B.

2. *By Magré and Novale.* 5 or 6 hrs. walking, exclusive of halts. In the important memoir mentioned in the introduction to this section, Sir Roderick Murchison has given an instructive section of the mountain rising W. of Magré, a village lying off the high-road, less than a mile from Schio. The lower part of the mountain near the village is formed of grey scaglia—the equivalent of our chalk—and in ascending from that side the traveller comes in succession on the outcrop of the overlying strata, which dip gently to the westward. The upper beds of red and white scaglia, containing characteristic fossils, are traversed by trap-dykes. These alternate with volcanic grit or tufa, and as he ascends he finds the latter deposit containing nummulites, and overlaid by the nummulitic limestone which is developed so extensively in this part of the Alps. It seems evident that the tufa beds have been formed from volcanic ejections in many successive periods of eruption during the latter portion of the cretaceous epoch, and the commencement of the eocene epoch. Striking across the hills to SW., several spots may be seen where eruptive rocks have been forced at a still later period through the nummulitic limestone. Keeping in the same direction, with the help of a guide acquainted with the locality, the traveller may visit the very interesting tertiary beds of the *Val*

Route D.

SCHIO TO RECOARO.

The distance between these places is trifling, but the district is so interesting to geologists that it seems desirable to call attention to it by noticing the paths here pointed out under a separate heading.

delle Fosse, nearly 1 m. from Novale in the valley of the Agno. These produce a great variety of vegetable remains, of which 74 species have been described and figured by Professors Visiani and Massalongo. The place whence these fossils have been extracted is of small extent, and is so much covered by vegetable soil that it is not easily found. Thence it is best to descend to *Novale*, a village on the l. bank of the Agno, about 1 m. N. of Valdagno (Rte. B), whence the post-road leads to Recoaro.

3. *By the Val degli Zuccanti.* About 3½ hrs. At some period subsequent to the deposition of the *scaglia* limestone, which is the geological equivalent of our chalk, a vast mass of igneous rock, of that variety of porphyry called pyroxene, issued from a crater near the present village of *Fongara*, S. of Recoaro, and flowed NE. across the existing valley of the Agno and that of the Leogra, terminating against a barrier of Jurassic limestone near Tretto. The course of this ancient lava-stream, and its action on the surrounding rocks, may best be studied in the *Val degli Zuccanti*, through which a path descends towards the Leogra from the ridge above *Rovegliana*, mentioned in Rte. B among the excursions from Recoaro. The most direct course is to follow the high-road to a point about 2 m. W. of Schio, and then with a local guide follow a path leading to the Val degli Zuccanti. This excursion may, however, be combined with a visit to Magré, and the section of the adjoining mountain above described. An examination of the stratified rocks in the neighbourhood of the porphyry will tend to modify the views of those geologists who have attributed to the outburst of igneous rock at Fongara the conversion into dolomite of the adjoining range of Jurassic limestone. It will be seen that the porphyry does exert some metamorphic action on the scaglia and the underlying grit, which corresponds to our greensand, and further that it has in places upheaved and fractured the adjoining beds; but its action in both respects, and especially the former, is limited to a very short distance from the actual line of contact. As mentioned in Rte. B, triassic fossils are found in abundance near the summit of the ridge overlooking the valley of the Agno, whence the traveller descends to Recoaro by Rovegliana.

ROUTE E.

MONTEBELLO TO RECOARO, BY ARZIGNANO AND CRESPADORO.

The mountain region lying between the Agno and the Adige is drained by torrents, often nearly dry in summer, that flow southward into the plain of Venetia. The most important of these, and the only streams that penetrate deeply into the mass, are the *Chiampo*, the *Illasi*, the *Squaranto*, and the *Pantena*. Of these the first named is that lying immediately W. of the Agno, and the valley which it drains is perhaps the most interesting to geologists of any in this part of the Alps. The mountains, which increase gradually in height as the traveller goes northward, exhibit in varied phases the traces of past igneous action. The most interesting of these are the masses of columnar basalt that probably owe their origin to subaqueous volcanic action, the basalt having perhaps been ejected in the state of highly heated semi-liquid mud. To the sudden destruction of the fish in a shallow sea, caused by such eruptions, we probably owe the extraordinary abundance of fossil fish for which the quarries of Monte Bolca have long been famous, and which have been so completely illustrated in the classical work of Prof. Agassiz. The fossil plants found in adjacent beds of the same eocene formation, nearly as remarkable and as well preserved as the fish, have been chiefly brought to light and illustrated by the late Signor Massalongo of Verona, whose early death has been a serious loss to natural science.

Arzignano, the first considerable village in the valley of the Chiampo, is about 6 m. from the Montebello station on the railway from Vicenza to Verona, and about 1 m. more distant from the Tavernelle station, which, in summer, is better supplied with vehicles. From Arzignano the road follows the l. bank of the torrent called *Chiampo*. Lignite has been worked in open quarries on either side of the valley. At Chiampo the geologist will leave the line of the main valley, and follow the track to *Vestena*. The latter village stands near the head of a glen traversed by a torrent from Monte Bolca. Columnar basalt is here developed on a large scale, especially at a place where the torrent, hemmed in between a serried mass of prismatic columns on either hand, falls over a ridge of the same formation. This spot, which is figured in Sternberg's 'Reise' (see introduction to this section), exhibits one of the finest examples of columnar basalt on the continent of Europe.

From Vestena the geological traveller will ascend to the famous quarries of *Monte Bolca*. The church of the village of *Bolca* is seen from a distance, but the ascent is rather long. It will be well to get some slight refreshment at the village inn before continuing the ascent to the quarries. It is not easy to obtain good specimens of fossils on the spot, as the quarrymen are accustomed to reserve them for regular customers. Apart from its fossils the

Monte Bolca is a singular mountain, well deserving a visit. On the NE. side is a large crater, whence streams of lava have flowed in various directions. Above this crater is a projecting mass of rock, which, on a nearer approach, is found to be formed of columnar basalt. On the western slope the surface stratum is formed of pozzolana. On the SW. side, at about two-thirds of the height of the mountain, are the famous quarries. The rock is a marly limestone with slaty cleavage, of eocene age, and the remains of fishes and plants, separated by a comparatively thin layer of stone, are found in the lowermost beds.

Returning towards the valley of the Chiampo by the village of Bolca, a steep descent leads thence in less than 1 hr. to *Crespadoro* (1,109'). Here the traveller bound for Recoaro has a choice of routes. The mountaineer will prefer to follow the valley northward for some distance, and, on reaching the hamlet of Langri, may follow a direction nearly due N. across the mountain ridge that divides him from Recoaro. The distance is not great, but the ascent is considerable, and 5 or 6 hrs. should be allowed for the walk from Crespadoro.

To the geologist it is probably a more interesting course to go from Crespadoro to Valdagno. The direct track, crossing a low pass (2,458'), leads to that place in about 2 hrs. It is, however, advisable to make a slight detour in order to visit the ancient crater of *Marano* on the ridge between Crespadoro and Castelvecchio. This is one of the largest of the ancient craters of this district. Two considerable lava-streams have flowed from it, one towards each of the above-named villages, through depressions that must have existed at the time of the eruptions. The eminences immediately surrounding the crater are composed of pozzolana, but in the crater itself is found a singular volcanic conglomerate *enclosing bivalve shells*. As a general rule, the volcanic rocks of this district are singularly bare of vegetation, and the botanist will find less to interest him than in the valleys next to be noticed.

Route F.

CALDIERO TO ALA, OR RECOARO, BY THE VAL D' ILLASI.

To the traveller wishing to study the geological structure of this district, and its singular volcanic phenomena, the valley of Illasi offers as many advantages as that of Chiampo, and the two main objects of interest—the basalt columns of Vestena and Monte Bolca—may be visited as well from Badia Calavena as from Crespadoro, while better accommodation is probably available at the former village.

Illasi is most conveniently reached from the railway station of *Caldiero*, whence it is about 4 m. distant. Several stately buildings were erected here in the last century by a member of the Pompei family, who united ample means with a professional study of architecture. The largest of these buildings—an immense villa in palatial style—is the residence of the present Count Pompei. Strangers are readily permitted to walk through the extensive grounds, laid out after the fashion of an English park; and those who have half an hour to spare will do well to ascend the hill included within the park, crowned by the ancient castle of the same family, which commands an extensive view of the surrounding country.

A good road is carried along the eastern side of the Illasi, passing *Tregnago* (1,091'), where there is a tolerable inn.

On the slopes on either side of this valley, and in the neighbouring valleys nearer to Verona, the botanist may gather many southern species of plants, rarely seen so near to the Alps. Among these may be mentioned *Coronilla scorpioides, Bupleurum rotundifolium, Asperula arvensis, Valerianella echinata,* and *Koeleria phleoides.*

The chief place in the valley is *Badia Calavena*, about 7 m. N. of Illasi. As already mentioned, this is a convenient starting-point for a visit to the basaltic rocks of Vestena, or to Monte Bolca. The walk is longer than from Crespadoro, but the ascent rather less considerable. Those who wish to visit the Monti Lessini (see next Rte.) may ascend from Badia to the village of Saline (2,903'), on the ridge dividing this valley from Val Squaranto, and cross that valley to reach the larger village of Cerro, where they may probably find better quarters. If bound for the valley of the Adige, or for Recoaro, the traveller will do best to follow the stream of the Illasi to its source. A few miles beyond Badia the valley assumes a more Alpine character, being enclosed between the *Monte Porto* (5,115') on the E., and *Monte Purga* (4,199') on the W. side.

The head of the valley, reached in 3¼ hrs. from Badia, is closed by the high dolomite crags of the group culminating in the Cima di Posta. The pass of Revelto leads on the l. hand to Ala on the Adige, and that of La Lora, on the rt., to Recoaro. See Rte. C.

petræa, long supposed to be confined to Monte Baldo. The chief place in Podestaria is *Chiesa Nova*, where it is said that a stranger may find tolerable quarters. From the summit of the plateau a path descends through a short steep glen to Ala on the Adige (§ 57, Rte. A).

For the traveller who may approach this district through *Val Squaranto*, the best chance of finding accommodation is at *Cerro*, a village on an eminence above the W. side of that valley.

ROUTE G.

VERONA TO ALA, BY THE MONTI LESSINI.

The mountain district lying between the upper valley of Illasi and the Adige is collectively known as the *Monti Lessini*. It is chiefly drained by the torrents Pantena and Squaranto, which fall into the Adige near Verona, and is most conveniently accessible through the valleys which bear the same names. The northern portion, towards the Tyrolese frontier, exhibits the peculiar plateau character which on a larger scale is found in the Sette Comuni (Rte. I). This is, however, more exclusively a pastoral district, having but a small population distributed in a few scattered hamlets. The highest summit of the district is the *Monte Tomba* (6,484'). Probably owing to its vicinity to so many places of special interest, this tract has been strangely neglected by all travellers, including the present writer, and he is able to give but scanty information respecting it. The larger portion of the plateau, lying within the province of Verona, is locally named *Podestaria*, and belongs to a few Veronese proprietors. The most interesting route for anyone disposed to explore this neglected tract is doubtless that through *Val Pantena*. The first considerable village is *Grezzana* (597'). On the limestone N. of that village the botanist may gather the very rare *Campanula*

ROUTE H.

SCHIO TO TRENT, BY THE VALLEY OF THE ASTICO.

Of the numerous streams that flow southward into the plain of Venetia, between the Brenta and the Adige, the most considerable, and that which penetrates most deeply into the mountains, is the Astico. This divides the group of peaks NW. of Schio, that culminates in the Pasubio, from the plateau of the Sette Comuni, described in the next Rte. This valley offers an agreeable and convenient way for a pedestrian going from Schio (or Vicenza) to the head of Val Sugana, or to Calliano in the valley of the Adige, either route being a tolerably direct course for Trent.

The traveller starting from Vicenza, who has no occasion to visit Schio, may

ROUTE H.—VALLEY OF THE ASTICO.

take a more direct course for the valley of the Astico, passing through *Tiene*, a thriving country town, and *Piovene*, a village picturesquely situated at the foot of Monte Sumano.

Starting from Schio, the easiest course is likewise by the road leading by S. Orso to Piovene; but the traveller who would escape from the heat of the alluvial plain that stretches E. and S. of Schio, will prefer a path that crosses the ridge between the Monte Valpiana and Monte Sumano. The way lies due N. from Schio, and the height of the pass is 3,112 ft. The geologist or the botanist will, however, prefer to either alternative the ascent of the *Monte Sumano*. This mountain is a sort of promontory, extending southeastward from the range of the Pasubio, and, though only about 4,300 ft. in height, is conspicuous from the neighbourhood of Vicenza by its bold conical form. It has long been known to botanists for the many rare plants formerly found there. Some of these have disappeared, or become very scarce under the teeth of cattle and goats, but it still will reward careful examination, especially if visited in the early summer.

In the memoir already frequently referred to, Sir R. Murchison has given a section of the rocks to NNW. of Sant' Orso – a village about 2 m. from Schio, close to the foot of the Monte Sumano, wherein the strata, from the lower neocomian to the newer tertiary are shown to have been folded over, so as to lie in reversed order, by the intrusion of a considerable mass of porphyry. The upper part of the mountain is formed of Jurassic limestone. According to local tradition, an altar to Pluto once stood on the summit of the mountain, and on the same site a monastery was afterwards raised, of which scarcely any traces are now visible. The view from the top will reward even those travellers who may make the ascent without any scientific object.

The NE. face of Monte Sumano, overlooking the valley of the Astico, is very steep, and those who do not desire a stiff scramble, will either descend by the rough path leading to Piovene, or follow the ridge to NW., until they reach the col, above mentioned, between this and Monte Valpiana, whence a tolerable path leads by Velo to the hamlet of *Seghe*. This place, which may be reached by a country road from Piovene, about 5 m. distant, stands at the junction of the Posina torrent with the Astico. A track goes eastward by *Arsiero* to the village of *Posina*, whence Roveredo may be reached by a fine mountain walk over the Monte Pasubio, and along the ridge of Col Santo (see Rte. A), or by an easier track, that leads NNW. from Posina over a pass but 4,004 ft. in height, to the head of the Val di Terragnolo.

For about 9 m. above the junction the valley of the Astico extends due N. Near the junction of the Assa torrent, descending from the Sette Comuni (Rte. K), the track crosses to the l. bank, and, after passing several poor hamlets, resumes its NW. direction a little beyond Zacolo. A walk of about 9 m. more will carry the traveller to the height of land near the village of San Sebastiano, whence the drainage flows partly to the Astico, partly westward to the Adige through Val Folgaria, and partly NE. through Val Centa to Val Sugana. The track through Val Folgaria leads to the Calliano station between Roveredo and Trent, and that through Val Centa, passing *Lavarone* (3,619′), will conduct the traveller to Pergine, and by the high-road to Trent. See § 59, Rtes. A and B.

Route I.

VICENZA TO BASSANO, BY ASIAGO. THE SETTE COMUNI.

The mountain district bounded on the N. and E. by the Brenta, on the W. by the Astico, and on the S. by the plain of Venetia, is in many respects unique in the Alps. The first striking peculiarity to be noticed is the fact that, with a single exception, no streams flow from it. Saving the torrent of the Assa, which carries off the rainfall of a small corner of this district, we have here an area of about 300 square miles, of which it is literally true to say that in ordinary weather it has no visible drainage. Elsewhere, in limestone countries, the course of streams is subject to interruption, as the water sinks into cavities and reappears at intervals; but here, except a few thirsty springs, and small muddy pools that insufficiently supply the wants of men and cattle, the surface-water sinks at once into profound crevices and subterranean channels, through which it finally issues to daylight on the outer verge of the district. This peculiarity in the structure of the country, by removing the chief agent that modifies the surface, has doubtless largely contributed to maintain its physical features unaltered. The greater portion may be described as an undulating plateau, varying in height from about 3,200 to 4,500 ft. above the sea-level. At its northern side, however, the plateau rises considerably into a range of lofty summits that present a very bold face towards Val Sugana. The highest of these is the Cima delle Dodici (7,651'), further mentioned in the next Rte.

The district distinguished by these singular physical features has, from a period of remote antiquity, been inhabited by a peculiar population, undoubtedly of German origin, as to whose ethnic affinities writers have advanced various speculative opinions. That commonly held among the inhabitants, but unsupported by any vestige of evidence, refers their origin to a tribe of Cimbri defeated by Marius in the neighbourhood of Verona. Better supported by some degree of historical warrant is the belief which identifies these people with a tribe of Allemanni, who settled in this region, under Theodoric, King of the Goths, about the end of the 5th century. Count Sternberg, in the work mentioned in the introduction to this section, has given several specimens of the dialect which at the time of his visit, in 1803, was commonly spoken by the people. Though marked by some peculiar words and phrases, and containing a good many others derived from the Italian, it is nearly allied to those of S. Bavaria and of the northern Cantons of Switzerland. During the last 20 or 30 years Italian has to a great extent supplanted the ancient dialect, which is now spoken only by a few of the older inhabitants.

The district has been known, from time immemorial, by the designation *Sette Comuni*, from the seven principal villages—*Asiago* (3.300'), *Gallio* (3,609'), *Roana* (3,288'), *Enego*, *Foza*, *Lusiana*, and *Rotzo* (3,128').

In addition to these there are 13 hamlets (contrade), and some smaller clusters of houses.

From a very early period the people of this district enjoyed local self-government, and virtual independence, while passing in succession under the nominal protectorate of the city of Vicenza, the Scaligers of Verona, the Dukes of Milan, and finally, in 1404, of the Venetian Republic. The first French invasion in 1796 seems to have spared this secluded district, and when Venetia was ceded to Austria by the treaty of Campo Formio the local privileges of the Sette Comuni were maintained, while the merely nominal annual tribute of 500 Venetian lire, previously paid to the Venetian Government, was increased to 25,000 lire, or about 500*l*. sterling. The local police, maintained by watchmen appropriately called '*Fazioni del quieto vivere*,' and the supreme control of public affairs, were vested in a '*Regenza*' composed of two representatives sent by each Comune. Their privileges included exemption from taxation, tolls, and customs duties, together with the right of pasturing cattle in the plain country in the provinces of Vicenza and Padua.

These privileges, together with the still more valuable rights of self-government, were swept away in 1805, when French rule was established over the former territory of the Republic.

Until lately the plateau of the Sette Comuni was accessible only by rough tracks, impracticable for carriages. A few years ago, direct communication with Vicenza was established by a tolerably good road which ascends, by many zigzags, the steep slope of the mountain above *Cogolo* in the valley of the Astico. The traveller who has reached that village from Vicenza, by a good road passing through *Tiene* (Rte. H), may probably prefer to walk the remainder of the way, a distance of about 10 m., to Asiago. After surmounting the first long and steep ascent, the road follows for a time the channel of a stream which, like most of those in this region, is dry except immediately after rain. But before long the road attains the plateau, and after some slight ascents and descent seaches

Asiago (Inns: Aquila d' Oro, and two or three others, not bad for so remote a place), the capital of the Sette Comuni, deserving by its population and the size of its buildings the designation of a town. A new church, unwisely commenced on a scale worthy of a wealthier community, remains unfinished. As may be expected from its position, the climate of the plateau surrounding Asiago is unfriendly to vegetation. The winter and spring climate is severe, and the sterility due to the deficiency of water has been increased by the felling of timber which once covered much of the surface. Rye, barley, and potatoes are the chief produce, but the main reliance of the population is on their live-stock and wool, for which there is an active demand. Instead of following the line of the new road to Asiago, the geologist may well take a somewhat longer route, which will give more insight into the structure of the country, and is at the same time more interesting in point of scenery. This is by the old horse-track, which quitted the valley of the Astico just above the junction of the Assa, and after a rapid ascent to *Rotzo* (3,128'), is carried at a great height above the N. bank of the last-named torrent to *Roana*. Here a steep descent, followed by an equally steep ascent, carries the track to the opposite side of the Assa, and in about 2 m. more the traveller reaches Asiago. The series of formations exposed may be thus enumerated in ascending order. 1. Dolomitic limestone probably belonging to the lias. 2. Oolite of variable mineral structure, the more compact beds containing *Diceras, Gryphæa, Nerinæa,* and other shells. 3. An arenaceous limestone, with impressions of *Neuropteris*, followed by a grey marly limestone with imperfect traces of large bivalves. 4. Oxfordian limestone, known to Italian geologists as 'Ammonitico Rosso,' containing many characteristic species of *Ammonites, Terebratula,* &c. 5. Neocomian, or 'Biancone,' with several species of *Crioceras, Belemnites, Ammonites,* and *Aptychus.* 6. Lower Chalk, or 'Scaglia inferiore,' with impressions of *fuci.* 7. Upper Chalk, or 'Scaglia superiore,' with flints in regular courses. 8. Nummulitic limestone, with *Cerithium giganteum,* of eocene age, identical with beds seen on the rt. bank of the Brenta near Bassano. The two last formations are better seen on the eastern side of the plateau than in the part N. of the Assa.

The most interesting excursions from

Asiago are those in the direction of Val Sugana, noticed in the next Rte.

A new road, which will probably be completed before the end of 1868, will lead from Asiago to Bassano in a SW. direction across the plateau, descending by *Conco* to join the high-road between Marostica and Bassano (Rte. L). For the pedestrian there is a rather shorter way by *Rubbio*. The chief temptation to choose either of these courses is the extensive view over the plain of Venetia which the traveller gains on reaching the southern verge of the plateau. Padua, and many smaller towns and villages, are laid out as on a map, and in very clear weather the towers of Venice are distinctly seen in the eastern horizon. Sometimes, even, the range of the Bolognese Apennine, rising in the far distance beyond the Enganean hills, closes the view southward.

On the whole, the most interesting way to Bassano is by Valstagna. A track passable for country carts is carried over the undulating plateau, and connects the chief villages together. The way to Val Stagna lies somewhat N. of E. to *Gallio* (3,609'), whence, after passing a cross that stands on a slight eminence, the track descends to Ronchi. To the l. is the bed of a stream wherein little or no water is seen except during wet weather, when it is sometimes swollen to a furious torrent. This leads to the narrow gorge which affords the only passage in this direction from the plateau to the valley of the Brenta. The descent is not rapid until, after passing a wayside *osteria*, where bread and tolerable wine are found, the track plunges into the narrowest part of the gorge, where the rocks on either hand almost overhang the passage, which serves as a bridle-path in dry weather, but after heavy rain becomes the channel of a furious torrent. The cleft is locally known as *Il Buso della Frenzena*, and among other rare plants the botanist may here gather *Cortusa Matthioli* and *Philadelphus coronarius*. In the same spot the first-named plant was discovered by Cortuso in the 16th century. Throughout the descent the path is extremely rough, and quite impassable when the waters take their course by this, instead of their usual subterranean route. Accidents have sometimes occurred to travellers unable to retreat in time from the track of the descending torrent. 2½ hrs. fully suffice for the descent, but 4 hrs. may well be allowed for the ascent from Valstagna to Asiago, especially if the traveller has not made a very early start, as the heat is often oppressive.

Valstagna is within 1 m. of Oliero, which is described in § 59, Rte. A.

Route K.

ASIAGO TO TRENT.

It has been already observed that the plateau of the Sette Comuni rises at its northern verge into a range of moderately high summits, which in the opposite direction overlook Val Sugana. The crest of this mountain range forms the frontier between that Tyrolese valley and the Italian province of Vicenza. Various paths lead across it to Val Sugana; and the traveller bound for Trent may easily reach that city in one day from Asiago.

1. By far the easiest course is that by *Val d'Assa*. As already observed, the *Assa* is the only permanent torrent that issues from the highland district of the

Sette Comuni, of which it drains but a small corner. The stream has excavated a comparatively deep channel, which must be traversed in going from Asiago to the neighbouring village of Roana. The pedestrian who follows the opposite bank will save some time by striking across the undulating plateau about due WNW. from Asiago. After passing above the small hamlet of Camporovere over a rounded eminence, he descends towards the Assa, and will find a beaten track that leads along the E. slope at some height above the stream. For fully 5 m. the valley is nearly straight, mounting gently a little W. of N. On the rt. hand is passed the opening of Val di Portole (see below), and about 1 hr. farther is a poor osteria called Ghertele. Here the *Assa* is formed by the junction of two minor torrents. The more direct, but more laborious, way to Val Sugana is by a track along the branch that flows from NW. In about 1½ hr. from Ghertele another poor place of refreshment, called Osteria delle Porte, is found near the summit of the pass, which, from the name of the adjoining summit, is known as *Passo di Manazzo*. A rapid descent leads down on the N. side, and takes the traveller to the W. end of Val di Sella, about ¾ hr. from Levico. The more frequented way from Ghertele is by the track following the western branch of the torrent. In ¾ hr. this leads to the Osteria del Termine, a rough inn, somewhat superior to those already mentioned. Although the watershed towards Val Sugana lies considerably farther W., the frontier of Tyrol here crosses the valley from N. to S., following a zigzag course to the head of the valley of the Astico. The way now lies through a broad upland valley, green with Alpine pastures, and woods yet spared by the woodcutter. To the hamlet of *Vesena*, which stands in the midst, many inhabitants of the neighbouring warm valleys resort in the summer, putting up with rough fare for the sake of the pure and fresh mountain air. There is a tolerable inn, but many visitors hire rooms in the few houses hereabouts, and carry with them necessaries not to be had on the spot. Due N. of the hamlet is the *Cima Vesena* (6,237'), commanding a fine view of Val Sugana and the surrounding mountains. The walk from Vesena to Levico is very agreeable, and the path fit for riding, which cannot be said of the other tracks from Asiago to Val Sugana. The highest point attained by the path is 4,662 ft. above the sea.

About 5 hrs., exclusive of halts, should be allowed for the walk from Asiago to Levico, whence the high-road leads to Trent (§ 59, Rte. A). The pedestrian who would reach Pergine by the W. side of the lake of Caldonazzo should engage a local guide at Vesena, who will put him on a track which much shortens the route to the village of Caldonazzo.

2. By the *Val di Portole*. After entering the Val d'Assa from Asiago by the course already described, the traveller, taking the upper path above the l. bank of the torrent, will reach the opening of Val di Portole at a moderate height above the streamlet that descends through the latter glen. After midsummer this is usually quite dry, and in autumn the few springs that exist at the head of the valley are also liable to disappear. After turning ENE. for a short distance, the ill-marked path through Val di Portole resumes its northerly direction, parallel to that of Val d'Assa. The ascent is very gradual, there being three successive steps, each with a *casera*, or chalet. The highest of these is but a short way below a depression in the ridge closing the head of the valley by which the track crosses to Val Sugana.

The pass is called *Porta di Portole*. The descent on the N. side towards Val di Sella is steeper than the ascent, but perfectly easy, and 1 hr. or less suffices to reach the road that leads through that valley to Borgo.

On several maps, the mountain W. of the Porta is marked as *Cima di Portole*, but, according to local information, that name properly belongs to the higher summit NE. of the pass, which is easily reached by keeping along the ridge. The summit (about 7,300'?) commands a fine view; but as it is overtopped by the adjoining Cima delle Dodici, the latter is to be preferred. Many rare plants are found on the Cima di Portole; but the vegetation is less Alpine in character than might be expected, doubtless owing to the dryness of the surface. During the ascent, many curious clefts and holes may be seen in the limestone rocks, and at intervals large circular depressions, from 20 to 30 ft. in diameter, and 10 or 12 ft. deep. If he intend to return to Asiago, the traveller may best descend from the E. side of the Cima di Portole into the head of *Val Galmerara*, an uninhabited glen, parallel to Val di Portole, whose stream (when it flows) joins that from the latter valley, a short way above its junction with the Assa. The shorter way is to return by that way to Asiago; but it is easy to traverse the ridge E. of Val Galmerara, and return by Val di Gallio.

3. By *Val di Gallio*. The mountaineer will prefer to both the above routes a rather more circuitous course, that will include the ascent of the *Cima delle Dodici* (7,651'), the highest summit of this district. This may be approached by the Val Galmerara, mentioned above, but more conveniently by the Val di Gallio, which is reached from Asiago by a path running somewhat E. of N., without traversing the village of Gallio. It is advisable to take a local guide, although the writer believes that there is no difficulty in the ascent. Though the aspect of this and the neighbouring summits towards Val Sugana portends a stiff scramble, it appears that in reality the descent on the N. side is easy. Instead of going directly down into Val di Sella, the lover of caverns may without much detour visit the *Grotto of Costalta*, but it is necessary to be provided with torches or other means for lighting it. A narrow and low entrance leads into an outer cavern or antechamber, whence another narrow passage ushers the visitor into the principal cavern, said to be 70 ft. wide, 93 ft. high, and 1,140 ft. long. Descending into Val di Sella, the traveller may either bear to the rt., to reach Borgo di Val Sugana (§ 59, Rte. A), or, keeping to the l., follow the road to Levico.

Those who wish to see more of the Sette Comuni than is included in the routes already described, are recommended to follow a track that leads NE. from Gallio to Grigno in Val Sugana, passing *Marcesina*. This district is well known to the sportsmen of the neighbourhood, as ptarmigan, and other birds not often seen so near the plain of N. Italy, are found there. Owing, no doubt, to the more compact nature of the rock, the ground is in places swampy, producing marsh plants, and among others the little northern shrub, *Andromeda polifolia*, which has not been seen elsewhere in Italy.

The inn at Marcesina may be reached in about 6 hrs. from the summit of the Cima delle Dodici, and an active walker may on his way ascend the *Cima delle Undici*, the adjoining peak, to NE., only a few feet lower than its rival. Instead of following the mule-track, which leads in about three hrs. from Marcesina to Grigno, the traveller may follow a path somewhat S. of E. from Marcesina to Enego, on the easternmost extremity of the plateau of the Sette Comuni, and immediately above the Gorge of Primolano, into which he may descend by a steep path. See § 59, Rte. A.

The names Cima delle Dodici and C. delle Undici have evidently originated at Borgo di Val Sugana, where these peaks mark the position of the sun at noon and 11 A.M. respectively.

Route L.

VICENZA TO BASSANO, BY MAROSTICA.

Carriage-road—22 English miles.

Though not strictly speaking an Alpine road, this deserves a brief notice here, as it connects the district of which Recoaro is the centre with those described in the following sections. Although the road is confined to the plain, and runs nearly the entire way at a dead level, there are few that offer more beautiful Alpine views, especially in the early spring, when the snow still lies deep on the higher summits, and the foliage of the mulberry and vine do not so far screen the view as they commonly do in the plains of Northern Italy. There is another road, fully a mile shorter—by Le Nove—but that by Marostica is more interesting, and is also that taken by the omnibuses that ply twice daily between Vicenza and Bassano. These vehicles travel tolerably fast, and have a cabriolet, or open coupé, from which a limited view of the country is obtained. For several miles from Vicenza the view of the Vicentine Alps includes all the principal summits mentioned in the preceding routes, excepting those forming the northern boundary of the Sette Comuni. A little N. of due W. is seen the great mass of dolomite crags above Recoaro, that enclose the head of the valley of the Agno, with the lower ranges that stretch far to the S. till they subside into the plain at Montebello, and San Bonifazio. To the rt. of the Cima di Posta is a very bold craggy peak—the Cengio Alto —and beyond it a deep depression, over which is carried the road from Roveredo, described in Rte. A. Farther to the rt.

is another high mountain mass, nearly flat at the top, but presenting a very bold front, with projecting jagged teeth of limestone rock. This is the mass whose highest summit is the Pasubio; thence extends due E., a range connecting the latter with Monte Valpiana, and nearer still the Monte Sumano, here showing a double peak, but easily recognised by its regular conical form. The opening to the rt. of Monte Sumano marks the Valley of the Astico, and the new road to Asiago, mounting in long zigzags the steep slope on the NE. side of the valley, is conspicuous from a distance. The outline of the great plateau of the Sette Comuni presents no marked features, and until the traveller approaches within a few miles of Bassano, he will find it difficult to distinguish the deep narrow cleft through which the Brenta issues into the plain. The plateau formation extends to the E. of that river, but the outline rises much above the general level into the flattened cone of Mte. Grappa, which is so conspicuous a landmark throughout the provinces of Vicenza, Padua, and Treviso. East of the Grappa is seen a vista of distant summits terminating, when the air is clear, with the bold outline of Monte Cavallo in Friuli.

About 7 m. from Vicenza the road crosses the Astico, here much reduced in volume, as the larger part of the stream is diverted from its course to supply canals of irrigation. After passing *Sandrigo* and *Schiavon*, at a distance rather exceeding 17 m. from Vicenza, the road reaches

Marostica, whose battlements, crowning the rock behind it, are seen at a distance of several miles. The little town stands on level ground at the base of a steep rocky hill; and the high walls, which are said to date from the rule of the Scaligers, are carried up the steep slope to the summit of the hill, so as to enclose its southern face along with the town. The effect is extremely picturesque.

From Marostica to Bassano the road is carried along the skirts of a range of tertiary hills, detached from the main mass of mountain which rises into the plateau of the Sette Comuni. Volcanic rocks protrude in many places and basaltic columns were formerly found near Marostica, but the spot is now concealed by rubbish. About 4 m. from Marostica the road enters Angarano—the suburb of Bassano lying on the W. side of the Brenta. See § 59, Rte. A.

SECTION 59.

VALLEY OF THE BRENTA.

THE absence of apparent regularity in the disposition of the mountain masses throughout South Tyrol makes it a somewhat arbitrary matter to divide this region into districts. In default of other criterion, the drainage of the country affords a guide to what is, to some extent, a natural division of the surface. Valleys whose torrents run together in a common channel are almost always more closely connected together than those separated even by comparatively low ridges. Although one of the chief valleys described in the present section offers (at this time) an exception to that rule, it has yet seemed most convenient to include within the same district all the mountain region whose drainage is united in the Brenta.

The main branch of that river originates in two lakes a few miles E. of Trent. For a distance of about 26 m. it flows through Val Sugana, a broad fertile valley, enclosed on the S. side by the range of the Cima delle Dodici, forming the N. boundary of the Sette Comuni, while on the N. side it receives several considerable torrents issuing from as many tributary valleys. After describing a considerable curve, convex to the N., the Brenta passes the Italian frontier at a point nearly due E. of its source. Henceforth its course, for nearly 20 m., is through a narrow defile, cleft through a once continuous range of limestone mountains. From the Italian frontier to the neighbourhood of Bassano, where the river finally issues from the mountains, its sinuous channel keeps a general direction to S. About 4 m. S. of the frontier the Brenta is united with the Cismone, a tributary which often carries down more water than the main stream. The Cismone rises in the beautiful valley of Primiero, and drains a great portion of the grand group of dolomite peaks that enclose it on the N. and E. sides. At the point where it reaches the Italian frontier it receives the Vanoi, another considerable torrent, flowing from the Canal di S. Bovo, whose waters are fed by the snow-fields of the Cima d'Asta, and the porphyritic range that divide this district from the Val di Fiemme. It appears convenient to include in this district the town of Feltre, with the fine group of rugged peaks, collectively known as Le Vette, rising to the N., as well as the lower mass to the SW., lying between the Brenta and the Piave, and culminating in the Monte Grappa. The valley of the Cordevole forms the eastern boundary of this district, but the description of that singular and beautiful valley may more conveniently be reserved for § 61.

Although calcareous rocks of Jurassic and cretaceous age prevail in this district, there has been extensive intrusion of porphyritic rock, especially on its N. border. Nearly isolated from the adjoining ridges, the granitic mass of the Cima d' Asta (9,193') rears its rugged summit between the head of the Vanoi glen and some of the tributary glens of Val Sugana. Popular prejudice throughout this district assigns the first rank in height to the Cima d' Asta. How this can have existed among people able to see that mountain and the Primiero peaks at the same moment, it is hard to imagine. Several of the latter are higher by fully 1,400 ft., and all considerably overtop it.

The scenery of this district is almost everywhere beautiful, and in many places rises to grandeur. Primiero, with its adjacent glens, can be reckoned inferior to none of the adjoining valleys for the weird beauty of its dolomite peaks. The village of Primiero will, when better known, be the most attractive spot for travellers in this district; unless the accommodation at San Martino di Castrozza be improved, when that place would offer the inducements of scenery even grander than that of Primiero, and considerably greater elevation. Excellent quarters are found at Levico, but it is too hot for most English travellers. The good inn at Caoria offers a convenient halting-place for a geologist wishing to study the granitic region of the Cima d' Asta.

Route A.

TRENT TO BASSANO, BY VAL SUGANA.

	Posts	Eng. miles
Pergine	1	7½
Levico	} 1½	{ 5
Borgo di Val Sugana		{ 8¼
Primolano	1¾	16
Carpenè	} 2	{ 10½
Bassano		{ 8
	6¼	55¼

Post-road, traversed by several public conveyances.

It is somewhat remarkable that the road from Trent to Bassano, leading directly to Padua and Venice, should have been so rarely selected by tourists, even before the opening of the railway from Trent to Verona. The haste which generally characterises the British traveller now naturally inclines him to prefer the rte. by Verona, since it offers him an economy of 4 or 5 hrs. Yet it is undoubted that the rte. here described is one of the most interesting and beautiful that can be chosen by a traveller entering Italy from the north. Several public conveyances ply in summer between Trent and Val Sugana. One of these, which goes to Borgo, corresponds with another vehicle between Trent and Primolano, and by a second change of carriage the traveller may continue his rte. to Bassano, but not without considerable delay. This inconvenient arrangement has existed since the last political changes, which have divided this and other neighbouring valleys between two rival nations. There is, however, a direct conveyance both ways, travelling slowly, but without change of carriage. In 1867, it left Trent at 2·30 P.M., and reached Bassano rather before 3 A.M. Travelling the opposite way, travellers left Bassano at 9 P.M. and reached Trent about 8·30 A.M.

For some years the project of a railway from Trent direct to Venice by this route has been much discussed. The difficulties are not very serious, and the new line would shorten the way from Northern Europe to all the Italian ports on the Adriatic by nearly 50 m.; but the present time is unfavourable to enterprises of this nature.

The road begins to ascend immediately on leaving Trent by its eastern gate, and very soon enters the gorge of the *Fersinà*, which leads to the low pass dividing the waters of the Brenta from those of the Adige. The old road was inconvenient, and scarcely safe for heavy carriages; but as this formed part of the network of military roads by which Austria sought to ensure her hold on Venetia, an excellent new road was completed some years ago. Of convenient width, and nowhere steep, it is carried through the narrow part of the gorge on a shelf obtained by blasting beneath overhanging rocks.

About 4 m. from Trent the valley of the Fersina opens out into a charming circular basin, enclosed by mountains of moderate height. Numerous villages with tall *campaniles* lie on the slopes, which bear evidence of rich cultivation; and the appearance of the population and of their dwellings speaks of general industry and consequent well-being.

[The *Silla* torrent, which flows southward out of the narrow glen, called Val di Pinè, passed on the l. hand, offers a short way to the Val Cembra (§ 60, Rte. B), which may be reached from hence in 4 hrs. After passing *Baselga* (3,157') the track lies by the little lakes of *Seraja* and *Piazze*, N. of which is the lonely Osteria di Varda. One path turning sharply to the l. through an opening in the porphyritic mountains, leads in ¾ hr. from Piazze to Spiazzo on the Avisio, while another track goes SE. over the ridge dividing Pinè from Palù.]

About 1½ m. beyond the bridge over the Silla the road crosses the Fersina for the last time. The mountain glen from which it flows is called *Val Canezza*, or Val di Palù, and by that way a path runs to cross the Kofeljoch, dividing this from Val di Calamen to (Rte. I).

At the foot of a rock of mica schist crowned by a picturesque ancient castle, stands the thriving town of

Pergine (Inns: Al Cavaletto, and several other clean-looking houses), 1,583 ft. above the sea. Just before the conclusion of the armistice between Italy and Austria, in 1866, the corps of General Medici, after having forced the Austrian positions at Primolano and Levico, had advanced to this place, and was about to attack Trent. The road from hence to Levico ascends gently to cross a depression in the rocky ridge that extends about 4 m. SSE. from Pergine and divides the Lake of Levico from that of Caldonazzo. After descending from the pass the high-road passes close to the small *Lake of Levico* (1,634'), amidst very agreeable scenery, but the traveller who does not object to a walk of 2 hrs. has a choice between two other more attractive routes. That most frequently taken by travellers goes due S. from Pergine along the W. shore of the larger *Lake of Caldonazzo* (1,411'), the principal source of the Brenta. This lies considerably lower than the Fersina near Pergine, and also than the Lake of Levico, and the more obvious course for the high-road would have been along either shore; but the actual line was doubtless preferred on account of the marshy nature of the soil, of late years corrected by draining. There is a pleasant track, keeping near the lake shore, to *Calceranica*, said to possess the most ancient church in the valley. A Roman inscription proves the former existence here of a temple to Diana. If bound for Levico, the traveller should keep along the southern shore; if he ascend to Caldonazzo (Rte. B), he will rejoin the high-road a little below Levico. There is another way by the W. side of the lake, somewhat longer, but commanding wider views of the surrounding scenery. This ascends somewhat from Pergine to *Susa* (1,744'), and thence keeps alongs the ridge, well planted with chestnut-trees, about 700 ft. above the level of the l. To his rt. the traveller has the pyramidal summit called *Terrarossa* (5,668'), which commands a fine view, but not equal to that from the Monte Scanupia (Rte. B).

On the whole, the most interesting way from Pergine to Levico is that by the E. shore of the L. of Caldonazzo. The lover of antiquities should visit the church of San Cristoforo, standing on a rock at the N. end of the lake, built, it would appear, on the foundations of a Roman temple dedicated to Neptune and Diana. Thence the track ascends, and keeps along the W. slope of the ridge already mentioned, that divides the Lake of Levico from that of Caldonazzo. The views of the latter fine sheet of water, backed by the Terrarossa, and the still bolder crags of Monte Scanupia, are charming. The lake contains much fish, and was formerly the haunt of wild swans; but the local sportsmen have extirpated the species. After passing the villages of *Ischia* and *Tenna* (1,861'), the traveller should not fail to follow the summit of the ridge, whence he will look down alternately upon the lakes that lie on either hand. At its southern end are seen the ruins of the castle of *Brenta*, which was destroyed first by Eccelino da Romano, and again, after being rebuilt, in some of the local wars constantly waged by the petty rulers of the adjoining valleys. The Roman road to Trent was carried along this ridge, and was defended by forts that stood on the sites of the Castles of Pergine and Brenta.

All the roads and paths here mentioned meet at the small town of *Levico* (1,657'), recently become a place of some resort on account of its mineral waters. There is an untidy inn, where the omnibuses from Trent put up; but immediately outside the town, on the W. side, is a large and well-built establishment, much frequented in summer by visitors who drink the acidulous waters, containing sulphates of iron, lime, and magnesia, with a minute portion of arsenic, or take baths whose water, derived from a different source, contains sulphate of copper in addition to the other substances above mentioned.

The waters are said to have very powerful tonic effects, but should not be taken without competent medical advice.

When the house is not full, no difficulty is made in accommodating travellers who intend to make but a short stay. A moderate charge, regulated by printed tariff, is made for rooms; and meals, supplied by a Trattore in the establishment, are paid for separately. Allowing for defects of attendance when the house is full, the accommodation is good—certainly superior to that at Recoaro. The waters issue from the slope of Monte Selva (4,463'), which rises immediately on the N. side of Levico. In the writer's opinion, the position of Levico is too hot to be agreeable in July and August; but in June and September, when there is less concourse of visitors, it offers agreeable and convenient head-quarters for many excursions, and especially for a geologist. Within a moderate walk he may examine the granite of the Cima d' Asta group (see Introduction, Art. Geology), the porphyry of the valleys of Palù and Pinè, the mica slate which is the prevailing rock close at hand, and the series of stratified rocks extending from the Trias to the Eocene, many of them well marked by characteristic fossils. The disturbances to which the stratified rocks have been subjected at many successive epochs, render the connexion of the strata obscure at many points, and require for their elucidation the eye of an experienced geologist.

After descending a gentle slope immediately outside Levico, the road is carried along the broad level floor of the main valley. It passes a hamlet called Masi di Novaledo (1,355'), but leaves on the l. the large village of *Roncegno* (1,723'), lying on the lower slope of a mountain, chiefly composed of Cima d' Asta granite.

[A cattle-track leads from Roncegno to the valley of Palù. Remains of ancient pavement are supposed to prove its Roman origin. From the summit of *Monte Fravort*, lying to the rt. of the track, a fine view is gained, including the whole of Val Sugana. Fravort is also easily accessible from Levico.]

The mountain population above Roncegno are of German origin, and speak, or rather did until late years speak, a dialect very similar to that of the Sette Comuni.

The upper part of Val Sugana deserves the notice of those geologists who refer the present form of the surface exclusively to meteorological agencies. In the first place the breadth of the valley is out of all proportion to the trifling streams which flow—or can at any time have flowed—through it. But especial attention should be given to the ridge (formed by the mountains Rocchetta and Armentara) which runs parallel to the Brenta in the middle of the main valley, although appearing from the road to enclose it on the S. side. The minor valley, lying between this and the main range of the Sette Comuni, is called *Val di Sella*. Its drainage flows mainly to NE., through the Moggio torrent, to join the Brenta just below Borgo; but the Moggio is separated only by a low, ill-defined ridge from the opening at the W. end of the valley, towards Levico. Hence this way may be easily taken by a pedestrian going from the latter place to Borgo, and as the level is considerably higher than that of the main valley, the temperature is sensibly cooler. There is a mineral spring in Val di Sella, 2,723 ft. above the sea, about 2 hrs. from Borgo, accessible for light carriages, with an inn near at hand, and several houses that are let in summer to visitors seeking fresh air. It is a convenient centre for some excursions, including the ascent of the Cima delle Dodici, and a visit to the Grotto of Costalta (§ 58, Rte. K).

Val Sugana abounds in ruined castles, each of which has been a witness to the centuries of border warfare, and ruthless violence between neighbours, that make up the mediæval history of the north-eastern frontier of Italy. Some of the most picturesque of these ancient buildings are seen as the traveller approaches Borgo. Immediately above the town, on the NE. side, is *Telvana*, once a stronghold of the powerful Counts of Caldonazzo, still partially inhabited. It is said to contain some curious frescoes. Looking down on Telvana from a commanding eminence are the more picturesque ruins of the castle of San Pietro, taken by the Vicentines in the 14th century. The view from it is admirable. There is a striking contrast between these remains of feudal power and the aspect of the flourishing town of *Borgo di Val Sugana* (Inns: Aquila; Post; both very fair, better than they seem). Although more than half the town was destroyed by fire a few years ago, the damage has been effectually repaired, and the new buildings give it a cheerful aspect. In the centre of a broad fertile valley, producing much wine, silk, fruit, wheat, and maize, and inhabited by an industrious population, this place shows many marks of prosperity. Much tolerably good wine is sent hence by mountain tracks to the higher valleys of S. Tyrol, and a good deal is exported across the Italian frontier. There are several mills for winding and spinning silk. Although 1,230 ft. above the sea, the climate is very warm in summer, and the character of the place completely Italian.

At the close of the campaign of 1866, General Medici—having on the previous day forced the seemingly impregnable position of the Austrians at Primolano—took Borgo after a sharp, but not very obstinate encounter with the enemy. Evening closed on this success of the Italians; but, without giving his troops time to rest, he pushed them on to Levico, and before midnight was master of that important military position, which was taken without firing a shot by a decisive bayonet charge. The merits of the Italian commander, and of his troops, in the operations which, two days later, were interrupted by the armistice, do not seem to have been adequately recognised.

Following the main road eastwards from Borgo, the traveller crosses in succession three torrents that descend to join the Brenta from as many converging valleys. The first of these is the *Zeggio*, flowing from *Val Zeggio*. This torrent originates on the NE. side of Monte Fravort, and flows eastward, till after passing round the rock on which stands the castle of S. Pietro, it turns southward to join the Brenta. The principal village is *Torcegno* (2,563′). Those of *Telve di sopra* (2,084′) and *Telve di sotto* (1,771′) stand on the slope close to the opening of the glen.

About 1 m. beyond the bridge over the Zeggio, the road, after passing the village of *Castelnuovo*, crosses the more considerable torrent *Maso*, issuing from the Val Calamento (Rte. I), and very soon after the *Chiepena*, descending from Strigno (Rte. G). The new road which here joins our route leads to Strigno and Tesin (Rte. F). About 200 yards beyond the junction is a fair country inn, at a spot called Le Barricate, convenient for a pedestrian awaiting the passage of some vehicle to take him up or down the main valley.

On an eminence above the Barricate stands the ancient castle of *Ivano*, which gave its name in the 12th century to a powerful family long since extinct. It is now one of the numerous Tyrolese castles belonging to Count Wolkenstein, who sometimes inhabits it in summer. The scenery now begins to assume a sterner and grander character as the mountains on either side approach the narrowed bed of the Brenta. The Cima Laste, rising precipitously above Ospedaletto, is a particularly striking object. The soil being reduced to mere gravel, or piles of debris, lying at the base of the rocks, cultivation almost completely disappears before the traveller reaches *Grigno* (857′), the last Tyrolese village, about 11 m. from Borgo, a poor place standing close to the opening of a narrow gorge through which the Grigno torrent descends due southward from the Cima d' Asta through the valley of Tesin. A steep mule-track ascends through the gorge (Rte. G).

At Grigno the Brenta fairly enters the great cleft in which it remains imprisoned for a space of 20 m., flowing SSE. as far as the junction of the Cismon, thence SSW. to Valstagna, and again SSE. to Bassano. For some miles, however, the scenery is of mediocre interest. A hot sun blazes down into an arid trench, where, except the high-road, there is little trace of human presence. At *Le Tezze*, a small hamlet, the Austrian custom-house is passed, and about ¾ m. farther the driver will point out a stone by the roadside which marks the ancient limit of the territory of the Venetian republic, now become the frontier of Italy. Immediately beyond it is the Italian customs frontier station. Goods are liable to further examination at the customs-office in Primolano; but little trouble is usually given to travellers. About 1½ m. from the frontier is the first Italian post-station.

Primolano (730′ ?—701′ Wolf). The poor little village, crowded into a narrow space between the impending rocks and the river, consists almost entirely of rough inns and *trattorias*. At the Post the traveller will find much civility and poor fare. The position of this village is remarkable. The Brenta runs southward through the narrowest part of the great gorge leading to Bassano, while on the E. side of the village a broad opening is seen in the mountain range, at a height of about 400 ft. above the river. This affords a passage for the road to Feltre, which ascends the short but steep slope in several long zigzags. The traveller who follows that road (Rte. D) will perceive that the depression E. of Primolano is orographically the western continuation of the valley of the Piave, though not traversed by any considerable stream.

On the W. side of Primolano, beyond the Brenta, a rough track ascends to Enego, one of the villages of the Sette Comuni.

The scenery of the defile through which the Brenta flows for 15 m. below Primolano, will be judged differently, according to the disposition of different travellers; but it is undoubtedly amongst the most singular and striking of the kind in Europe. It may be said to want variety, for the rocks on either side, rising from 3,000 to 3,500 ft. above the stream, nowhere admit a view of more distant summits, and the meagre soil does not produce luxuriant vegetation; but, such as it is, it would be hard to cite another instance of a defile so long, so rugged, and seemingly so hopeless. Cattle-tracks lead up to the high plateau of the *Collalti* at Cismone and Solagna, but, for a distance of 11 m. between those places, the rocks are accessible in but three or four places to a goat, or a practised mountaineer. On the opposite side of the river the Sette Comuni can be reached only by the precarious path up the bed of the torrent of Val Stagna, mentioned in § 58, Rte. I.

About a mile below Primolano the traveller should not fail to observe in the face of the vertical rock on his l., at a height of about 80 ft. from the ground, the entrance to a large cavern. Smoke-stains on the rocks, and the remains of masonry, at once show that it has served for human habitation; but he will be surprised to find that this is the famous rock fortress of Covolo (from the German Kofel), which at times has sheltered a garrison of 500 men. It appears to have been used as a stronghold at a very early period, probably before the descent of the Longobards into Italy. An internal spring of fresh water, and secure magazines for stores, seemed to make it impregnable, as access was obtained only by means of a rope let down from the mouth of the cavern. Yet it has been repeatedly taken in time of war. After the valley had passed into the hands of the Venetians, the right of garrisoning the cavern was still conceded to the Emperor of Germany, and was held by the Austrians until 1798, when the stronghold was for the last time taken by the French under Augereau.

About 1 m. farther the road reaches the junction with the Brenta of its most considerable affluent — the Cismon — which issues from a gorge still more contracted than that of the Brenta. Vast quantities of timber are annually sent this way from the valleys of Primiero and San Bovo, and here formed into rafts that are floated down to Bassano, and thence to Venice. About ½ m. S. of the junction is the village of *Cismone* (590'), standing a little to the l. of the road. The pedestrian, already acquainted with the scenery of the main valley, may enjoy a mountain walk with little loss of time, by following the cattle-track that mounts from Cismone to the plateau above the E. side of the valley, and taking a course nearly due S., till he descends to Pove, about 2½ m. N. of Bassano; or, if he start early enough, he may take the ascent of the Grappa (Rte. C) in his day's walk. The plateau over which his route lies is called the *Collalti*, and is similar in character to the Sette Comuni, described in the last §, but far less extensive. It further differs in having no permanent population; as the herdsmen who resort thither in summer descend in winter to the villages of the main valley.

About Cismone the traveller will observe the first patches of tobacco-ground. The privilege of cultivating this plant, subject to rigid excise regulations, was first granted to the inhabitants by the Venetian republic, and has been continued under successive governments. Throughout the distance of 8 m. between Cismone and Carpenè there is scarcely a house or trace of cultivation to be seen. The floor of the valley is abandoned to the Brenta, which though low in summer pours down a vast mass of water in the full season, while on either side the rocks rise in mural precipices of vast height. The finest scenery is near Val Stagna, where the valley bends from SSW. to SSE. Though still very steep, the mountains here present a more broken outline. Projecting masses are crowned by narrow terraces, above which other towers and ramparts of rock are seen to rise; while here and there some tree finds space to fix its roots. In approaching Carpenè and Val Stagna the traveller will be puzzled to account for the appearance of numerous lines of masonry, rising in places to a height of many hundred ft. above the stream, sometimes appearing to adhere to the face of the precipices, sometimes carried along slopes of the steepest debris. These give evidence of the industry and enterprise of the inhabitants. Each of these constructions has been raised in order to procure a plot of ground, often measuring but a few square yards, whereon to grow tobacco. The walls of rough masonry enclose narrow terraces, whither earth is borne on the backs of men and women. To each plot, often accessible only by a ladder, the cultivator resorts frequently, and in dry weather carries up buckets wherewith to water each individual plant. In favourable seasons the leaves grow to a prodigious size.

Val Stagna (522′) is a considerable village, the first that has been seen on the rt. bank of the Brenta, and opposite to it, connected by a handsome stone bridge, is *Carpenè*, where the omnibuses usually halt for a few minutes. Here the traveller may cross to the rt. bank of the river, if he wish to visit on his way the Grotto of Oliero. The road to Bassano along that bank, though very narrow, between Val Stagna and Oliero, is easily passable for light carriages.

The road from Carpenè is somewhat hilly for 2 or 3 miles, as it crosses the bases of several buttresses that descend from the Collalti to the Brenta. After passing several smaller places, the road traverses *Solagna*, a large and thriving village that stretches some way along the bank of the Brenta. Here the defile at length begins to open out, and it is evident that we are approaching the point where the mountains finally subside into a plain. Passing under a steep rock the road leaves the banks of the Brenta, and ascends a little to gain the level ground, some 80 ft. above the bed of the river. For nearly 2 m. the road is confined between stone walls, enclosing olive gardens and vineyards, when a sudden turn presents to the eye an extremely picturesque view of Bassano. The city is still guarded on the N.
side by the ancient ivy-grown wall which in winter screens it from the cold winds. At intervals rise the towers that recall the rule of Eccelino da Romano, and at the foot of the wall all the ground slopes steeply towards a flat alluvial basin of richly cultivated ground. The road passes round the eastern verge of this basin, and finally enters

Bassano (Inns : Mondo ; Sant Antonio, both very fair and better than they seem). Though ill-built, and not boasting a sing'e handsome street, the interior of the town is quaint and picturesque; while the view from the promenade along the city wall, and the adjoining Caffè dei Fossi, exactly facing the opening of the defile of the Brenta, should on no account be omitted. It may be remarked here that the Venetians, carrying into their provinces of terra firma the peculiar phraseology of their city, called the principal valleys of the Venetian Alps canals! Thus the valley of the Brenta, as far as the Venetian frontier, is commonly known as Canal di Brenta, and the same nomenclature prevails through the greater part of Friuli.

Bassano boasts of a Museum more rich and complete than that of many more important cities, which it owes to the liberality of private donors. The Picture Gallery includes many works of the Da Ponte family, natives of the town from which they took their common designation, and of others of the Venetian school. The library contains nearly 60,000 volumes. The collection of prints is especially rich, containing many valuable and rare engravings. A complete set of casts of the works of Canova, along with the drawings, works on art, and MSS. of that celebrated sculptor, was presented by his brother the late Bishop of Mindo. A very valuable collection of minerals and fossils was given to the Institution by the late Cav. Parolini. In addition to the specimens collected by the founder in Italy, Greece, and Asia Minor, or purchased in various parts of Europe, it includes a large series of rocks collected by G. B. Brocchi, also a native of Bassano, and the series of Subapennine fossils on which was founded the classical work of the same eminent geologist. The botanist will be interested in examining the Herbarium of Parolini, and another, not in such good condition, but very rich in the plants of this part of the Alps, formed by G. Montini, a good local botanist.

The castle built by Eccelino da Romano, now partly in ruins and partly inhabited by the *arciprete*, or rector, stands by the NW. gate of the town, and is a very picturesque object.

The covered wooden bridge connecting Bassano with the suburb of Angarano on the W. bank of the Brenta is deservedly a favourite object with artists, who seldom fail to introduce it into views of the town. A similar structure built by Palladio was carried away in the last century by a flood of the Brenta, and the next bridge on the same site was blown up by the French. The readers of military history are familiar with the masterly but audacious operations by which the first Napoleon in 1796 here completed the destruction of Wurmser's army, already defeated at Lonato and Castiglione, and forced that veteran general to seek shelter for the remains of his force within the walls of Mantua. Few visitors to Bassano omit to visit the garden formed by the late Cav. Parolini. The entrance is in the suburb called Borgo Leon, and admission is readily given on application to the gardener. It includes a very numerous collection of herbaceous plants, partly arranged as a botanical garden, but most visitors are more attracted by the grounds, very well laid out, and commanding picturesque views of the ancient walls, and the range of the Collalti. The collection of *coniferæ* includes many fine specimens of trees that do not flourish in Britain, and amongst others the botanists will observe with interest a knoll planted with *Pinus paroliniana*, a curious tree, with contorted trunk, discovered by the late owner of the garden on the Trojan Mt. Ida.

The principal piazza of Bassano is 470 ft. above the sea, while the mean height of the Brenta at the bridge is but 397 feet.

Many interesting excursions may be made from Bassano. Of these the more considerable—such as that to the Sette Comuni, to Possagno, and the ascent of the Grappa — are noticed elsewhere. One, which should on no account be omitted, is that to the *Grotto of Oliero*, on the rt. bank of the Brenta, about 7 m. from Bassano. A few hundred yards from the village of *Oliero* is a recess in the mountain, enclosed by precipitous rocks, where copious streams of beautifully clear water issue from two caverns. It appears certain that by far the largest portion of the drainage of the Sette Comuni finds its way to this outlet. No other stream of any importance flows from the extensive plateau, and the volume of water here issuing, having been protected from evaporation, is much greater than it would have been if it had flowed above ground. From a remote period the waters of the Oliero were used to work several paper-mills. One of these, till very lately belonging to the Remondini family, supplied paper to the printing-office which for fully 80 years made the name of that Bassanese family familiar to the literary world, while the prints issuing from the same establishment were spread throughout Europe, and beyond its bounds. No serious attempt seems to have been made to explore the grottoes until their late proprietor, Cav. Parolini, penetrated in 1832 into the outer one. He also planted the environs with much taste, made winding walks up the steep side of the mountain above the grotto, and rendered the spot more accessible and more attractive. After entering the cavern on flags laid in the bed of the stream, visitors enter a small boat which can carry 5 or 6 persons, and passing over a small subterranean lake of considerable depth, land at the farther end. The guides climb up with torches, and illuminate the stalactites that hang from the roof. On the whole, though not of large dimensions, this is one of the most interesting caverns known to the writer. It does not appear possible to penetrate into the farther cavern, but it is well worth while to approach close to the entrance by a path along the S. side of the stream.

An excursion of especial interest to the botanist and the geologist may be made from Bassano to the hills of San Michele, lying within a short distance of Angarano, on the W. side of the Brenta. They are composed of tertiary strata, which have undergone considerable disturbance, in part owing to the intrusion of igneous rocks since their deposition.

The neighbourhood of Bassano possesses an extremely rich flora, and the botanist may here reap an ample harvest. The hills of Angarano, the neighbourhood of Oliero, the Collalti, but most of all, the rocks above the l. bank of the Brenta between Cismone and Solagna, produce many rare species, a few of which are noted in the following list:—*Anemone trifolia, Isopyrum thalictroides, Eranthis hyemalis, Epimedium alpinum, Mœhringia Ponæ, Cerastium sylvaticum, Linum narbonense, Genista sericea, G. radiata, Medicago carsciensis, Saxifraga petræa, Eryngium amethystinum, Seseli glaucum, Ferulago galbanifera, Carpesium cernuum, Centaurea alpina, C. rupestris, Leontodon crispus, L. incanus, Chondrilla prenanthoides, Phyteuma comosum, Campanula carnica, C. Alpini, C. sibirica, Lithospernum graminifolium, Lamium orvala, Euphorbia carniolica, Limodorum abortivum, Iris graminea, Veratrum nigrum, Carex Michelii, Hierochloa australis, Festuca spectabilis.*

ROUTE B.

ROVEREDO TO LEVICO.

The traveller approaching Val Sugana from the Lake of Garda, or from Verona, will probably pass through Roveredo, and will have a choice between two easy and agreeable routes to Levico—one practicable in a light carriage, the other on foot or horseback. If he should have no occasion to halt at Roveredo, he should take his railway-ticket to either of the stations mentioned below.

1. By *Vigolo*. Char-road—about 12 m. It will be prudent to order a carriage from Levico to meet the traveller at the rly. station. From the *Matarello* station, on the rly. between Roveredo and Verona, a char-road is carried due E. through a deep depression between the bold summit of Monte Scanupia, so conspicuous from Trent, and the summit called Terrarossa, which overlooks the Lake of Caldonazzo. A very short glen leads up to the summit of the pass, very near which, but on the Val Sugana side, is *Vigolo* (1,902′? but Mr. Holzmann found 2,287′). On a neighbouring height stands the castle of Vigolo, an ancient stronghold, which passed into the possession of the Bishops of Trent, and afterwards into private hands. This is a convenient point for the ascent of *Monte Scanupia* (7,027′), which offers the attractions of a very fine view, with many rare plants. The little valley through which the road descends to *Calceranica* is called *Val Vattaro*. For the way thence to Levico, see Rte. A.

2. By *Val Folgaria*. *Val Folgaria*, a favourite summer retreat of the people

of Roveredo, pours its torrent into the Adige at Calliano (§ 57, Rte. A). From the rly. station, the traveller will be directed to the track which mounts steeply the narrow part of the valley, passing the ancient castle of *Beseno*, and it is not till he has ascended to a height of nearly 3,000 ft. above the Adige that the valley widens into an upland basin, with swelling downs of meadow and Alpine pastures. There are many scattered dwellings, chiefly belonging to wealthy inhabitants of Roveredo. The traveller may choose among various pleasant paths, one of which passes by *La Villa di Folgaria* (3,760′). The ascent of Monte Scanupia may be easily made from this side. A gentle ascent leads to the summit of the pass (4,476′? probably less) that separates this from the head of the Valley of the Astico. The watershed is ill defined, and mere undulations of the ground, rather than definite ridges, separate the head of this valley from Val di Terragnolo on the S., and Val Sugana to the E. A track, passing *San Sebastiano*, leads the traveller to the head of *Val Centa*, a little glen through which a pleasant path descends to *Caldonazzo* less than 2 m. from Levico. The distance from Calliano to that place is about 20 m.

Route C.

BASSANO TO FELTRE, BY POSSAGNO.

	Italian geog. miles	English miles
Possagno . . .	9¼	10¾
Fener . . .	6¼	7¼
Feltre . . .	9¼	10¾
	24¾	28¾

Although this road offers much agreeable scenery, its attractions cannot be compared with those of the defile of the Brenta from Bassano to Primolano, and the road from the latter village to Feltre by Arsie. That is the course taken by the slow country diligence or omnibus that plies daily, leaving Bassano at 4 A.M.; and the road by Possagno is chiefly taken by those who are drawn to that village by its association with the name of Canova. Most travellers will prefer to engage a carriage from Possagno and back, and then proceed to Feltre by Primolano.

On the E. side of Bassano the outer range of the Alps, including the Collalti, and the more lofty mass of the Grappa, subsides into the low country so abruptly that there is scarcely an undulation of the ground between the plain of Venetia and the base of the steep continuous slopes that vary from 3,000 to 5,000 ft. in absolute height. Farther E. the base of the range is, as usual in mountain countries, defended by outworks, formed by the tertiary hills of Asolo, whose structure has been illustrated by Sir R. Murchison in the memoir here frequently referred to. Rather more than 2 m. from Bassano a square campanile, on a swelling knoll to the rt., marks the church of *Romano*, the birthplace of the redoubted Eccelino. On the l. hand, opposite Romano, is the opening of a short glen of the wildest and most rugged character, called *Val di Santa Filà* (Felicità). About 2 m. farther the road leaves to the l. the village of Borso (Rte. D), whence the ascent of the Grappa is usually made. Crossing some rather deep trenches cut by the autumn and spring torrents, and passing the village of *Crespano*, the road traverses a fine bridge whose cost was defrayed by a legacy left by Canova, and then ascends to a sort of low pass between the tertiary hills of Asolo on the rt., and the stern range of the Grappa and Boccaor on the l. Before long the so-called Temple of Possagno comes into view. It stands in a commanding position on the N. side of the little *Val d' Urgana*, which extends eastward from hence to the Piave, collecting into a single bed a number of minor torrents. Canova's house, the principal building in the village. now the property of a lady, niece of the great sculptor, is freely shown to strangers. It has been in great part converted into a museum, wherein, besides casts of most of his works, there are several unfinished statues, and a fine monument to the daughter of a Spanish nobleman who was unable or unwilling to pay for the work when completed. It is known that Canova, like many other eminent men, mistook his real vocation, and took more satisfaction in the productions of his easel than those of the chisel. The pictures preserved here, and others which may be seen at the Villa Rezzonico, near Bassano, do not give any countenance to this delusion. Not content with the sister arts of painting and sculpture, Canova wished to distinguish himself also in architecture, and at the same time to leave to posterity a monument of his piety and attachment to his birthplace. With this view he designed a great church of circular form, in which he sought to combine the doric portico of a Greek temple with the cupola of the Pantheon at Rome. The work was commenced in his lifetime, the superintendence of details being entrusted to a local architect, who completed the building after the sculptor's death. It stands on the slope, at some height above the village, and 928 ft. above the sea level. Opinions may differ as to the fitness of the buildings for a church, but apart from its destination it must be regarded as a fine structure. The road to Feltre keeps along the base of the mountains, not following the torrent of Val Urgana, and on reaching the Piave turns northward to the village of *Fener*. The height of the bed of the Piave is here 626 ft., or 229 ft. more than that of the Brenta at Bassano. In the dry gravelly bed of the river the botanist may gather *Leontodon Berinii*, which is known only in similar stations between this river and the Isonzo. After following the rt. bank of the Piave for about 8 m., the road leaves the river-bank to ascend, at first by the rt., afterwards by the l., bank of the *Sonna* torrent, which leads to

Feltre (Inns: Vapore, very fair; Aquila d' Oro), a small town, claiming to be reckoned among the most ancient in Europe. It stands on a rather steep slope, above the junction of the *Curmeda* torrent with the Sonna, the ancient castle called La Rocca (1,085′), and the cathedral (1,051′), being much above the level of the main street. Among other citizens of note, Feltre has produced Panfilo Castaldi, who has been claimed, on very slender grounds, as the inventor of printing with movable types, and Frate Bernardino. a monk who established the first *Mont de Piété*, an institution which still exists in the town.

Although at no great distance from the peaks of the so-called Vette di Feltre, it is not conveniently situated for excursions. Those summits are better reached from Primiero. (See Rte. E.)

Route D.

BASSANO TO FELTRE, BY MONTE GRAPPA.

9 to 10 hrs. walking, exclusive of halts.

The traveller who does not object to a moderately long day's walk, may enjoy some varied scenery, and a very fine view, by taking a nearly direct line from Bassano to Feltre across the summit of *Monte Grappa* (5,817'), the highest summit of the outer range of the Alps rising immediately above the plain of Venetia. Additional interest will be felt by the botanist, who may collect many rare plants, characteristic of this region. If the excursion be made from Bassano, a very early start is advisable, as the ascent of the long unbroken treeless slopes of the Grappa, after the sun has acquired power, is a trying process. The easiest way is to ascend from *Borso*, a village a little to the l. of the road to Possagno, nearly 5 m. from Bassano; but the botanist and the mountaineer will prefer a rather more arduous sheep-track that ascends the steep S. face of the mountain from Crespano. The summit commands a considerable Alpine panorama to the N., but the chief interest of the view is in the opposite direction, as this summit overlooks the greater part of the plain of Venetia, and there is no other point so well situated for a general view of the lagoons, which in clear weather are seen as though laid out upon a map. The Monte Cesen, rising on the E. side of the Piave, is at about the same distance from Venice; but it is lower by at least 700 ft.

The shortest way from the summit of the Grappa to Feltre is to keep nearly due N. until you descend into the head of the *Val di Seren*, a long glen running a little E. of N., and drained by the *Stizzone* torrent. Thenceforward a track leads along that stream. The *Stizzone* is the chief of the torrents which, uniting near Feltre, form the Sonna. On reaching the village of *Seren* (1,268'), near the opening of the glen, where the stream turns eastward towards Feltre, the traveller may follow a track by the rt. bank, but it is a shorter course to cross to the opposite bank, and there join the high-road, at a point nearly 5 m. from Feltre.

A notice of the road from Primolano to Feltre is found in the next Route.

Route E.

BASSANO TO PRIMIERO, BY PRIMOLANO AND FONZASO.

Carriage-road to Fonzaso, mule-track to Pontetto, carriage-road thence to Primiero.

	Eng. miles
Primolano	18½
Fonzaso	10½
Pontetto	10
Primiero	7
	46

The beautiful valley of Primiero must long since have acquired celebrity, were it not for the fact that it lies out of the track of ordinary tourists, and is comparatively difficult of access, especially from the S. side. The Austrian Government has recently achieved the construction of a military road from Predazzo in Val di Fiemme, which has opened the valley to travellers of every class; but even before this inducement had been offered, many English tourists had during the last few years been attracted towards one of the finest—in the writer's opinion the finest—valley of the Dolomite Alps. For the first introduction to Primiero, English travellers are indebted to the very interesting work of Messrs. Gilbert and Churchill, often referred to in the following sections. The mountaineer will desiderate further information as to the higher summits than he will find in that volume. It should be understood that although the most direct for travellers from the S. side, the route here described is the most difficult for nervous persons, unable to walk a few miles, owing to the steepness and roughness of the bridle-track between Fonzaso and the Tyrolese frontier. The way by Agordo, noticed in Rte. K, is doubtless easier.

At Primolano, where the road to Feltre leaves the main line for Val Sugana (Rte. A), the new road ascends by several long zigzags the very steep, but short, slope that leads up to the level of the broad valley which extends hence to Feltre, being the orographic prolongation of the valley of the Piave. The geologist will find it difficult to reconcile the actual course of the rivers here, as in many other parts of the Eastern Alps, with the views of those who refer the existing valleys and ridges mainly to subaërial erosive action. The new road is known as La Scala di Primolano, but the name *La Scala* was anciently given to an adjoining castle erected by the Scaligers, and now in ruins. Having attained the summit level at Fastro (1,160′), the road traverses undulating rocky ground, without any running stream in either direction, passes the village of Arsiè (1,076′), and descends about 150 ft. to cross the Cismone. This river, after issuing from the defile above Fonzaso, mentioned below, traverses the broad valley, and escapes southward through the still narrower defile from which it flows out at Cismone (Rte. A). The road to Feltre is carried NE. for a short distance, and then turns due E., over the nearly level floor of the valley, which seems to be partly filled up by recent sedimentary deposits, either of marine or freshwater origin. Against the supposition of some geologists that the valley of the Piave from hence to Belluno was at one time a lake, it may be objected that the deposits of gravel which cover the surface, or remain in the form of terraces on the flanks of the valley, though sensibly level to the eye, are not truly horizontal. [From the point where the road to Fonzaso leaves the main line the distance to Feltre is about 8 m. A little way beyond *Arten* the Stizzone descends from the Grappa into the valley, and turns eastward. After receiving several minor torrents it assumes below Feltre the name Sonna, and finally joins the Piave near *Sanzan* (737′).]

The diligence from Primolano to Feltre usually makes the detour of about 1½ m. by *Fonzaso* (1,032′), a large and thriving village, with a poor country inn (Sant' Antonio), and another (Angelo), which perhaps deserves a preference. Fonzaso stands at the very base of the steep stony slopes of the Monte d' Avena, which produce a strong, rather rough, wine, for which there is much demand.

There is a road, passable for a light *carrettina*, from Fonzaso to *Lamon* (2,060′), a village above the rt. bank of the Cismone, only 6 m. from the Tyrolese frontier. By writing, or sending beforehand to Primiero, a vehicle may be found in readiness at the frontier to carry travellers to that place. But the track from Lamon crosses the ravine of the Cismone, thereby involving a long descent and ascent, and besides this the Italian customs authorities require that luggage should pass by the frontier station at Zorzoi. The consequence is that nearly all the traffic passes by the l. bank of the Cismone, and the so-called Via dello Schener from Zorzoi to Pontett. It is not easy to find mules suitable for ladies at Fonzaso, and the way is in part so rough that they do better to walk if possible. The best course for those who cannot do so, is to write beforehand to Primiero to order one or more horses from the landlord of the Aquila Nera. Each horse may go in harness with a *carrettina* (a small vehicle carrying two passengers and the driver) as far as the frontier, and be used with a saddle between that place and Fonzaso. Bonetti, the landlord above mentioned, promises to have in future at least one side-saddle for lady visitors. On leaving Fonzaso, the pedestrian should not attempt to take the track close by the l. bank of the Cismone, but follow the narrow and rough char-road along the slope of the hill, till in less than 1 m. he enters a gorge enclosed between steep rocks, whereon *Phyteuma comosum* grows abundantly. The gorge soon opens out, and before long the road descends towards a new bridge over the Cismone, whence it ascends to Lamon. The way to Zorzoi keeps to the E. side of the valley, and mounts from near the bridge to a point about 1,800 ft. in elevation, whence the traveller gains for the first time a general view of the surrounding mountains. It is seen that the basin extending northward for 3 or 4 m., was at a comparatively recent period filled to a great depth (at least 500 ft.) with drift and alluvial gravel, and that since that period the Cismone, and other minor streams, have cut deep ravines through this incoherent deposit. The presence of erratic blocks from the head of the valleys of the Cismone and Vanoi on the surface of the plateau shows that the glacier, which must have once filled the lower valley, failed to clear away, or to excavate deeply, the deposit over which it had advanced.

The traveller very soon has practical experience of the results of the geological operations here referred to. The Ausore torrent, descending from the Vette di Feltre, crosses his route, and necessitates a steep descent by a vile stony path, and an ascent of nearly 700 ft. to reach the village of *Sorriva* (1,982'). This is particularly trying to beasts of burthen, and the greater part of an hour is here consumed in performing a distance not exceeding ½ m. in a straight line. From Sorriva to *Zorzoi* is a very pleasant walk over the level plateau, with fine views of the surrounding mountains, and occasional glimpses of the deep trench excavated by the Cismone. The mountain on the opposite side of the valley, rising N. of Lamon is *Monte Coppolo*, sometimes visited by botanists, but its flora is not comparable for variety to that of the Vette di Feltre, of which some summits are seen at no great distance on the rt. *Zorzoi* is the last village on the Italian side of the frontier, and therefore the customs station. It has a very poor *osteria*. The diluvial plateau, over which the track has passed for some distance, has been excavated by torrents, and disappears as the valley north of Zorzoi gradually contracts to a defile. The track mounts gently along the slope of the mountain, and is then carried nearly at a level for a considerable distance. Nearly at the highest point reached by the path it passes the ruined tower of *Schener*, once used for levying toll from passengers, which has given its name to this road. The path is not bad, but as it is rather narrow, and often carried along precipitous rocks, almost overhanging the bed of the Cismone, nervous persons are not comfortable in riding over it. Near Schener the track from Lamon mounts to join our route. A stream descending from the rt. has cut a deep trench in the side of the mountain, and the path is forced to make a considerable circuit, and thenceforward with some undulations descends towards the level of the Cismone. The scenery is throughout charming. For some time the traveller has before him the *Monte Tatoga*, shaped like a gigantic wedge, and cut off from the mountains on either side by a deep cleft. Through that on its W. side flows the Vanoi, descending from Caoria (Rte. H), while the Cismone washes its eastern base. About ½ m. above the junction of the two streams the path, keeping always to the l. bank of the Cismone, reaches the frontier, called Pontetto, from a small stone bridge over a torrent descending through a ravine on the rt. hand. There is a wretched *osteria* on the Italian side; but, on crossing the bridge, the traveller finds a well-built house kept by a guardaboschi. Since the separation of Venetia from Austria the house was occupied by custom-house officers, but in 1868 they are removed to another house, and a stranger may count on finding tolerable accommodation, and much civility from the landlord.

On reaching the Tyrolese frontier the traveller is surprised to find an excellent road, completed in 1866, leading from this point to Primiero. Unfortunately there is little prospect of the road being continued along the much more difficult ground intervening between this and Fonzaso. With the passage of the international boundary ensues a change in the character of the scenery. The defile opens out somewhat, and allows space for the road along the l. bank of the stream. Huge erratic blocks of porphyry are perched on the steep slopes, composed of fine angular fragments of dolomitic limestone, and when detached from their resting-places by rain or frost, roll down into the bed of the Cismone. For about 2 m. the road follows the l. bank, about due N., a small church on a lofty pinnacle of Monte Tatoga being here a conspicuous object. After crossing the Cismone by a new stone bridge the road turns to NE., and the valley of Primiero opens out before the traveller. The principal group of dolomite peaks is not immediately seen; but the summits enclosing the head of Val Noana, rising above the intervening range of Monte Tase, are already attractive objects. Passing the first group of houses, called *Tauferi*, whence the beaten track to Canal di San Bovo (Rte. G) ascends to cross the ridge of the Gobera, the road soon reaches *Imer*, the first of the group of villages that make up the district of Primiero. This stands opposite the opening of Val Noana, a remarkable glen, further noticed among the excursions in this neighbourhood. It should be observed that among the people of the valley the name Primiero is employed collectively for the entire district, and that the application of that name to the chief village, though general among strangers, is not sanctioned by local usage.

A short way beyond Imer is the second village, called *Mezzano*. Here, and throughout the valley, the stranger is struck by the appearance of comfort and prosperity which seems universal among the population. Though surrounded by barren mountains, there is a moderate breadth of good land in the bottom of the valley, whereon heavy crops of maize are annually raised. Of course the chief reliance of the population is on their dairy stock; and Primiero butter is advantageously known in Venice, and other Italian cities. The road winds round the base of the mountain on the l. hand, and then approaches the banks of the rushing Cismone; but it is only when within a few hundred yards' distance that the traveller gains a view of the slender pointed spire that marks the chief village of the valley, locally known as

La Fiera (2,349′). The traveller will find good quarters and attention at the Aquila, kept by Bonetti, surnamed Moro —charges not unreasonable, but not so cheap as a few years ago. He must not expect in this remote place all the appliances of advanced civilisation, but will find several clean and comfortable rooms, and tolerably good and abundant food.

A party intending to remain here some weeks might probably arrange for board and lodging on economical terms. There is another inn on the opposite or W. side of the main street, kept by a family, also named Bonetti, whose delinquencies are chronicled in Messrs. Gilbert and Churchill's book. As they have since suffered by seeing all English visitors go to the rival house, the writer is inclined to believe in the sincerity of their repentance, and promises of amendment.

Primiero was celebrated in the 15th and 16th centuries for its silver mine, long since exhausted. The only evidence remaining of its former wealth is a massive silver remonstrance, 2 ft. in height, presented by the miners to the parish church. This is worth a visit, being a characteristic specimen of early German pointed architecture. Opposite to La Fiera, on the E. side of the Cismone, is the village of *Transacqua*, with the adjoining hamlet of Ormanico. The parish church contains a picture of St. Mark, of which the head has been attributed to Titian.

Iron mines are still worked at Primicro; but the increasing cost of fuel, and the expense of carriage in a valley not accessible by wheel vehicles, has interfered with their prosperity.

A short description of the valley, and a notice of some excursions not included among the following routes, may be acceptable. Further information will be found in a lively article by Mr. Leslie Stephen in the 4th vol. of the 'Alpine Journal.'

The *Valley of Primiero*, from the base of Monte Tatoga to Siror and Tonadico, the highest villages, is enclosed on either side by comparatively low, rounded, pine-covered ridges. That on the NW. side is formed of crystalline slate, and at one point, not far from the track to Canale, granite makes its appearance on the surface. The opposite ridge, collectively called Monte Tase, is partly formed of limestone, and partly of red porphyry, which forms the rugged mass rising E. of Transacqua. Immediately above the village of La Fiera the valley divides. The main branch of the Cismone, descending from nearly due N., receives a torrent from the NE., issuing from *Val di Canale*. In the fork between these two branches rises the wonderful group of dolomite peaks, which must ever make this one of the most extraordinary of mountain valleys. Whatever fantastic forms that rock may assume elsewhere, they are here surpassed in boldness and strangeness. Of the five or six highest, all much exceeding 10,000 ft. in height, there is but one at all easy of access. The others are either mere towers or obelisks of rock, with sheer vertical faces, or else, as the highest peak, fashioned like a ruinous wall, abruptly broken away at one end, and cleft at frequent intervals along the ridge by chasms that appear perfectly impassable. In rock-climbing it is never safe to declare any place impracticable without actual trial. Narrow ledges and clefts often give footing on a seemingly impracticable declivity. The writer's impression as to the inaccessibility of the Primiero peaks, though confirmed by several of the most experienced mountaineers, has been falsified by the successful ascent of two of the highest. As most of the higher summits lie nearly in a line from N. to S., they are not seen to advantage from Primiero. One alone —the *Sas Maor*, the southernmost of the group—suffices to rivet the attention of the beholder. A much lower summit, the Cima Cimedo, which may be likened to a massive buttress, adorned by hundreds of pinnacles, stands between the spectator and the Sas Maor; but as the latter towers above it to a vast height, the general effect is rather increased than otherwise. There is no satisfactory information, or at least none published, respecting the height of these summits. There can be no doubt whatever that the

Cimon della Pala, partly seen from Primiero, at the head of the main valley on the rt. hand, is the highest peak. The measurement of the Austrian 'Kataster' is 10,643 ft.; while the height attributed on the same authority to the *Palle di San Martino*, not visible from Primiero, is 10,969 ft. It is possible that the error here arises from a transposition of names, as on that supposition the figures correspond pretty well with the relative height of those summits. The *Cima di Fradusta*, SE. of the Palle di S. Martino, is about the same height, while a broad topped summit farther E., seen from Primiero above the Val di Canale, may be a few feet higher. The summit E. of the head of Val di Canale, is the *Croda Grande* (Sasso di Campo of some maps), 9,091 ft. in height, according to the Kataster, but higher by 700 or 800 ft. The *Sas Maor* falls somewhat below the highest of its companions, but the height of 8,323 ft., given in the second edition of Schaubach, is ludicrously below the mark, as it cannot fall much below the limit of 10,000 ft. Some dolomite peaks which elsewhere would attract attention rise above the head of Val Noana, locally called *Val Asinozza*. The highest is apparently that called, *par excellence*, *Il Piz*. In the opposite direction, about due W. of Primiero, rises the granitic mass of the Cima d'Asta (Rte. H), which comes into view whenever the traveller rises high enough to overlook the ridge bounding the valley on that side. It is strange that the popular belief in the supremacy of that peak extends even to the people who live at the foot of much loftier summits.

Few places offer a greater variety of interesting excursions than Primiero. Strangers must not expect to find here professional guides. Travellers contemplating ambitious excursions must bring competent guides with them. Of the local men the best is probably Giuseppe Brentel. An old man, nicknamed Moidele, who is sometimes recommended to strangers, knows the country, but is unable to keep up with even the most moderate pace. Two hunters, both named Colesel, also deserve mention. One of them, designated Colesel Rosso, is very useful as a porter. He is stunted and unprepossessing in appearance, but honest, and very strong, and will carry 50 or 60 lbs. of luggage, day after day, over rough ground, not expecting more than 2 florins daily. The men hereabouts are used to carry heavy weights, and an older man who acts as carrier between Primiero and Fonzaso may be trusted to carry the same burden between those places.

The inevitable excursion from Primiero, a mere stroll, is that to the castle of La Pietra, noticed in Rte. K. A slight detour to a plain square shooting-lodge standing near the entrance to Val di Canale, will give some idea of the scenery of that singular glen. This is the residence of Count Welsberg, the present representative of a very ancient Tyrolese family, once lords of the entire valley.

An excursion highly to be recommended, which is within reach of very moderate walkers, is that to *Val Noana*. The lower part, for a distance of about 1 hr. from its opening opposite Imer, is a defile of the grandest character. About 2 hrs. farther the Noana torrent receives an affluent descending from the Alpe di Neva, where there is a large dairy establishment. This lies but a short way from the *Passo della Finestra*, over which a circuitous track leads to Feltre. The main glen, above the junction of the Neva, is called *Val Asinozza* a wild recess, enclosed at its head by the bare dolomite rocks of Il Piz and Monte Asinozza. The best way to visit Val Noana is to enter it by a rough cart-track recently made for the carriage of timber and charcoal, connected with the main road through the valley of Primiero by a bridge near Mezzano. The track is carried for some way close to the Noana torrent, in the jaws of the defile. This begins to open out when Val Noana turns to NE., parallel to that of Primiero. If not anxious to reach the Neva Alp, and the Passo della Finestra, the traveller will do well to take the first track to the l., and mount the ridge of Monte Tase, keeping, however, to the Noana side of that ridge, till he has passed the junction of its two upper branches. Rather beyond the point where it would appear expedient to strike NNW. across the ridge of Monte Tase, in order to return to Primiero, he will find a well-made track, carried nearly at a level for a considerable distance up Val Asinozza, at a great height above the torrent. The alp at the head of that glen is devoted exclusively to sheep, and the mountaineer's mid-day luxuries, milk and butter, are not to be found. Returning over the ridge of Monte Tase fine views are gained of the Cima d'Asta, and part of the Primiero dolomites. A guide is almost necessary for this excursion, as most of the paths on Monte Tase are very faintly traced, excepting one leading to Mezzano.

§ 59. VALLEY OF THE BRENTA.

Another excursion, recommended to moderate walkers, is to ascend westward from *Siror* (the last village on the Cismone, less than 1 m. from La Fiera) to the little *Lake of Calaita* (about 6,000'?). This rests on a small plateau, drained by a torrent that runs SW. through the *Val di Lozem* to join the Vanoi near the village of Canale (Rte. G). The traveller may follow the track along the torrent to Prade, returning to Primiero by the Gobera; but he will gain finer views by following the ridge dividing Primiero from Lozem, and thence descending to Mezzano. The interest of this excursion will be much increased by ascending from the Lake of Calaita to the summit of *Monte Arzon* (about 8,700'?), a mountain nearly due W. of Primiero, equidistant between the great dolomite peaks, the Cima d' Asta, and the porphyry range forming the boundary of the Fiemme district.

An excursion of the highest interest, strongly recommended to all tourists, but especially to the botanist, is the ascent of the *Pavione*, or *Col di Luna** (7,877'), the highest summit of the *Vette di Feltre*. This, which is the summit seen to the rt. in viewing the Vette from Primiero, may be reached from Feltre or Fonzaso; but the interest of the expedition is much increased by following the course here suggested. It is rather a long day's walk for moderate pedestrians, but fair quarters for the night are found at the Agnerola Malga, of which the botanist will not fail to avail himself, if he would gain necessary time for gathering the many rare plants found on the mountain.

From the SW. end of the craggy range of the Vette di Feltre extends to NW. a broad rounded ridge, partly covered with pine forest, partly green with Alpine pasture and mountain meadows, cut off on three sides by deep valleys, above which it rises in steep cliffs. This is the *Monte Vederne*, under whose W. and N. faces the new road is carried from Pontetto to Imer. Its eastern face overlooks the deep gorge of the Noana mentioned above. The direct way from Primiero is by a track through the fields from Mezzano, leading to a bridge over the Cismone immediately below the junction of the Noana torrent. A beaten track, known as Strada della Vederne, begins to ascend through pine forest close to the bridge, and after reaching an oratory about 1,000 ft. above the torrent, is carried southward above the gorge of the Noana. The way is throughout very beautiful, and there seems to be no reason why ladies should not ride as far as the Agnerola Alp, dismounting at one or two awkward places. Rather more than 1 hr. from the foot of the mountain the track is joined by a goat-track which mounts directly from the gorge of the Noana, and that course is recommended to active pedestrians not already acquainted with the grand scenery of the defile below. A little farther a point is reached where the wall of rock overhead forms a semicircular enclosure and a little streamlet springing over the edge falls into a basin. The obstacle is surmounted by a wooden gallery supported on beams driven into the rock: for a few minutes the way lies through a rocky cleft, and then emerges on a slope of fine mountain meadow. *Echinospermum deflexum* grows near the gallery, and many other rare plants are seen by the way. A short ascent through pine forest now leads to the green pastures that cover the ridge of the mountain. A little to the rt. is the *casera of Agnerola* (5,147'). This offers better accommodation than usual in such places, having a bedstead full of clean dry hay, separated from the common room by a

---

* The name Col di Luna has been supposed to indicate a pass, from the word Col being taken in the sense it commonly bears, derived from the local dialects of the Western Alps. In this region it must be understood to be the Venetian form of the Italian word *Colle*—hill or mountain. It recurs frequently in the Venetian Alps, and the Italian Tyrol; and if it has anywhere got into use to indicate a pass, it is only in the same sense as many passes in Switzerland and Savoy are designated by the word Mont: e.g. Mont Cenis, Mont Genèvre, Mont St. Gothard.

partition. When not required by the owner, who sometimes comes to visit the establishment, this is at the disposal of strangers. About 150 cows are pastured here, and the services of six or eight men are required; yet there is no drinkable water near at hand, and one of the men daily descends a distance of 1 hr., and remounts laden with a small barrel of the precious liquid. The position of the Agnerola Alp is charming, and an evening is pleasantly spent in breathing the pure air and enjoying the view, unless the traveller prefer to seek rare plants at the base of the rocks of the Pavione. This rises SE. of the alp in the form of a pyramid, girdled by two steep rocky belts that from a distance seem difficult of access. Below the lower range of rocks is a declivity clothed with pine forest, and in part with *Pinus mughus.*

The ascent of the peak, though sufficiently steep, does not offer the slightest difficulty. There is no need to make a considerable detour to the rt., as counselled by the herdsmen. Keeping but a little to the left of the straight course, any one used to mountain climbing will reach the summit in about 2 hrs. from the *casera.*

The view is at once varied and extensive. The coast of the Adriatic from Chioggia beyond Venice to the mouth of the Isonzo, is better seen than from any other Alpine summit, excepting, perhaps, the Monte Cavallo (§ 63, Rte. I). The dolomite peaks of Primiero are not seen to the best advantage, but the supremacy of the Cimon della Pala over his nearer rivals here admits of no doubt. Most of the higher summits of Cadore may be distinguished, along with many a minor peak not to be identified without minute local knowledge.

This mountain is known to botanists as one of those in the range of the Alps that produces the richest harvest of rare plants. A few of these only can be enumerated here:—*Anemone baldensis* and *A. narcissiflora, Ranunculus Seguieri* and *R. Thora, Delphinium montanum, Papaver pyrenaicum, Arabis pumila, Alyssum Wulfenianum, Cochlearia brevicaulis, Alsine lanceolata* and *A. graminifolia, Cerastium tomentosum* (this and the last on the rocks above Aune), *Phaca frigida* (highest peak), *Potentilla nitida, Saxifraga petræa, Valeriana elongata, Ptarmica oxyloba, Scorzonera purpurea, Pæderota Ageria* and *P. Bonarota, Pedicularis rosea, Primula Facchinii, Cortusa Matthioli* (abundant), and *Avena Hostii.* On rocks at the base of Monte Vederne may be gathered the rare *Asplenium Seelosii.*

In descending from the summit, various courses are offered to the traveller's choice. He may turn ENE. to the col (7,185′), between the Pavione and *Monte Pietina* (the next peak in the range of the Vette), and by a circuitous but agreeable track, known to the herdsmen, finally get down to the middle part of Val Noana. If bound for Feltre, the shortest and easiest way is to bear at first SE., then S., along the slopes of *Monte Lamen,* and finally, by going down steep grassy slopes, reach the col (3,472′) between Aune and *Pedevena* (1,206′). A beaten track leads from the col to the latter village, which is only 2 m. from Feltre. Whatever the traveller's destination may be, if he be a lover of extraordinary scenery, or a botanist, he should prefer to every other course the path to *Aune,* a small village lying in a recess at the SSW. side of the mountain, unless he choose to reverse the route here suggested, and ascend from that side. A little below the top, he should descend a rather long slope of steep debris (producing some of the rarest plants above enumerated), which leads to a stony hollow where there is one of the few springs of water to be found on the mountain. Thence the course lies westward, nearly at a level, and even ascending slightly above the rim of the formidable precipices, whose existence is not suspected till they are seen from below. The track leads to a *casera,* whence an easy path leads to the Agnerola Alp. If he be not accompanied by a local guide, one of the herdsmen should be engaged to put the traveller ou the path leading down the precipices to Aune. When once found, it is impossible for him to lose it, and further guidance is not needed. It will be some time before he will be aware of the formidable character of the precipices amongst which he is engaged. The path is carried to and fro along ledges and under overhanging rocks, so that it is impossible to guess what its ultimate direction may be. With many another scene of the kind present to his memory, the writer does not recollect any frequented path that surmounts such hopeless-looking precipices. Difficulty there is none; but at one point, unavoidable, though slight, danger is incurred for a few moments. The track passes at one place along the foot of a precipice, about 1,800 ft. in height, which actually overhangs its base. The cattle feeding on the slope above, sometimes set stones in motion that fall on, or close, to the path.*

If returning from Aune to Primiero, the traveller may take the beaten track by Servo to Zorzoi, or avoid the village of Aune, and follow a rough path along the N. side of the valley, till after many ups and downs, he descends in about 3 hrs from the summit to Zorzoi to rejoin the Schener track to Primiero.

Practised mountaineers who may halt for awhile at Primiero will naturally give some attention to the great dolomite peaks, which are its chief attraction. Such travellers usually select their own route, but it may be well to point out that the broken plateau, which on the NE. side seems to connect together the mass of the dolomite peaks, is accessible through the main branch of the Val di Canale (mentioned above), and from that side the Cima di Fradusta is accessible as well as from the side of Pravitali. There is no difficulty in passing along the plateau by the N. side of the Palle di San Martino to the Passo delle Cornelle (Rte. L), and so descending to San Martino di Castrozza and Primiero.

On the whole, the finest expedition for a moderate mountaineer, anxious to make acquaintance with the highest peaks of this district, is to ascend through the *Val di Pravitali* (misprinted Travitali in Mr. Stephen's paper in the 'Alpine Guide'). This is a singular gorge narrowed above to a mere cleft that is passed on the l. hand in ascending the Val di Canale. In about 4½ hrs. from Primiero the climber issues from the cleft upon a little grassy plain almost completely enclosed by lofty peaks. In one direction a small glacier leads up to the *Cima di Fradusta*, the most easily accessible of the Primiero peaks; to the S. rises another summit, hitherto nameless, now called Cima di Ball (probably about 10,000'), climbed by Mr. Stephen, separated by a deep trench from the Sas Maor. N. of the same spot is the *Palle di San Martino*, the third in height of this group, which has hitherto resisted all attempts to scale it. Mr. Stephen made a rather difficult descent from the col between the lastnamed and the Cima di Ball into the main branch of the valley above Siror; but on a subsequent occasion took a more interesting way over the rough plateau that stretches from the Fradusta to the Cimon della Pala, descending by the Passo delle Cornelle (Rte. L), to which he was led by the stone-man erected by Mr. Tuckett's guides.

---

* The writer is accustomed to believe that in such places the risk of injury is much diminished by carrying an open umbrella over his head.

Route F.

PRIMIERO TO PREDAZZO IN FIEMME, BY SAN MARTINO DI CASTROZZA.

A new char-road now open for traffic.

	Hrs. walking
San Martino di Castrozza	3½
Paneveggio	3
Predazzo	3
	9½

Since the opening of the road to Primiero from the Val di Fiemme, that way is naturally chosen by travellers arriving from the N. side. Although the whole distance is easily accomplished in one day, it is a better plan to halt at Paneveggio and enjoy the charming walks that are found in the neighbourhood. If the accommodation at San Martino di Castrozza were improved, all mountaineers would select that place as head-quarters for expeditions among the higher peaks.

As mentioned in the last Rte., the upper end of the valley of the Cismone, sometimes called *Val di Castrozza*, stretches for about 12 m. nearly due N. from its junction with the Val di Canale. Beyond the village of *Siror*, standing at the lower end, less than 1 m. above La Fiera, there are scarcely any permanent dwellings in the valley. On the east side the steep slopes at the base of the great range of dolomite peaks are mostly covered with forest, save where landslips, avalanches, or torrents, have torn away the surface, and exposed the soil, composed of comminuted fragments of dolomite. On the opposite side the slope is rather less steep, but is also to a great extent covered with forest. The shortest way to Siror is by the path that is carried along the l. bank of the Cismone from the bridge at La Fiera. The path above Siror by the E. side of the valley leads directly to San Martino, but the new road ascends along the opposite side above the rt. bank of the torrent. This way is rather longer, but rewards the traveller by noble views of the great peaks that tower above the valley.

San Martino di Castrozza (4,912') is an ancient hospice, formerly belonging to a religious community, now leased to a farmer, whose numerous family and farm-servants occupy a large part of the building. Another part is reserved for a priest, who officiates here in summer, so that the space available for travellers is very limited. There is but a single separate bed-room, comfortless and ill-lighted, and meals are taken in the common close and crowded room which serves for the inmates and passing wayfarers. A single woman, one of the family, cooks for and waits upon all, and though she does all in her power for strangers, the result is discomfort and privation. This is the more unfortunate as there are few spots in the Alps more thoroughly enjoyable in fine weather, or where a few days might be passed so agreeably, if a moderate share of creature-comforts were to be found. The new road passes about 100 yards from the hospice, and the drivers halt there. Of the many excursions that might be made from San Martino, we may here mention the Passo delle Cornelle, noticed in Rte. L, and those to the Lakes of Colbricon, and to the Monte Castellazzo, mentioned below. On no account should the traveller fail to gain the wonderful view of the dolomite peaks which is obtained from the heights on the W. side of the valley. The most favourable point is probably a summit (Monte Tognazzo) which may be reached in ½ hr. from the Tognola Alp. (Rte. H.)

The valley of the Cismone extends for about 1 hr. above San Martino to the base of a massive wall of rock that bars the valley across. At its E. end this abuts against the base of the Cimon della Pala, while on the l. hand it is divided by a narrow gap from the Monte Cavalazzo. The road winds up the E. slope of the latter mountain to the plateau that lies between it and the head of Val Travignolo. This highland tract is locally known as *La Costonzella*, which name is given to the pass. As the ground is perfectly easy, the pedestrian need not keep near to the road. If pressed for time he may take a path passing by the Casera di Rolle, or else bear to the rt. over swelling pastures. The views are already very fine, but no traveller having an hour to spare should omit to make a slight detour in order to approach the base of the *Cimon della Pala*. This may best be described as a shattered wall of dolomite, about 11,000 ft. in height. When seen from the S. and SW., the crest shows as a broken ridge, cut into teeth by deep chasms, surmounting a broad and nearly vertical face of rock. But from the NE. side scarcely anything is in view save the extremity of the wall, surmounted by two enormous coping-stones, in the shape of masses of unshattered rock, each several hundred ft. in height. The uppermost is pyramid-shaped at the top; but the point visible from this side is certainly not the highest. To see it to full advantage the traveller should bear to the rt. from the track to Paneveggio, and ascend to the upper part of the plateau, above the wall of rock that bars the head of Val di Castrozza, overlooking a savage hollow through which the drainage of the snow-beds, and of two small glaciers, descends to Val Travignolo. Involuntarily the Alpine traveller will compare this with the most sublime scenes of a similar character to be found elsewhere in the Alps, and especially with the view of the Matterhorn from the ridge of the Hörnli. The height of the two peaks from the apparent base is about equal, but the Cimon is undeniably the more slender, and, so to say, the more incredible of the two. Daring as is the form of the Matterhorn, it suggests the idea of stability; whereas it is easy to conceive that a trifling accident, the yielding of a single stone in its masonry, might set this gigantic fabric toppling over into utter ruin. It is needless to say that the absence of great glaciers, and extensive snow-fields, makes the general character of the view very different.

The mountaineer who does not object to rough ground may follow the stream through the above-mentioned hollow till he strikes the path leading from the Venigia Pass to Paneveggio (§ 60, Rte. E). The shorter and easier way is to return to the track which was left near the summit-level, 6,657 ft. in height.

The scenery of *Val Travignolo*, towards which the track now descends, offers a striking contrast to that which has been so recently left behind. The easily disintegrated porphyry rock, which here prevails, forms mountains with rounded outlines, whose slopes are covered with extensive pine forests. In 3 hrs. from San Martino the traveller will easily reach *Paneveggio* (5,160'). A large building here, originally constructed as a hospice on the same plan as that of San Martino, has, like it, passed into the hands of a family of peasants. The house has of late been partly rebuilt, and supplies very fair accommodation for a few travellers.

Val Travignolo—one of the chief lateral valleys of Val di Fiemme—is further noticed in § 60, Rte. E. An easy walk of 3 hrs. leads from Paneveggio to Predazzo in Fiemme.

There is another route, a little shorter, but much rougher, than that above described, between San Martino di Castrozza and Paneveggio. Turning westward from the hospice along the S. side of a large meadow, the traveller will easily find a broad track that mounts gradually to NW. through pine-forest till it reaches a large *casera*, lying in a hollow traversed by a slender rivulet. This leads up to another higher and much wilder stony basin, partly filled by fragments of rock fallen from the surrounding heigths. The track keeps the bottom of the hollow, and then mounts the ridge at its upper end, forming the water-shed between the Cismone and the Travignolo. This is the *Passo di Colbricon*. Several small lakes or Alpine tarns lie in hollows of the mountain on the right of the pass. This is incorrectly represented in all the ordinary maps, where the track is made to pass by the lakes. To reach the lowest and largest of these it is necessary to turn sharply to the rt. from the summit of the pass, and cross some rough ground. Keeping onward through the forest below, and E. of the lake—a haunt of the cock of the woods, now rare in this district—it is easy to reach the Casera di Rolle, and return that way to San Martino. The beaten track from the Colbricon pass leads by Paneveggio to Predazzo, but there is a rather shorter way, avoiding Paneveggio, and following for some distance the l. bank of the Travignolo.

Travellers bound for the Val di Fassa may follow a mountain track from Paneveggio to Moena, and enjoy glorious views by the way.

For excursions from Paneveggio see § 60, Rte. E.

Route G.

BORGO DI VAL SUGANA TO PRIMIERO, BY CANALE DI SAN BOVO.

Carriage-road to Pieve di Tesin, about 9 m.; thence to Primiero 7½ hrs.

Although this involves a longer ride, or walk, than the route to Primiero by Fonzaso (Rte. E), it is perhaps to be preferred by nervous persons, as the track is throughout safe and tolerably easy. In spite of the necessity of crossing three ridges, one of them being of considerable height, much traffic passes this way, especially since the separation of Venetia from Tyrol. It is not uncommon to meet trains of mules laden with wine, and other produce of the warm region, bound for the Canal di S. Bovo and Primiero. In approaching Primiero by this way from Bassano, it is expedient to engage a vehicle at Primolano for La Pieve di Tesin (4 to 5 fl. with one horse); unless the traveller prefer to mount on foot through the gorge of the Grigno.

Starting from Borgo there is a direct road from Castelnovo to Strigno, but in approaching from the south side the high-road is left at the Barricate. (Rte. A.)

Strigno (1,491′) is a well-built village, with every appearance of comparative wealth and comfort. It has lately been connected by a new and tolerably good road with the valley of Tesin. This winds up the hill above Strigno, leaving to the N. the old steep track, and finally gains the ridge (about 3,000′) that divides the valley of Tesin from Val Sugana. A gentle descent leads to the principal village of the former valley, called

La Pieve di Tesin (2,862′). The inn (al Sole) is of humble and unprepossessing appearance, but there is a pretty good room on the second floor, and the traveller will find tolerable food, civility, and very moderate charges.

The population of Tesin is concentrated in three villages, La Pieve, *Castello* (on the l. bank of the Grigno torrent), and *Cinte*, a little below La Pieve, on the rt. bank. In the last century, when the Remondini printing-office in Bassano was one of the most considerable in Europe, some natives of this valley undertook the business of selling books and coloured prints in foreign countries. Starting as hawkers, they spread themselves over Europe, and many of them established shops in Germany, Russia, and elsewhere. In course of time other branches of trade were added, and although this sort of adventure is less fortunate in the present day, it has not ceased. Many people of Tesin still seek to gain a living in distant countries, and some return with an independence to close their days in their native valley, or in the milder climate of the adjoining Val Sugana. The name *Tesin* properly belongs only to the open basin at the lower end, where the above-named villages stand on the *scaglia* (indurated marl of the chalk period), with some traces of overlying eocene beds. It will be observed that the depression over which the road from Strigno reaches Tesin extends in the opposite direction (or ESE.) to Lamon, in the valley of the Cismone, and thence to Fonzaso; while the *Grigno* torrent, which drains the valley, runs due S. through a narrow cleft in a lofty mass of dolomite rock to Grigno in Val Sugana (Rte. A). By that way, but at a great height above the stream, runs the mule-track to Primolano.

Above La Pieve the Grigno soon enters the granitic region, whose centre is the Cima d' Asta, and the valley is called *Val Malene*, until, a few miles farther N., it divides into the two glens of Tolvà and Sorgazzo (Rte. H).

The way to Canal di S. Bovo and Primiero is known as La Strada del Brocon. It is necessary to descend from La Pieve to the rather deep trough which the torrent has excavated in the scaglia, and then follow a rough cart-road along the opposite or l. bank of the stream, gradually ascending until, nearly 1 hr. from La Pieve, the track turns NE., away from the valley, and commences the long ascent leading to the pass. The path winds in snake-like fashion along the slopes some way N. of the summit of *Monte Agaro*, crossing several minor ridges. Not far from the summit refreshments may be found at the Osteria del Brocon. From the summit level of the *Brocon* (5,994') a great part of the Primiero valley is seen over the ridge of the Gobera. The first village reached is *Ronco*, whence the track descends to cross the Vanoi; then mounting the opposite bank, in the fork between that stream and the torrent from Val di Lozem—in 5½ hrs. from La Pieve—the traveller reaches

Canale (about 2,340'), the principal village in the valley of the Vanoi, locally known as *Canal di San Bovo*. The inn here has been improved and enlarged.

If Primiero may be truly called a secluded valley because of the badness of the track leading from Zorzoi, the same epithet may still more justly be applied to that of San Bovo. The portion extending from Canale to the junction of the Vanoi with the Cismone may be said to be practically impassable. A wood-cutter's track along the steep flank of Monte Tatoga is considered to be dangerous, and there is not, or was not lately, any bridge whereby to cross either stream near their junction. There is a track by the rt. bank of the Vanoi; but it is crossed by several unbridged torrents, impassable after rain, and is besides so rough and bad that it is never used save by the inhabitants of two or three scattered houses, or by an occasional smuggler. Communication with Feltre, and with Primiero, is carried on exclusively by the track crossing the ridge of La Gobera, while the only moderately easy way from the W. is that of the Brocon. For several months in each year these passes lie deep in snow, and exposed to the severity of winter blasts.

The upper part of the Canale di San Bovo is described in Rte. H.

The track from Canale to Primiero passes by *Prade*, only ½ m. from the former villages, at the opening of Val di Lozem. Here commences the ascent of the *Gobera* (3,340'). This is a depression in the range that bounds the valley of the Cismone on the W. side, corresponding nearly to the junction of the dolomite of Monte Tatoga with the crystalline slates. The top of the pass is only about 1,000 ft. above the valley on either side. In 1½ hr. from Canale the traveller reaches *Tauferi*, also called Masi di Imer, and may descend directly to Imer, following a terrace path to the l. that with a slight descent leads to *La Ficra*, the chief village of Primiero.

The pedestrian, who can afford a détour of 2 or 3 hrs., instead of keeping the ordinary track, should follow the torrent from Prade through Val di Lozem to its source in the Lago di Calaita; and in descending to Siror will enjoy a grand view of the opposite range of dolomite peaks. (See Rte. E.)

Route H.

SAN MARTINO DI CASTROZZA TO BORGO DI VAL SUGANA. ASCENT OF THE CIMA D' ASTA.

The shortest way in time, if not in distance, from the head of the Cismone valley to Borgo di Val Sugana is no doubt that by Primiero, and by the beaten track passing Canale and Tesin, described in the last Rte. The mountaineer will, however, prefer to take on his way the ascent of the Cima d'Asta, the crowning summit of the granitic region on the N. side of Val Sugana. If the height and importance of this mountain have been exaggerated in popular estimation, it yet undoubtedly offers one of the finest panoramic views in this part of the Alps, some fine rugged scenery in its middle region, and some special interest to the geologist and mineralogist.

The glen leading to the *Passo di Tognola* (6,654?), over which a moderately frequented track goes from San Martino di Costrozza to Canale di San Bovo, is well seen to the SW. from the neighbourhood of the hospice, and is marked by a large *casera*, standing on the summit of the pass. The only precaution necessary to find the way is to be careful to cross from the l. to the rt. bank of the torrent descending from the pass by a bridge which will be found a little below the junction of another stream issuing from a more northerly branch of the glen. This latter glen leads also to Caoria, but involves a circuit of $1\frac{1}{2}$ m. In the damp wood through which the torrent brawls, the botanist will notice some British plants not common in the Southern Alps, such as *Comarum palustre* and *Pedicularis palustris*, with others less rare here, but prized by the British collector, e. g. *Moneses grandiflora, Goodyera repens, Carex capillaris,* and *Polypodium rhæticum*. Soon after the forest comes to an end the traveller reaches the pass, whereon stands the large Casera di Tognola. The views of the dolomite range are very limited if the pedestrian has kept to the path, but a summit easily reached in $\frac{1}{2}$ h. from the *casera* (Cima di Tognazzo?) offers a magnificent view when the peaks are uncovered. The descent on the SW. side lies through *Val Sorda*, a glen inhabited only by a few herdsmen in summer. The upper end is rather dreary, but some fine scenery is traversed during the descent. On reaching the base of the slopes on the l. side of the valley it is advisable to cross to the rt. bank, where the torrent is swollen by the drainage of a boggy tract. After a considerable descent the track passes a *casera*, deserted during the hot season, and soon after seems to come to an end on the rt. bank, in a place where farther progress is impossible. A wooden bridge has been swept away, and (in 1867) its place was supplied merely by a single trunk thrown across the stream, with the untrimmed stumps of the branches sticking out in all directions. A good track is now carried along the l. bank, but soon rises to a great height above the stream. At one place, in the midst of a pine-wood, a path descends steeply towards the torrent, and leads to Caoria by the bottom of the valley. The upper track is, on the whole, to be preferred; it mounts gradually above a wide slope of mountain meadow, and then runs nearly at a level along the brow of the mountain, till the traveller finds himself on a considerable eminence above the Canale di San Bovo, immediately above its highest village. *Caoria* (2,711′). The traveller, whose expectations should be slender on reaching a spot so completely out of the way of all traffic, will be surprised to find at the house of Lorenzo Pezza, a prosperous inhabitant of the valley, a clean and comfortable inn, a hospitable reception from the host and his daughters, with extremely moderate charges. Butcher's meat is not common in such a place; but fowls, eggs, fresh butter, and potatoes, ought to satisfy his wants. Trout from the neighbouring lake sometimes complete the entertainment. Caoria is connected with Canale (see last Rte.), about 5 m. distant, by a narrow but tolerable road, which is continued some way up the valley, in the opposite direction, for the conveyance of timber, charcoal, butter, and other produce of the neighbouring mountains.

At the head of the valley, the principal source of the Vanoi, rising on the W. side of the Cima d'Asta, flows to NE., and curves gradually so as to describe a semicircle round the N. side of that mountain. The uppermost segment is called *Val Cia*; the next portion, for about 5 m. above Caoria, is called Val Caoria; and it is only below that village, where it takes a nearly direct course to SSE., that the valley assumes the name *Canal di San Bovo*. The traveller will be surprised to behold a large lake, more than a mile in length, lying half-way in the valley between Caoria and Canale, which is not to be found (so far as the writer knows) on any map, and is not mentioned in guide-books, even so recent and so complete as the second edition of Schaubach.* It owes its origin to a series of great landslips, which commenced in 1819, reached a climax in 1823, and continued with diminished force during several subsequent years. The debris borne down from the flanks of the valley dammed the stream of the Vanoi, and formed the lake. A flood, accompanying the berg-fall of 1823 quite destroyed Canale di Sopra, enumerated by Schaubach among the existing villages of the valley.

A chamois hunter of Caoria (name forgotten), well acquainted with the *Cima d'Asta*, acts as guide, and his services would be almost essential to anyone wishing to ascend the mountain by one side, and descend by the other; but, with fine weather, a moderate mountaineer will have no difficulty in combining the ascent with his day's walk to Tesin, in case (as happened to the writer) the aid of a guide should not be available. For about 3 m. from Caoria the way lies up the main valley; at first by the rt. bank, afterwards by the opposite side. Near the second bridge over the Vanoi the writer found two specimens of the rare little fern *Botrychium matricarioides*. Avoiding a track laid down on several maps, the traveller should not quit the main valley till he reaches a wooden bridge just *above* the junction of the torrent from *Val Regana*. A tolerable path mounts a rather steep declivity, partly grown over with pine and beech-wood, till it attains the first step in the wild and picturesque glen of Regana. A first *casera*, empty in summer, is passed, and then another ascent leads to the upper alp, with a small *casera*, about 2¼ hrs. from Caoria.

Val Regana mounts nearly due S. to the *Passo di Regana*, a depression on the E. side of the Cima d'Asta, at the head of Val Tolvà, the eastern branch of Val Malone. The great granite ribs of the Cima d'Asta descend steeply into the head of Val Regana, but between them are two lateral openings, the first of which, though tempting, is to be avoided. The true course for the ascent of the mountain is to follow the rough and faintly marked track leading up towards the pass, as far as the foot of the last slope, where the head of the valley is completely covered by the debris fallen from the surrounding heights. A low face of granite rock, like the wall of a

---

* It is referred to by Messrs. Gilbert and Churchill.—' The Dolomite Mountains,' p. 451.

small house, marks the most convenient spot for commencing the ascent. On the rt. side of it is a faintly marked goat-track, for goats here monopolise the higher pastures. The ascent is now straight forward, steep throughout, but nowhere difficult; and after a climb of about 2,500 ft., the traveller reaches the verge of the basin which occupies the upper level of the mountain on this side. It presents a scene of the wildest character. Bare rock, and large patches of snow, occupy the surface, and around the basin rise the topmost ridges of the mountain. At the first moment a stranger may hesitate in his choice between 3 peaks, of nearly equal apparent height; but before long he will ascertain that the centre one of the three considerably overtops its rivals. Its surface is covered from the top to its base with large granite blocks lying at a high angle, but with moderate caution there is no difficulty in the ascent, and in 4 hrs.' moderate walking from the casera, the traveller will reach the summit.

The measures of the height given on different authorities differ widely. That of the Austrian 'Kataster' is 9,337 Eng. ft.; but Herr Trinker, the most competent authority, prefers the result found by Weiss—9,132 ft. The view is at once very extensive and interesting; nearly all the higher peaks of the dolomite region are well seen. Among the more distant summits, the Sorapis — more commonly known as Croda Malcora—is conspicuous, and beyond the limits of S. Tyrol some peaks of the High Tauern range, especially the Gross Venediger. Of the nearer mountains the most remarkable is the rugged range of porphyritic summits dividing the Val di Fiemme from the tributaries of the Brenta. Immediately round the base of the mountain the spectator looks down upon several comparatively broad and open valleys, partly covered with forest, with wide patches of open pasture. Here and there some distant casera may be descried, but it will appear strange that no village or hamlet is in sight nearer than Castello di Tesin, fully 10 m. distant as the bird flies. There is scarcely another instance in the Alps of a district at least 20 m. in length, by 15 m. in breadth, traversed by many comparatively deep and not unproductive valleys, wherein there is not a single hamlet, and scarcely a permanent dwelling. The thinness of the population has tended to the preservation of bears, and many other wild animals, and has favoured the growth of legendary stories, and fanciful tales, wherein this mountain has played a similar part to that of the Untersberg in the Salzburg country.

In viewing the mountain from its highest peak the horse-shoe form attributed to it by a writer in the new edition of Schaubach is seen to be an illusion. The summit lies at about the meeting-point of many ridges that converge towards this as a centre. Those who approach it from one or the other side are apt to leave out of account the portion that remains unseen. From the topmost ridge the traveller looks down on two small lakes or tarns, which remain half frozen and partly covered with unmelted snow late in July. It is obvious that a slight fall in the mean temperature, which would permit the accumulation of névé in the basin on the side of Val Regana, would soon give rise to a considerable glacier. The W. face of the peak seems to be the steepest, and though a descent may probably be effected, the prospect did not appear certain. If accompanied by a guide, the traveller will naturally descend towards Tesin by *Val Sorgazza*, the W. branch of Val Malene; but if alone, he might lose much precious time in seeking the way.

The beautiful *Primula glutinosa* is extremely abundant, but the flora of the mountain is singularly poor. Scarcely a dozen species of flowering plants are to be found on the peak.

The granite of Cima d'Asta is fine grained, and very unlike that of western Tyrol. In some places it is traversed by veins of dark rock resembling serpentine (?). Fine crystals of quartz and garnets are found here.

About 2¼ hrs. suffice to descend from the summit to the *Passo di Regana*. This commands a fine, though limited, view. The valley of the Grigno stretches southward in a straight line, backed by the mountains of the Sette Comuni. Little more than ½ hr. suffices to reach the Malga di Tolvà, where a crust of bread preserved in the traveller's pocket is converted into a delicate luxury by excellent milk and butter. Thenceforward for many miles the path lies by the E. or l. hand bank of the upper valley—locally called *Val Tolvà*—usually at some distance from the torrent. The scenery is agreeable, and the path pleasant, being unusually free from stones. At about ⅔rds of the way to Tesin the stream from Val Sorgazza joins that from Val Tolvà, and the valley is thenceforward called *Val Malene*. A new cart-road is being carried along the l. bank of the stream. At a place where this road is connected by a wooden bridge with a similar road along the opposite bank, the traveller, if bound for La Pieve, should cross to the rt. bank. The road now gradually rises above the bed of the stream, and, having entered the zone of secondary rocks, winds round several ravines cut by torrents in the yielding strata. The villages of Castello and Cinte are seen from a distance, but it is only after crossing a tract of level cultivated ground, and turning sharply to the rt., behind a spur of the mountain which screens the village from the N., that the traveller, in 3 hrs.' steady walking from the Pass of Regana, reaches La Pieve di Tesin (Rte. G).

In case clouds, that too often hang round the mountain tops, should dissuade the traveller from undertaking the ascent of the Cima d'Asta, he may enjoy a very agreeable walk from Caoria to Borgo di Val Sugana, or to Tesin, by following the stream of the Vanoi to its head in *Val Cia*. This route to Borgo may easily be taken on horseback by a lady who does not object to a ride of 8 or 9 hrs. As already mentioned, the Vanoi, in its course from the head of Val Cia to Caoria, describes a semicircle round the Cima d'Asta as its centre. This form of the valley gives much variety to the views that are gained on the way. Starting in a NW. direction, the traveller finds himself facing nearly due S. when, after a long but gradual ascent, he attains the head of the valley, between the stern granitic rocks of the Cima d'Asta and the rugged porphyritic mass of the *Cima di Lagorei* (8,574'). Here he has a choice between two paths, one lying to the rt., and the other to the l., of the granitic summit named *Centello*, which rises directly in front. The more frequented, and by far the easier way, is that to the rt., leading over an easy pass to the glen of *Conseria*. The track lies over crystalline slate, which is here interposed between the granite mass of Cima d'Asta and the porphyry range of Lagorei and Montalon.

Val Conseria is one of several minor glens whose waters unite to form the *Maso* torrent, which joins the Brenta about 2 m. E. of Borgo. The first torrent which joins that of Conseria issues from a short glen (named Val Sorda) that drains the S. side of Cima di Lagorei, and the E. side of the neighbouring summit of *Montalon*, a mountain which has yielded many rare plants to the diligent investigation of Dr. Ambrosi of Trent. The next affluent on the E. side descends from the mountain named Ciolara. Below the junction the valley takes the name Val di Campelle, which it retains only till, about 4 m. lower down, it joins the considerable torrent that descends to SE. from Val Calamento (Rte. I), and the track from that valley joins our path. A humble mountain inn stands at *Pontarso*, the spot where the paths meet. Thence a beaten track runs along the rt. bank of the Maso torrent. The shortest way to Borgo is by *Telve*, a village mentioned in Rte. A.

The track that mounts SE. from the head of the Val Cia to a pass between the Centello and Cima d'Asta descends to Tesin through *Val Sorgazza*, the E. branch of Val Malene. The scenery is fine, but the path is rough, and said to be fit only for practised mountaineers.

Route I.

BORGO DI VAL SUGANA TO CAVALESE IN VAL DI FIEMME.

Most travellers who unite a visit to the valleys of Fiemme and Fassa (described in the next §) with Val Sugana and the Sette Comuni, follow the new road from Cavelese to Neumarkt, and thence go by rail to Trent, and by the high-road to Borgo, described in Rte. A. There are, however, several easy passes which enable the pedestrian to go in one day from Borgo to Cavalese, and others connecting that place, or Predazzo, with Caoria. The attractions of agreeable scenery are increased in the case of those who may take an interest in the geological structure of the country, or in its rich and varied flora.

We give here a brief notice of the more frequented paths.

1. *By the Forcella di Cadino.* This, the most direct way from Borgo to Cavalese, is reached through the Val di Calamento. The way to it is by Telve, and thence by the track along the rt. bank of the Maso, mentioned in the last Rte., to the Osteria di *Pontarso*. The path there leaves the northern branch (or Val Campelle) to the rt., and for about 2 hrs. follows a direction near due NW. through *Val di Calamento.* On the way is the Osteria di Pupille (4,087′), another humble mountain inn, opened in summer to supply refreshment to wayfarers. At its head the glen bends round to W., and ultimately to WSW. If he were to follow the track over the ridge in that direction the traveller would reach the head of the valley of the Fersina (Rte. A), locally named Palù. The way to Fiemme is by a path that mounts NW. to the *Forcella di Cadino* (6,712′), a depression in the range connecting the *Cima di Ciolara* on the rt., with the Pizzo Croce to the l. From the summit the *Val di Cadino* extends nearly due N. to its junction with the Val di Fiemme. Another *osteria*, at a spot named Tabiai, is found about half-way down the Val di Cadino. The path is on the rt. side of the torrent, and on reaching the junction of the latter with the Avisio, it turns to the rt. and keeps to the S. side of the main valley till, after passing the opening of Val di Moëna, it descends to a bridge over the Avisio just below Cavalese, which is reached in 10 hrs. from Borgo.

2. *By Montalon.* As mentioned in the last Rte., Montalon is a porphyritic summit, rising SW. of the Cima di Lagorei, remarkable for its rich and varied flora. The botanist will not find time to examine it carefully in the course of a long day's walk, but will be tempted to seek night-quarters in some neighbouring *casera*. The ordinary traveller may choose this way for the sake of a route, somewhat more laborious than that by Cadino, but certainly more interesting.

The way follows the northern branch of the Maso torrent through Val Campelle (see last Rte.), and instead of turning to NE. through Val Conseria, to reach the pass leading to Caoria, mounts through *Val Sorda* (not to be confused with the more important glen of that name NE. of Caoria). The summit of *Montalon* (about 8,300'?) lies to the l. in ascending the glen. On attaining it the traveller may choose between a longer, but rather easier, way, which descends through *Val di Stuato* to join Val di Cadino about 2 hrs. above its junction with Val di Fiemme, or a rougher, but shorter way, through *Val di Moëna*. This glen may be reached directly by the track which mounts through Val Sorda, leaving to the l. hand the summit of Montalon.

3. *By the Passo di Sadole.* The traveller who is willing to give two days for the walk from Borgo to Predazzo in Val di Fiemme may best proceed on the first day to Caoria, by some one of the paths mentioned in Rtes. G and H. From that place he may reach Predazzo in 6 hrs. by the *Passo di Sadole* (6,785'). He follows the track along the Vanoi for about 1½ hr. above Caoria, till he reaches the opening of *Val Fossernico*, a lateral glen through which a torrent descends from the *Pizzo di Val Maor*. From hence the path to Sadole ascends in a northerly direction, and is said to be practicable for beasts of burthen. Instead of descending directly to Predazzo, a path may be taken which winds round to the westward, and descends into *Val Cavillonte*, one of the tributary glens of Val di Fiemme, which opens into that valley about half-way between Cavalese and Predazzo. A mineral spring in Val Cavillonte has of late acquired local reputation, and is much visited by people from the neighbouring valleys. The accommodation is said to be rough, but it may be found convenient head-quarters for a naturalist wishing to explore the neighbouring range of porphyry mountains.

The writer has no information respecting another pass from Caoria to Fiemme which lies on the E. side of the Pizzo di Val Maor. It is considerably longer than the path by Sadole, and appears to be rarely used.

§ 59. VALLEY OF THE BRENTA.

ROUTE K.

PRIMIERO TO AGORDO, BY THE PASSO DELLA CEREDA.

In the preceding routes the chief roads and paths leading into this district from the N., W., and S. sides have been described. It now remains to notice the passes connecting it with the beautiful valley of the Cordevole, described in § 61. The account of this route in the earlier editions of this work was based on erroneous information, which has been corrected by obliging correspondents.

For about 20 minutes, the track from Primiero follows the branch of the Cismone that descends from Val di Canale—passing *Tonadigo*, with two or three poor-looking inns. A short way beyond that village the remarkable castle of *La Pietra*, already visible from Primiero, is seen near at hand. It is difficult by description to give the effect of this singular pile, perched on the summit of a rock, and so completely isolated that it has long ceased to be accessible. The object sought by castle-builders in general has here, with the assistance of the natural decay of the rock, been attained too completely. Some 30 years ago, Count Welsberg, the owner of the castle, succeeded with the help of ladders in effecting an entrance; but since that date it has been finally abandoned. Just under the crag on which the castle is built, the very stony track leading to the pass turns away nearly due W. from the Val di Canale. The ascent is not long, but rather uninteresting; and it is with satisfaction that the traveller finds himself at the top of the *Passo della Cereda* (4,503'). Near the summit there is a choice between two paths both leading to Agordo. The way to the l. goes by Sagron, and is somewhat shorter; that to the rt. passes by Gosaldo, and is the more interesting. The undulating ground over which the winding track is carried does not slope towards Agordo, as might be expected; and the drainage is carried southward through the *Mis* torrent to join the Piave near Bribano. It is characteristic of the structure of the Dolomite Alps that so low a pass should be found in the immediate neighbourhood of such lofty peaks; for the Sasso di Campo on the N., and Il Piz on the S., must both approach near to the limit of 10,000 ft. After passing *Gosaldo* the path begins to mount to NNE., to pass a second low col between the Monte Luna and the Gardellon, two prominent points in the ridge projecting from the Sasso di Campo and thence descends into the glen of the Sarzana torrent to reach *Frassenè* (3,612'). The walnut extends up to the level of the latter village. The track then keeps to the l. bank of the Sarzana, passes Voltago and descends to a bridge over the Cordevole about ¾ m. from Agordo.

The other track descends gently from the Passo della Cereda to *Sagron*, and then by a steep and rough path (not good for ladies to ride) down to the quicksilver mines. For about 1½ m. below the mines the track descends along the Mis till that torrent turns abruptly to ESE. to join the Cordevole near the opening of the Canal di Agordo (§ 61, Rte. C). At this point a short tributary glen descends from the NE. to join the main valley of the Mis. The name *Val Imperina* is sometimes given to this glen, and sometimes, more correctly, to that which on the opposite side of the ridge descends (also due NE.) towards the Cordevole. The path lies above the rt. bank of the first-mentioned torrent to the ridge dividing it from Val Imperina, and then descends by the hamlet of Riva, and bearing nearly due N., takes the traveller down to the high road close to the Ponte Alto about 1 m. from Agordo. The way by Sagron is reckoned 7 hrs. walking, and that by Gosaldo from ½ hr. to 1 hr. more.

[By far the most interesting way for a mountaineer going from Primiero to Agordo is by the Val di Canale, and the pass at its head—called by Mr. Tuckett, *Passo di Canale*. It was first crossed by Mr. Tuckett, who was benighted on the S. side, and recently (1872) by Mr. Holzmann, whose accurate notes are here used. In 1¾ hr. from Primiero the last *sennhütten* in Val di Canale are reached. Keeping first for ½ hr. close to the l. bank, and then for 1 hr. chiefly by the E. slope of the glen, the traveller attains the highest shepherd's hut. A steep ascent of 40 min. nearly due N. and then for 25 min. more nearly NW. leads to the summit of the pass, lying between the Sasso di Campo (or Croda Grande) and the Cima di Canale. This overlooks the head of the *Val d'Angoraz*, the uppermost southern tributary of the *Val di San Lucano*. As the direct descent appears impracticable the way now bears to the W., and then turns towards the N. to reach a depression in a ridge projecting from the *Coston di Miel*— 150 ft. higher than the actual pass. From this point the last-named peak, commanding a very wide view, may be climbed in less than 1 hr., going and returning. The descent from the depression above mentioned is at first N., then bearing towards E., and in 1¼ hr. from the summit attains a small green plain, below which is a faintly traced path. 1½ hr. more suffices to reach the opening of Val d'Angoraz, and to meet the track descending from the *Forcella Gesurette* leading to the *Val delle Cornelle*. The *Val di San Lucano* is entered a little above Pra. A beaten track then leads in 1¼ hr. to Taibon, in the valley of the Cordevole, 25 min. above Agordo. See § 61, Rte. C.]

Route L.

SAN MARTINO DI CASTROZZA TO CENCENIGHE.

The hunters of Primiero have long been aware of the possibility of attaining the ridge connecting the Cimon della Pala with the Cima della Rosetta, at a point ENE. of S. Martino di Castrozza. They now and then effect a passage from thence to the head of Val di Canale, by the N. side of the Palle di San Martino, and so return to Primiero. The practicability of effecting a pass over the same ridge from San Martino to Gares and Cencenighe was first established, as the writer believes, in 1865, by Mr. Tuckett, who then crossed with several companions, and recrossed from the Cencenighe side in 1867. The writer has been on the summit of the ridge in unfavourable weather, but saw enough to make him agree with Mr. Tuckett's designation of this as a '*most romantic pass.*' The name *Passo delle Cornelle* was suggested by the name of the glen leading thence to Gares, which the writer willingly adopts in the absence of any recognised local name. Mr. Tuckett estimates the height at 9,150 ft., but the writer ventures to think this estimate too high by 150 or 200 ft. This excursion, though it involves some rough walking, is quite free from difficulty to any practised mountaineer, and requires but a moderate day's walk. The distances may be reckoned 3½ hrs. from San Martino to the summit; 3 hrs. thence to Gares; and 2½ hrs. from Gares to Cencenighe—all exclusive of halts. The way from San Martino to the summit is sufficiently obvious to any mountaineer, and the only hint required is to keep well to the l. close to the precipitous rocks that extend nearly to the summit of the pass. A sort of track will be found, except towards the top, as sheep climb up to seek shelter from the noon-day sun. The summit is a comparatively broad ridge marked by a stone-man raised by Mr. Tuckett's party. It produces a considerable number of Alpine plants, all reduced to the most stunted proportions. With regard to the NE. side of the pass, the reader will be glad to have the following note, with which the writer was favoured by Mr. Tuckett, who describes the ascent from Cencenighe by *Forno di Canale,* in Val di Biois (§ 60, Rte. E). In case of need, a decent country inn is found at Forno.

'A good broad track leads gently up, in about 1¼ hr., from Forno di Canale to *Gares.* A little farther up, after traversing some broken ground and a wood, the stream (which is seen in front pouring in a fine cascade from the narrow gorge giving admittance to the Val delle Cornelle) is crossed to its rt. bank by a bridge. The path (improved in 1867) zigzags up the face of the mountain till it reaches the level of a ledge, and then, turning to the rt., passes along the latter till the mouth of the ravine is reached (¾ hr. from *Gares*), immediately above the point where the torrent takes its final leap. Crossing the stream, the way lies by a new path along the l. bank of *Val delle Cornelle,* among masses of débris which in some places almost choke the gorge, to a level, torrent-ravaged, and desolate-looking plain (1¼ hr. above *Gares*). An excellent spring on the W. side of this hollow, at the foot of the slopes of the *Pian di Campido* (a mountain NE. of the Cimon della Pala), affords a good halting-place for lunch. Looking back, the valley of Gares, set as in a frame between the frowning portals of the Val delle Cornelle, forms a striking and beautiful picture. To the plain succeeds a series of steep gorges alternating with small terraces, until, in 1½ hr., the valley widens out considerably somewhat below the junction of its two uppermost branches, separated by a spur from the Palle di San Martino, which mount respectively to SE. and SW. By traversing the open space diagonally to its W. side and following the latter branch, which is very narrow, and bounded by cliffs of moderate height, the broad plateau forming the watershed is gained without difficulty.' [F.F.T.]

In descending towards Gares it is best to keep as near as possible to the bed of the gorge. Avoid a cattle-track that bears to the l. a little above the desolate plain mentioned by Mr. Tuckett. The Cima di Rosetta, a prominent point in the range S. of the Passo delle Cornelle, and commanding a very fine view, is easily accessible in 20 min. from the top of the pass.

A traveller bound for Agordo need not descend to Cencenighe. A little above Gares a path mounts to SE. leading to a pass called *Forcella Gesurette,* at the head of the Val di Sanbucano, which opens at Taibon near Agordo.

THE DOLOMITE ALPS OF SOUTH TYROL.

SECTION 60.

FASSA DISTRICT.

While the district surrounding Primiero, described in the last section, and many of the most beautiful tributary valleys of the Piave, noticed in § 61, are even now known to but few travellers, it has been the fortune of the region whose centre is the valley of Fassa, to have attracted at an early period the attention of men of science, and of not a few other visitors. Although the latter includes some amongst the grandest and most impressive scenes of the Dolomite Alps, it certainly does not in this respect surpass the adjoining districts mentioned above. Yet (so imperfectly were the Alps known until very recently) it was supposed that the dolomite scenery deserving a traveller's attention was confined to a small portion of the district now to be described. The key to its topography is to be found in the course of the Avisio torrent, fully 60 m. in length from its chief source N. of the Marmolata to its confluence with the Adige near Lavis. Within that space the valley is known by three different names, and is spoken of as if divided into three distinct valleys. The uppermost is *Val di Fassa*, or *Fassathal*, the middle part is *Val di Fiemme*, or *Fleimserthal*, and the lower end is called *Val Cembra*, or *Zimmerthal*. The course of the Avisio is mainly SW. or W., but in Val Cembra it is about SSW., or nearly parallel to the adjoining track of the Adige, until it approaches Lavis, when it turns WSW. to join the latter river. In its long course the Avisio receives but two considerable torrents through the lateral valleys of Travignolo and San Pelegrino, the other tributaries issue from short lateral glens, or hollows, in the mountains that enclose the main valley.

Westward and northward of the valleys of Fiemme and Fassa, a rather extensive mountain district, including some of the most interesting scenery of this region, extends towards the Adige and the Eisack. This tract also is drained by short and inconsiderable streams, there being but two lateral valleys of any consequence—the Karneidthal and Grödnerthal—on the way from Lavis to Brixen, a distance of nearly 70 m. Besides the basin of the Avisio, and the country lying between it and the Adige and Eisack, we also include in this section the Gaderthal, or Abteithal, with the tract lying in the rt. angle formed by that valley and the Grödnerthal. The boundaries of this district are therefore easily traced. It includes the basin of the Avisio and the adjoining region drained by the Rienz, Eisack, and Adige, between Bruneck and Lavis, and on the E. is limited by the valley of the Cordevole.

It would exceed the bounds of this work, even though the writer should feel himself competent to the task, to discuss the many intricate questions that have been suggested by the singular geological structure of this region. In adjoining districts reference has been frequently made to the appearance here and there of eruptive igneous rocks, but there is no part of the Alps where the phenomena connected with ancient volcanic action can be studied on so great a scale as here. It is clear that this continued for a long period (even long in geological language) to be a centre of volcanic action; and some progress has been made towards establishing the sequence of igneous rocks originating at successive periods of eruptive activity. The labours of two generations of geologists have resulted in the overthrow of the theoretic views of one of the earliest, and the ablest, of the writers in this district—the late Leopold von Buch. The most complete account of the geology of this region is found in the important work by Richthofen, mentioned in the introduction to this work. The writer may venture to say here that the important part attributed by many modern writers to the granitic mass of the Cima d' Asta in regard to the orography and geological history of this and the adjoining district of Val Sugana, appears to rest upon very questionable theoretic views; and that the existence of two defined axes of elevation —one running from N. to S., the other from ENE. to WSW.—and supposed to intersect in the so-called, Sella Plateau, is by no means clearly established. The writer has throughout this work pointed out those broad features in the orography of the Alpine region, that appear to him to prove irrefragably the existence of forces acting on a great scale upon the earth's crust; but in the region now described the indications of such action seem to him to be completely masked by local phenomena, exhibited on a gigantic scale. Besides the prodigious mass of eruptive rocks, properly so called, of which the red porphyry forms the larger portion—constituting the ranges that enclose the lower part of the valley of the Avisio, and extending in one direction beyond Botzen, on the other to the head of Val Sugana—the part played by so subordinate a constituent as mere volcanic ashes and scoriæ excites wonder by the vastness of its volume. The greater part has been more or less consolidated by aqueous action into tufa beds which are often 2,000 ft. in thickness. But in the more elevated positions, where the materials have not undergone the prolonged action of water, the effect of weathering is to bring back the surface to its original condition. There are spots where the traveller, fixing his eyes only on the objects immediately surrounding him, can scarcely believe that he is not ascending the cone of a modern volcano. Several of the highest dolomite peaks of this region stand round the head of the Val di Fassa, yet the traveller, whose curiosity and interest are mainly directed to these, will be disappointed to find that they are visible only from comparatively few spots in the main valley. Although scenery of the highest order is close at hand, there is no place in the valley offering views at all equal to those found at many places more easy of access in the adjoining districts. An active traveller will, however, not object to gain the most varied enjoyment of grand scenery at the cost of a little labour, but it must be owned that the chief attractions of the valleys of Fassa and Fiemme are for the lover of natural science. If this be to the geologist a battle-ground, rendered classical by the importance of the questions disputed, and of the combatants, it is the Eldorado of the mineralogist, the botanist, and the entomologist. Of the many rare minerals it is usually possible to purchase fine specimens at Predazzo and elsewhere.

The flora of this and the neighbouring valleys has been investigated by an indefatigable native botanist, the late Dr. Facchini, and by many scientific visitors. Dr. Ambrosi, of Trent, the possessor of the herbarium of Facchini, will, it is hoped, complete our knowledge of it, by terminating his *Flora del Tirolo Meridionale*, of which two volumes have already appeared, unfortunately in a form too bulky to be convenient to the traveller.

The comparatively frequent visits of strangers have led the inn-keepers in Fassa and Fiemme to adapt their prices to the supposed means of visitors, rather than to the ordinary rates of South Tyrol. A traveller remaining some days should make a distinct agreement as to prices.

Lying along or near to the frontier, between the German and Italian races, the population here is of mixed origin,

In the main valley the Italian tongue prevails, even among people of German descent. In most of the short glens that fall towards the Adige, and all those that are drained into the Eisack and the Rienz, the German element prevails. To this there is a remarkable exception in the Grödnerthal (Rte. G), and the adjoining parts of the Gaderthal, where a population of southern origin has retained a dialect having much affinity with the Romantsch of the E. of Switzerland, being based upon Latin, though very unlike any existing Italian dialect.

The best head-quarters in the main valley are found at Predazzo, Vigo, and Campidello—the latter being superior in point of scenery, quite sufficiently comfortable. Tolerably good quarters, though rather rough, are found at Ratzes and Seiss. Accommodation of a humble kind is also found in several villages in the Grödnerthal and Gaderthal, but St. Cassian, which is as attractive a place to the palæontologist as Predazzo is to the mineralogist, is very ill provided.

It is now pretty generally known that the crowning summit of the Dolomite Alps is the *Marmolata*, but its height is far from being exactly determined. (See the ascent of that mountain in Rte. A.) The other dolomite peaks belonging to this district are surpassed by many of those of Primiero and the Ampezzo district. The most noticeable are the Langkofel (10,392′) and the Rosengarten (10,163′).

The map prefixed to this section is founded on imperfect materials; none other being available for some portions of the district included in it. The portion N. and W. of Primiero is especially defective.

Route A.

TRENT TO CAPRILE, BY THE VALLEYS OF FIEMME AND FASSA. ASCENT OF THE MARMOLATA.

	Hrs. walking	Eng. miles
Neumarkt (by railway) .		22
Cavalese (by road) . .	6	18
Predazzo	2¾	8¼
Vigo	3½	10¼
Campidello . . .	2¼	6¾
Fedaya (by foot-path) .	3	8
Caprile	3	8
Total from Neumarkt	20½	59½

A post-stellwagen plies between Neumarkt and Cavalese, and another lighter vehicle between Cavalese and Vigo. The road from Vigo to Campidello is very rough. Ladies might ride nearly all the way from Campidello to Caprile, but will not easily find animals that can be trusted.

It must appear strange to anyone viewing the map of this district, that the way from Lavis to the upper valley of the Avisio should not follow the course of that stream. In point of fact, however, not one person in a hundred bound for that destination ever passes through the Val Cembra (noticed in Rte. B); and this holds true more especially since a good road has been opened from the valley of the Adige to Cavalese, the chief place in Fiemme. The *Auer* (Ital. *Ora*) station on the rly from Trent to Botzen is nearer to Cavalese by 2 m. than that of *Neumarkt* (Ital. *Egna*), but most travellers prefer the latter because it is much better supplied with vehicles, and is the starting-place for the post-omnibus, which takes 3½ or 4 hrs. to reach Cavalese. The traveller who reaches Auer or Neumarkt late in the day should on no account sleep at either of those places in the hot valley of the Adige, but at the hamlet of *Kaldisch*, about half-way to Cavalese. 'Beautiful position; good and cheap inn.' [F. L. L.] On one side of the road is passed the village of *Truden* (Ital. *Trodena*), 3,671 ft. above the sea, a favourite *sommerfrisch* resort of the natives of the adjoining places in the Adige valley. After a long ascent, the road reaches the summit-level, whence a comparatively slight descent leads to the Val di Fiemme. The road passes *Carano*, where there is a sulphureous spring used for baths, and 1½ m. farther reaches

Cavalese (3,292′), a small but well-built and apparently thriving town (Inns: Ancora, good and reasonable; Uva, not recommended). The lover of art should not fail to visit the ancient gothic church, standing on rising ground, with a marble portal that appears to be still older than the existing church. The paintings and statues, of various dates, are all by natives of the valley, many of whom have attained to eminence as artists. The most interesting is a fresco representing the battle of Lepanto, by Francesco Furlanell of Tesero. The picture over the altar in the chapel of the Rosary is by Antonio Longo, a former parish-priest, who was distinguished as a painter and architect. Under the shadow of lime-trees above the church is a stone table, with stone seats around it, which was long the meeting-place of the notables of the valley.

German writers claim the population of the valley of the Avisio as mainly belonging to the Teutonic stock, although an Italian dialect, not much differing from that of Venetia, has prevailed here for many centuries. It is certain that from a remote period they maintained virtual independence, paying a small annual tribute to the Bishops of Trent. Whether from sympathy with their German neighbours, or dread of the encroachments of the Venetians, they sided with the empire in the many local conflicts with the troops of the republic, and in later times fought vigorously against the French. The local annals record that when, about the year 1300, the people of Feltre attempted to take by force some tracts of Alpine pasture on the confines towards Primiero, the sturdy men of Fiemme asserted their rights by sacking and burning the offending city.

In Val Cembra, and the portion of Fiemme below Cavalese, cultivation is limited by the narrowness of the valley and the steepness of the slopes, and Val di Fassa is an Alpine valley with a severe climate. The intermediate tract between Cavalese and Moëna is comparatively fruitful, and maintains a numerous population, scattered among frequent villages. On the S. side the range dividing this from the valleys of the Brenta and the Vanoi is formed exclusively of red porphyry, which there attains its greatest elevation in the Alps —the *Cima di Lagorei* reaching 8,575 ft. (For the passes leading to Val Sugana, see § 59, Rte. I.) On the opposite side of the valley the dolomite begins to show itself. The westernmost point (?) in the dolomite range is the insignificant *Monte Cucal* (5,579′), N. of Cavalese, separated on the NE. side by the porphyritic summit of the *Zangenberg* (8,198′) from the steep dolomitic ridge of *Latemar* (8,983′). The road from Cavalese runs nearly at a level along the N. side of Val di Fiemme by *Tesero* (3,267′) and *Ziano*, and then crosses the Avisio to reach

Predazzo (3,277′), the chief place in Fiemme, after Cavalese. This is the most attractive spot in the valley to the geologist and mineralogist, and in the stranger's book at the Nave d' Oro, a very fair inn, the names of many of the most eminent scientific men of Europe were, and perhaps are still, to be seen. Already, in the last century, the Vicentine geologist, Count Marzari Pencati, called attention to the fact that granite was here to be seen overlying secondary limestone. It is impossible within the space here available to explain the grounds upon which geologists have based the conclusion that the present site of Predazzo stands about the centre of an ancient crater, from which six well-marked species of igneous rocks were ejected during successive periods of activity. The earliest of them was syenite, to which followed a variety of granite, in which tourmaline takes the place of mica, and then four varieties of porphyry, the latest of which approaches in structure and appearance to syenite, and contains large crystals of orthoclase. The traveller who feels interest in the subject will doubtless provide himself with Richthofen's important work, already referred to, and should also refer to the writings of Cotta and other German geologists who dissent from some of the conclusions there announced. The valley seen above Predazzo in approaching that place from Cavalese is Val Travignolo, through which lies the way to Cencenighe, described in Rte. E, and to Primiero, noticed in § 59, Rte. F. The valley of the Avisio here turns aside from its previous course; and the road, which returns to the rt. bank, henceforth runs NNE. as far as Campidello. Nearly opposite Predazzo a track mounts NW. to the *Sattel Jöchl* (7,520′), on the E. side of the Zangenberg, and leads either to Deutschenofen, or to the Karneidthal (Rte. D). The valley above Predazzo is enclosed between masses of igneous rock which screen from view the much higher dolomite range of Latemar. At *Forno* (3,703′), a coarse limestone, apparently belonging to the Muschelkalk, is for the first time seen in the bed of the valley, separated by a mass of porphyry (*melaphyre*) from sandstone beds which are referred to the Lower Trias. The boundary between Fiemme and Fassa is reached at

Moëna (3,873′), a large village with two tolerably decent-looking inns. Collections of minerals for sale are, or were, kept here by Felicetti Medil, and J. B. Zachia. A line of depression, which seems to have some orographic importance, here traverses the valley of the Avisio. To the east the Val di San Pelegrino stretches about 9 m. between ranges mainly composed of igneous rock, and leads over a comparatively low pass, connecting this with the valley of the Cordevole (Rte. E). In the opposite direction a short and steep ascent leads to the Caressa Pass (Rte. D), which marks a wide gap between the dolomitic ranges of Latemar and Rosengarten. After passing Moëna the road ascends continuously along the rt. bank of the Avisio. Those who do not intend to halt follow the lower road near the river, which passes by *San Giovanni* (4,362′). Another road, bearing to the l., and ascending the swelling slope above the stream, is the way to

Vigo (about 4,550′), the chief place in Val di Fassa. Outside the village is the inn kept by Antonio Rizzi, which affords good rooms, very fair food, and the attention of the host and his family; but native simplicity has been corrupted by intercourse with strangers, and the host is grasping, and not very reliable. Those who remain some days should make an agreement with the landlord. Among other things he is apt to charge too high for horses and vehicles. The proper price for a one-horse vehicle to Predazzo is 3 fl., and to Cavalese 6 fl. This is the best head-quarters for excursions in Val di Fassa; but strange to say, all the higher summits are concealed from view, and the scenery of this part of the valley, as compared with the adjoining region, may be pronounced tame. The nearest point from which a stranger can form any conception of the grand objects close at hand is the *Sasso dei Mugoni*, rising W. of Rizzi's inn. Passing the church of Sta. Giuliana, and ascending through a larch wood, a path bears to the rt. on approaching some cliffs, behind which is the desired summit. A far more complete panoramic view, including all the higher peaks of this district, is gained from the *Sasso di Dam*, a summit rising above the N. side of the Monzoni glen, mentioned below. It is most conveniently reached from Pozza, the village standing at the opening of that glen. The height is probably about 8,600 ft. In the writer's opinion, the most impressive scenery in this district is enjoyed by mounting from Vigo into a hollow, or *cirque*, called *Vajolet*, which penetrates deeply into the mass of the *Rosengarten*

(10,163′). The stream issuing from it passes fully 1½ m. to the N. of Vigo, but by following it along a very rough path, the traveller cannot miss his way to the centre of the *cirque*. It is not so regular in form as some spots to which that designation is given, but for grandeur and variety of rock-scenery it has scarcely a superior. To enjoy it fully, and to measure the vast scale of the fabric, the traveller should by a stiff climb reach the ridge at the E. end, which is accessible (seemingly only at one point), and gives a view in the direction of Botzen, looking down a wall of precipice fully 3,000 ft. in height.

The naturalist will not fail to make at least one excursion into the *Monzoni* glen, which opens about 1 m. above Vigo. Crossing the Avisio to *Pozza* (4,270′), where the parish-priest, Sig. Pescota, has, or had, a fine collection of minerals for sale, the traveller follows a good path which for some distance mounts very gently, somewhat S. of due E. After about 3 m. the valley forks. Through the longer branch runs a path leading to the head of Contrin (Rte. F). Much more interesting to the naturalist is that which lies to the right in ascending the valley. The traveller will have already observed large erratic blocks of a peculiar syenite, scattered over the limestone deposits of the lower part of the glen. This syenite comes from a high mass culminating in the *Riccobetta* (8,634′)—known to German writers as *Monzoniberg*—which lies between the SE. branch of Monzoni and the Val di San Pelegrino. Between the Riccobetta and the valley of the Avisio is a dolomite peak, best known as *Sasso di Loch* (8,658′), which conceals the Riccobetta from view in the main valley. The rarest minerals of this district, such as Vesuvian, gehlenite, fassaite, zeylanite, &c., are found near the junction of the Monzoni syenite with the dolomite. The mountaineer who climbs the ridge of the Riccobetta a little E. of the summit, may descend into Val di San Pelegrino by a very long slope of grass beginning a short way below the ridge of the mountain, and so steep that caution is advisable. Here is found *Cirsium flavescens*, one of those permanent hybrids characteristic of that genus.

There are many men at or near Vigo who are ready to act as guides—expecting 3 fl. a day—but beyond a knowledge of the paths, they are of little use. The writer does not know of any man in the valley who has the least claim to be counted as a mountaineer, unless it be a *guardaboschi*, at or near Campidello, whose character did not stand high in the estimation of his neighbours. Few districts in the Alps can boast of so rich a flora as that of the valleys of Fiemme and Fassa; but several species, once supposed to be nearly confined to this valley, are now known to be widely spread throughout the Dolomite Alps. The following very rare plants may be noted among those of the dolomite mountains, especially of the Rosengarten:—*Saxifraga Facchinii, Valeriana elongata,* and *V. supina, Artemisia lanata, Campanula Morettiana,* and *Androsace Hausmanniana.* Among the plants confined to syenite, or porphyry, may be enumerated *Silene Pumilio, Saxifraga cernua, Pedicularis asplenifolia, Androsace helvetica, Primula nivijlora, Juncus arcticus,* and *Sesleria tenella.*

Above Vigo and San Giovanni, the road leading to the head of the valley is narrow and rough, so that little time is gained by taking a vehicle to Campidello, where it comes to an end. After passing the small village of *Pera* (4,316′), with a small inn kept by Ricci, the road crosses the torrent from Vajolet (see above), and about 2 m. farther reaches *Mazin* (4,488′), in a very picturesque situation, at the opening of a short glen (called Vajol?) which runs into the mass of the Rosengarten, and must be well worth exploring. Bearing to the rt. from that glen, a path mounts to the *Antermoja Pass*, leading to the upper end of the *Duronthal* (Rte. C). This is a short cut in distance, but scarcely in time, for a traveller going from Vigo to the Seisser Alps. About 2½ m. beyond Mazin is

Campidello (4,814′), standing at the opening of the Duronthal, through which descends the frequented track from the Seisser Alp (Rte. C). This place has the finest position in the valley of the Avisio as a centre for excursions in the adjoining valleys. From the village and its immediate neighbourhood, fine glimpses are gained of the surrounding peaks, and it stands at the meeting-place of the paths leading to several passes. With ampler accommodation, it would, doubtless, become a place of frequent resort. Of two small inns, that (Al Mulino) kept by G. Bernard is well managed and fairly comfortable—the best head-quarters for mountaineers in this valley.

Among other excursions the traveller may well follow the path by Gries leading to the Pordoi Pass (see Rte. I). Before reaching the summit he should bear to the right till he attains the western ridge of Monte Padon, which commands a noble view of the Marmolata. Gio. Batt. Bernard is the best guide here, and might be taken as porter even on an arduous expedition.

Above Campidello the scenery of the head of the Fassathal constantly increases in beauty and grandeur, and occasional glimpses of the Marmolata keep the traveller's attention constantly on the alert. Leaving on the l. hand the hamlet of Gries, the track passes *Canazei*, and for a short distance pursues a SSE. course, till after passing *Alba* (5,080′), at the opening of *Val di Contrin* (sometimes called Val Fredda), the easterly direction is resumed throughout the head of the valley. A short way beyond Alba is *Penia*, the highest hamlet. The track soon after crosses to the rt. bank of the torrent, and a rather steep ascent leads up to the broad green basin which lies immediately on the N. side of the Marmolata, and receives the torrents from two of its glaciers, here uniting to form the stream of the Avisio. The scenery of the Fedaya Pass may be truly called unique in the Alps. Its nearest counterpart will be sought among those famous passes in the Bernese Oberland that approach the bases of the great peaks. But, if it must be owned that the Wetterhorn and the Eiger, as seen from the tracks of the Scheidegg and Wengern Alps, are still grander objects than the Marmolata, there is something in the contrast between the idyllic repose and seclusion of the Fedaya basin, and the intense sternness of the Marmolata, for which the writer is unable to suggest a parallel. A further notice of the mountain is given below. Leaving on one side a small cluster of *casere*, where tolerable night-quarters are found by a traveller intending the ascent of the Marmolata, and passing a very small tarn, the track reaches the summit of the *Fedaya Pass* (6,884′) at the E. end of the basin, and rising but little above its level. The frontier between Italy and Tyrol is here passed, as the valley of the Cordevole, except at its extreme N. end, belongs to the Italian province of Belluno. The path (steep in places) descends to SE. amid very beautiful scenery, through a short glen called *Val Pettorina*; and as the traveller passes round the E. side of the Marmolata range, hitherto unseen portions of that peak come into view. After joining a cattle-track that descends from Val Ombretta (Rte. F), the path descends to enter the *Serai* or gorge of *Sottoguda*, one of the most remarkable in the Alps, which, by some strange chance, has remained almost unknown to travellers, and is not even named in the last edition of 'Schaubach,' usually very complete and well informed as to this district. For more than half a mile the torrent rushes through a cleft, varying from 12 ft. to about double that width, and the walls on either side rise so vertically, that but a narrow strip of sky is visible, and is in places almost completely concealed by bushes clinging to the rocks. Through this the path is carried, partly along the stream, but mainly on a stage suspended above it, crossing from side to side ten or twelve times. After issuing from this extraordinary defile, the path passes Sottoguda (4,254'), a small group of houses with a miserable inn, and descends thence to *Rocca* (3,881'). In 1 m. farther it reaches

Caprile, described in § 61, Rte. C.

The ascent of the *Marmolata* is an expedition which will be attractive to all practised mountaineers who may visit this district. Although the writer, in company with Mr. J. Birkbeck and Victor Tairraz of Chamouni, arrived within a few feet of the summit of the second peak of the mountain in 1860, the weather was so utterly unfavourable that his acquaintance with the mountain is mainly derived from the narratives of Dr. Grohmann, who reached the same peak in 1862, and made the first ascent of the highest summit in 1864, and from notes kindly communicated by Mr. Tuckett, who effected the second ascent in 1865. The name Vedretta Marmolata, often given to the mountain because its northern declivity is covered with névé, or glacier, should be rejected.

The description given by Mr. Churchill, who likens the form of the mountain to a wooden case for stationery, vertical on one side, and sloping at a high angle on the other, conveys very well the impression gained when the mountain is viewed in profile from the W. or E. side. To speak more accurately, the mountain may be described as a ridge extending from E. to W. with two central peaks, divided by a comparatively slight depression, and flanked by two attendant summits, one on the E. the other on the W. side. On the S. side the ridge falls in a range of precipices, in great part nearly vertical, and averaging about 3,000 ft. in height. On the N. side four massive buttresses project from the main mass, and between these three tongues of glacier, fed by the continuous slope of névé that covers the range on this side, descend towards the basin of Fedaya. Viewing the mountain from the N. side—the most favourable point being the Forcella di Padon (Rte. I)— the eastern flanking peak, called *Saranta* (9,947'), is seen to the l.;

thence the snow-ridge rises continuously to the Marmolata di Rocca, or second peak, which, according to the 'Kataster' measurement, is 402 ft. lower than the W. peak. Separated from the latter by a well-marked depression in the ridge, is the westernmost summit near Penia, called by Dr. Grohmann, Vernel; but the writer doubts whether that name is known in the Val di Fassa. The most direct and easiest course for the ascent seems to be that taken by Mr. Tuckett. Approaching the base of the peak by the central tongue of glacier, which is that nearest to the Fedaya châlets, he ascended thus until the rock-buttress on his rt. hand disappeared beneath the névé, and then bore to the rt. until he reached the lower part of the trough or couloir which divides the two main peaks. Finding the rocks on his rt. hand to be unexpectedly easy, he climbed up them, and so reached the topmost *calotte* of névé, when the actual summit was easily attained. Under favourable circumstances, the expedition seems to be free from all serious difficulty, but it would be unwise to attempt the ascent without at least one guide well used to ice-work, a qualification not possessed by any of the natives of Fassa. The 'Kataster' measurement of the highest peak is 11,466 ft., while a careful barometric determination by Dr. Grohmann gives only 11,045 ft. As the 'Kataster' measurements do not inspire complete confidence, and a single barometric measurement is subject to many chances of error, it is allowable to infer that the height of this crowning summit of the Fassa Alps is not yet satisfactorily determined. In a second ascent, accomplished in 1869, Mr. Tuckett, who reached the summit in 6¼ hrs. from Caprile, ascertained beyond a doubt that this peak surpasses the Cimon della Pala, and the other Primiero peaks, a point on which doubt had been thrown by Dr. Grohmann.

Route B.

LAVIS TO CAVALESE, BY VAL CEMBRA.

Fully 10 hrs. steady walking. At least 30 m.

The *Val Cembra*, or *Zimmerthal*, is so difficult of access that it is rarely traversed, except by the inhabitants of the villages that are perched on the heights above the river, which has cut a deep trench through the porphyry rock that prevails throughout this lower part of the valley of the Avisio. It is not, however, without attractions in point of scenery, and cannot fail to afford objects of interest to the naturalist. Those who would avoid the most laborious and hottest part of the way may take the path leading from the high-road between Trent and Pergine by Baselga and the Lake of Pinè (§ 59, Rte. A), and so reach *Spiazzo*, on the l. bank of the Avisio. That is one of the few places where it is possible to cross the river without great delay, and the traveller may join the main track on the rt. side of the valley near *Valda*. Another course is to start from Salurn and take a mountain-path that leads across the porphyry ridge dividing that place from Valda. There is a char-road from Lavis as far as Valda, and a bridle-track thence to Cavalese. Little or no time is saved by taking a vehicle, especially in ascending the valley. The distances are much greater than they appear on the map, owing to the many ravines cut by torrents in the porphyry slopes, each of which involves a detour.

From Lavis the road at once begins to ascend above the rt. bank of the Avisio, winding along the slopes with a general direction but little N. of E. After passing *Lisignano*, which commands a fine view, the road, in 3 hrs. from Lavis, reaches

Cembra (2,186'), the chief place in the valley, with a tolerably good inn (bei Lanziger), and a church, which does credit to so remote a place. Henceforward the valley ascends towards NE., but the road winds in every direction, owing to the roughness of the ground. Passing Faver, the road (in about 1½ hr. more) comes to an end at *Valda* (2,562'). Between these two villages Spiazzo is seen at a much lower level on the opposite bank, at the junction of the torrent from *Val Regnana* with the main stream. Grumes, Grauno, and some small hamlets are passed before reaching *Capriana*. At this village, and at *Val Floriana*, on the opposite bank, Val Cembra comes to an end, and the traveller enters Val di Fiemme. As far as Predazzo (see last Rte.) the direction henceforward is but little N. of E. Passing Altrey, the track for the first time approaches the Avisio at *Molina* (3,312'). This place, where there is said to be a good country inn, stands at the point where the *Pradajathal* pours its torrent into the Avisio from the N., and the more considerable stream from Val di Cadino joins the river from the S. By that way the most direct path from Borgo di Val Sugana reaches Cavalese (§ 59, Rte. I). From Molina the direct way to Cavalese is by Castello, but, by a slight detour, the carriage-road from Neumarkt (Rte. A) may be joined at Carano.

Route C.

BOTZEN TO CAMPIDELLO IN FASSA, BY THE SEISSER ALP.

	Hrs. walking	Eng. miles
Atzwang (high-road)	2½	8
Völs (bridle-track)	1¼	2½
Campidello (by Seisser Alp)	7½	20
	11¼	30½

The favourite way to approach the Dolomite Alps from the N. is that here described, and deservedly so, as it offers the attractions of scenery as singular as it is charming. Fine weather is, however, an essential condition. A walk or ride across the Seisser Alp in rain or snow, with the surrounding peaks veiled in cloud, is as little tempting as any expedition that can be suggested. As will be seen below, the way from Völs to Campidello admits of many variations; but, supposing the traveller not to diverge widely from the direct course, the time allowed is enough for a steady walker, clear of halts, except for the way across the summit of the Schleren.

The easiest course for reaching Völs from Botzen is to hire a carriage, and follow the road to Steg, whence a rather steep path mounts direct to *Völs* (2,862'), a village perched on a mountain terrace nearly 1,500 ft. above the Eisack. It has a very fair inn (Weisses Kreuz) which may serve as starting-point for the ascent of the Schleren (see below). Those who wish to avail themselves of the railway will take their places from Botzen to *Atzwang* (§ 49, Rte. A). In mounting from that place, the traveller bound for Seiss or Ratzes leaves Völs on his rt. hand, and joins the main track about ½ m. from that village. Ladies can obtain horses (? as to side-saddles) at Atzwang, or, if they prefer it, may be drawn in a sort of sledge which slides along the blocks of stone with which the track is paved. Guides are generally found ready to proffer their services both at Atzwang and Steg. They are content with 2 fl. a day, and generally ask no more than ½ fl. for showing the way to Seiss or Ratzes. Anton Bergler is recommended to botanists, as he knows the habitats of a good many rare plants, and is an agreeable companion. Josef von Metz, of Seiss, is also well recommended. Although a guide may not be absolutely necessary, it is judicious to take one; there are many paths, and it is easy to miss the direct way, especially in going to Ratzes. The writer knows of no guide here who can be relied on for difficult expeditions.

Nothing can be more charming than the track from Völs to the Seisser Alp. It winds along the gentle slopes that stretch up to the base of the Schleren, amid alternations of patches of pine forest with clumps of deciduous trees, and occasional openings of the greenest mountain meadow. After going some way NE. the track bears to the E., and the pinnacles of the Schleren become more and more dominant as the traveller approaches their base. When the defile of the Eisack between Klausen and Botzen was impassable to travellers, a frequented track was carried along this side of the valley. It is not surprising that at the time when vague popular traditions of heroic adventure were consolidated in the earliest German '*Heldenlieder*,' the marvellous scenery of this district should have become associated with legends that do not seem more marvellous. The 'crystal castle' of 'King Laurin the dwarf' was in the interior of the Schleren, and the 'Grüne Tan,' commemorated in those poems, was the forest of Hauenstein, that once extended from the base of the mountain to the verge of the defile of the Eisack. Before long the ruined castle of Hauenstein, the home of Oswald von Wolkenstein, the warrior and *minnesänger*, is seen rising above the forest. The traveller here has to choose his course. To the E. and SE. he sees before him an undulating ridge of moderate height, locally called *Puflatsch*, which is merely the outer declivity of the great plateau of the Seisser Alp. Due E. on undulating ground N. of the Puflatsch is the village of *Seiss* (3,264'), with two very fair country inns, of about equal pretensions. To the rt., or SE., is a hollow recess, 2 or 3 miles deep, almost completely overgrown by forest, at the head of which stand the *Baths of Ratzes* (4,172'). The place consists of three small houses nestling at the very base of the pinnacles of the Schleren, almost lost in the forest, so that visitors who stray from the beaten track are sometimes hard set to find their way when within a few hundred yards of the establishment. It is fair to warn the stranger, who may be tempted by the more than Arcadian beauty of the position, that he must expect more than Arcadian simplicity, and some deficiencies from the standard of modern civilisation. The baths are resorted to by farmers and small shopkeepers from the adjoining towns and villages, who willingly put up with the roughest sleeping accommodation. The food supplies are uncertain; but a traveller with mountain appetite will generally find sufficient nourishment. The people of the house are civil and obliging; but when it is full, as happens not rarely in summer, their good intentions cannot do much for the traveller's comfort. He who would spend some days in the immediate neighbourhood of the Seisser Alp and the Schleren, must choose between Ratzes and the next village inns of Seiss; but, if merely on his way from Völs to the Fassathal, he need not halt at either place. His shortest way is by an intermediate path that joins the cart-track from Seiss half-way in the ascent; but the writer recommends him to pass by Ratzes, if he does not fear a slight detour, or else a steep and rough ascent from that place, which leads up to the Seisser Alp near the point where the cart-track reaches the summit.

Postponing a notice of the Schleren, which is *par excellence* the mountain of this neighbourhood, it is necessary to say something of the Seisser Alp, so frequently referred to by all travellers who have visited this region. As the name denotes, it is an *alp*, or mountain pasture, but of extraordinary dimensions, measuring about 36 m. in circuit. The surface is an undulating plateau, with a mean elevation of from 5,500 to 6,000 ft., rising on its N. side towards the Grödnerthal, and on the NW. towards Ratzes, into a range of hills, chiefly formed of augite porphyry, that reach or surpass the level of 7,000 ft. On the SW. side the plateau is bounded by the dolomite range of the Schleren and Rosengarten, and to the SE. rises the still loftier mass of the Langkofel and Plattkofel. Between the latter and the Rosengarten, the S. limit of the plateau, marking the watershed between the Eisach and the Avisio, is formed of volcanic rocks, rising to a height of between 7,000 and 7,600 ft. The plateau, which is lower in the centre than towards the verge, would be converted into a lake if there were not an opening in the rim on the side of the Grödnerthal, through which passes the greater part of the drainage. The corner near the base of the Schleren is drained by a torrent, called Tschippitbach, that passes close to the Baths of Ratzes. One of the first facts that strike the traveller in a region where the strata are almost uniformly permeable, is the marshy character of the vegetation on the more level parts of the plateau. On further examination he will find that this arises from the nature of the superficial deposit. It is a tufa formed of volcanic ashes, that have been subjected to marine action, either at the time, or subsequent to the date of their original ejection. When the traveller in this district finds a tenacious soil, causing paludose vegetation, he may usually, though not invariably, attribute the effect to the presence of the same deposit. When he finds this deposit covering the greater part of the space lying between the Schleren and the head of the Gaderthal, and in many places appearing to be 2,000 ft. in thickness, he will infer the vastness of the scale of the ancient volcanic action of which one centre was probably at the Seisser Alp itself.

The great 'alp' supports in summer a large population, partly engaged in tending 1,200 or 1,300 head of horned cattle, and partly in making hay on portions of the plateau reserved for that purpose. It is said that there are 300 sennhütten and 400 hay-sheds. The former number is probably an exaggeration, and the more so as only a portion of the stock consists of dairy cows. The surface of the plateau is not altogether bare. There are many clumps of pine timber on the slopes, which help to diversify its aspect.

Nothing can be more charming than the walk over the Seisser Alp when favoured by weather. The *Langkofel* (10,392′), and *Plattkofel* (9,702′), which rise in front as the traveller steers towards the pass leading to Campidello, are unfailing objects of interest. The latter is accessible without serious difficulty from Seiss, or, more conveniently, from Sta. Christina in the Grödnerthal (Rte. G). The Langkofel looks as if it might long continue to defy all attempts at an escalade.

The rough cart-track, used for carrying down cheese, hay, &c., mounts from Seiss along the W. face of the *Puflatsch* (7,127′), and is joined on the way by a beaten path from Ratzes. But there is no difficulty in mounting through the forest from that place and joining the track about ¼ hr. below the point where it reaches the level of the plateau. When this has been attained there is no need to follow paths, as the traveller may take his own course, provided he keeps the true direction. The botanist will find many interesting plants, of which the following are seen in marshy ground:—*Thalictrum alpinum, Knautia longifolia, Kobresia caricina, Eriophorum alpinum, Carex capitata,* and *C. microglochin.* On drier spots, rising above the general level, several of the species given below in the Schleren list may also be found. In about 6 hrs. from Völs the summit of the pass leading to Fassa is attained. It is at the SW. side of the broad gap between the Plattkogel and the Rosengarten range, near to a NW. outlier from the latter. It is called *Mahlknecht Pass* on the German (Seiss) side, and *Molignon* in Fassa, and is 7,016 ft. above the sea. The name Mahlknecht properly belongs to a house, a sort of châlet inn, nearly ½ hr. below the summit on the Seisser Alp side, where the traveller willingly halts to enjoy a mountain luncheon, ennobled by the surrounding scenery. The way towards the Val di Fassa lies through the *Duronthal,* and though quite free from difficulty, is considerably steeper than on the other side. The glen makes a bend a little S. of due E., soon reaching a group of *Pinus cembra. Sedum villosum, Lomatogonium carinthiacum,* and other rare plants may be gathered by the way, and many species usually confined to the high Alpine region descend to the lower end of the glen. In 1½ hr. from the Mahlknecht the traveller reaches Campidello, and if he has not halted too long by the way, may easily go on to Vigo, or even Predazzo, on the same evening. (See Rte. A.)

Few travellers will take this route without accomplishing the ascent of the *Schleren* (8,405′). The panoramic view from the Rittnerhorn (on the opposite side of the Eisack defile) is more complete; but this is in many respects more interesting, and by ascending this, which is perhaps the most easily accessible dolomite summit in this region, the stranger gains the opportunity of making a nearer acquaintance with the singular structure of these mountains. The name is often applied to the entire range, which extends from WNW. to ESE., nearly at rt. angles to that of the Rosengarten; but is locally confined to the mass forming its western extremity, and immediately overhanging Ratzes. This is separated by a slight depression from the E. end of the range, appropriately named *Rosszähne*, as its shattered towers of rock seen from a distance bear some resemblance to a row of horse's teeth, of unequal size, loosely set in a jaw-bone of rock. On its N. and NW. sides, the Schleren shows precipitous faces of rock, broken here and there into detached pinnacles and towers that are characteristic of the dolomite formation; and the range extending thence to the Rosszähne falls everywhere steeply towards the Seisser Alp. On the S. side, the range is far more easy of access, and the central portion subsides in comparatively gentle slopes towards the Tierserthal (Rte. D). The geologist cannot fail to be struck by the regular order in which the sedimentary strata have been deposited in a district where there is such complete evidence of volcanic action on the largest scale, and where the forms of the mountains suggest the belief in violent disturbances of the earth's crust. In ascending the mountain from Völs, or Seiss, or Tiers —by three different sides—he will pass over the same series of formations, including nearly all the subdivisions of the trias, beginning with the Gröden sandstone at the base, and terminating with the Raibl beds which form a small patch at the summit. However extensive the changes that have supervened in the mineral character of these beds, their nearly horizontal stratification, and uniform thickness, show that since the period of their original deposition they have suffered no considerable disturbance. The same conclusion is enforced elsewhere in this district, but is nowhere better seen than here.

The easiest way to the summit of the Schleren is that from Völs. There is a tolerably good path, and ladies may ride nearly all the way. In 1864, a hut was erected to supply refreshments by the way, but the writer has not heard whether it has been kept open in subsequent years. There is another easy, but rather circuitous, way from Tiers (Rte. D). Having gained the ridge between the Schleren and the Rosszähne, the latter way turns to the l. and follows the ridge to the summit.

The way from Seiss is to follow the beaten track to the Seisser Alp, and then turn sharply to the rt. It is necessary to cross the Tschippitbach before reaching the base of the slope, immediately to the L of the crags of the Schleren. Here a beaten track is found, frequented by native visitors, who often pass the night in an adjoining *senn hütte*, in order to reach the summit earlier. On reaching the ridge of the mountain, a little chapel or oratory is seen, erected for the shepherds who pass the summer on the mountain, and turning to the rt., a short ascent leads to the top. From Ratzes, the ordinary course, involving a wide detour, is to join the track from Seiss to the Seisser Alp. The mountaineer will much prefer a steep scramble through the forest by the N. side of the impassable cleft of the Tschippitbach. The path has been carried away in places, and, unless improved, can scarcely be recommended to ordinary travellers. There was a more difficult, and rather shorter, way from Ratzes, by the very steep slopes above the S. side of the gorge of the Tschippitbach. Bearing to the l., the ordinary track above mentioned was joined about halfway in the ascent. Still more arduous, and fit only for a practised and steady cragsman, was a way that led nearly directly from Ratzes to the upper plateau of the Schleren by narrow ledges on the face of the seemingly hopeless precipices. It was discovered by noticing the passage of chamois, and called Gams-steig — here pronounced Gammets-steig. In 1864, the writer was assured that this way, and that by the slopes S. of the Tschippitbach, had both been rendered unapproachable by landslips that had been caused by a storm in that year. Another course, also reserved for practised cragsmen, is through the Klamm. This is seen from the track between Völs and Seiss as a deep gash, cleft, as though by Roland's sword, into the centre of the mountain. The climb is said not to be very difficult, but the fall of a rock or other slight accident might easily make it impracticable. The summit of the Schleren shows distinctly the plateau character, though it is deeply excavated by the Klamm and other lesser fissures. The highest point is rather far from the edge of the plateau, so that the view does not extend to the nearer valleys. The outline of the Rittnerhorn panorama, given in this volume, will assist the traveller in identifying many of the distant summits. The Gross Glockner is not seen, being apparently masked by the Antholzer Alps. Nor did the writer notice the Pelmo (counted in the panorama by Schaubach), which is very finely seen from the Rosszähne. The Adamello, Ortler, and Oetzthal Alps are all well seen, but the SE. horizon is concealed by the Rosengarten range. Besides admiring the view from the summit, the traveller should not omit to approach the verge of the Klamm, and that of the precipices facing towards Ratzes and the Seisser Alp. An active walker may easily take the Schleren on his way from Völs to Campidello in a day's walk of about 10 hrs., excluding halts. Those who have time may combine the Rosszähne with the Schleren in the same excursion. The height attributed (on what authority?) to the eastern tooth—9,172 ft.—appears to the writer considerably above the truth, and he estimates the difference between this and the Schleren at between 300 and 400 ft. For the greater part of the way, the ridge is quite easily followed; but at the E. end there are some awkward places. The face of the Rosszähne towards the Seisser Alp is fluted into a series of furrows by the action of the weather. There are several places where the ascent is sufficiently easy, but caution should be used in descending. It is not a place where any but a very experienced climber should go alone; especially when the rocks are covered with ice, as the writer found it at his last visit, on Aug. 13, 1864. Though a part of the panorama is lost, the writer prefers the view from the Rosszähne to that from the Schleren. Especially striking is the view into the gorge of the Tschaminbach, and that of the Rosengarten range, here near at hand. It would doubtless be possible for a mountaineer to reach the Rosszähne by the Tschaminbach from Tiers (Rte. D), and the excursion would be full of interest.

There is no mountain in the Alps that has acquired so great a reputation among botanists for the richness of its flora, and the number of rare plants it produces, as the Schleren, and there is, perhaps, none that deserves its reputation so well. At the same time it may be here remarked that many species once supposed to be peculiar to this and a few other spots, are now known to be spread throughout the Dolomite Alps, extending hence to the sources of the Isonzo, and even beyond those limits. The following list includes the more interesting plants of the Schleren range (including the Rosszähne). An asterisk is prefixed to those characteristic species found on nearly all the dolomite peaks of this and the adjoining districts:—*Ranunculus hybridus, R. Seguieri, *Aquilegia Bertolonii, * Papaver pyrenaicum, Arabis cœrulea, * A. pumila, Draba tomentosa, D. incana, Cochlearia brevicaulis, Capsella pauciflora, Dianthus glacialis, *Alsine austriaca, A. lanceolata, *Cherleria imbricata, Phaca alpina, Oxytropis Halleri, Astragalus purpureus, * Potentilla nitida, * Saxifraga squarrosa, * S. Sedoides, S. Facchinii (Rosszähne), Valeriana supina, *V. elongata, Gnaphalium carpathicum, *Achillea clavenæ, * Ptarmica oxyloba, Artemisia spicata, * Senecio abrotanifolius, Saussurea discolor, Leontodon Taraxaci, * Crepis incarnata, * Phyteuma comosum, * P. Sieberi, Campanula Morettiana, Lomatogonium carinthiacum, Gentiana prostrata, G. tenella, * G. imbricata, * Pæderota Bo-

narota, Tozzia alpina, Pedicularis rosea, Androsace helvetica, A. Hausmanniana, *Primula minima, Juncus arcticus, Carex rupestris, C. incurva, C. reclinata, *Sesleria sphaerocephala, Asplenium Seelosii (above Hauenstein), *Woodsia hyperborea, W. glabella* (?) Besides the localities for fossils mentioned by Richthofen and others, the writer has observed that the steep rocks of the Rosszähne, on the side facing the Seisser Alp, are in some places extremely rich in marine testacea.

Route D.

VIGO TO BOTZEN, BY THE CARESSA PASS.

Within the last few years a road has been opened through the Karneidthal from Botzen to Welschenofen, which deserves to be generally known. In many parts of the Alps it would of itself suffice to draw tourists from a distance, but it has been almost overlooked amid the manifold attractions of this beautiful district. It has the further recommendation that it supplies a deficient link in the most direct and easiest route between Vigo, the favourite headquarters of tourists in the Fassathal, and Botzen. Before the completion of that road, travellers followed a circuitous course, either by Deutschenofen or by Tiers, to avoid the diffi-

culties of the Karneidthal. As the walk by either of those places offers agreeable alternatives to the pedestrian, they are further noticed below.

1. By the *Karneidthal*, 4 hrs. on foot (or rather less) to Welschenofen. About 15 m., by road, thence to Botzen. The *Caressa Pass* (5,966′) is a broad opening in the irregular range of dolomite peaks that extend along the NW. side of the Avisio from near Predazzo to Campidello. It is especially remarkable in descending through the Val di San Pelegrino (Rte. E); and this broad opening, between the great peaks on either side, seems to point this out as one of the main portals between the secluded Valley of Fassa and the outer world. *Moëna* (Rte. A) stands immediately below the opening of the pass, and close to the junction of the little torrent that descends from it to the Avisio. There is, however, a good path from Vigo, mounting diagonally along arid slopes composed in part of Gröden sandstone; and as the latter place stands higher than Moëna, the pass is reached in about the same time. At the top is an opening, fully ½ m. broad, between the N. extremity of the Latemar range and the *Kälbleck* (about 8,600′), a rugged point, not very difficult of access, which forms the southern extremity of the Rosengarten range, being followed to the N. by the Rothewand. The view from it is not very extensive; but the Primiero dolomites and the Cima d'Asta are well seen. A broad track that runs NW. from the summit of the Caressa Pass, leads to Tiers (see below). The way to Welschenofen lies only a little N. of true W., and presently enters a depression, soon converted by the action of the torrent into a deep cleft. The rough path descends steeply on the W. side of the cleft. In 4 hrs.' easy walking the traveller reaches

Welschenofen (3,868′), standing in an open basin where several mountain streams unite to form the *Karneidlach*. Of three or four rough inns the Krone is said to be the best. From this place, or from Tiers, the naturalist may best explore the great western face of the Rosengarten and Rothewand, so conspicuous from Botzen, which for combined height and length may be counted one of the greatest walls of rock in the Alps. Johann Plauk, of this place, is recommended as a guide. At Welschenofen commences the remarkable road spoken of above. The traveller, by paying high, may generally procure a horse and light country vehicle here, but if pressed for time may do well to accept the terms offered by Rizzi, the landlord of Vigo, who sends a horse across the pass with the traveller's luggage, and after a rest at Welschenofen forwards him in an einspann to Botzen, at the rather high rate of 15 fl. The road, which is throughout narrow, and in places very steep, is fit only for the lightest vehicles. For the first hour the scenery, though pleasing, is not very remarkable. The red porphyry mountains that enclose the valley offer the accustomed contrast between masses of parched rock and a luxuriant vegetation which finds nourishment in the fissures. After passing Birchbrücke, about 3 m. below Welschenofen (inn seems better than any at that place), where a torrent that descends partly from the Latemar range, partly from the Schwarzhorn (see below), joins the Karneidbach, the valley narrows gradually, and before long the road enters the defile which, until pierced by the new road, opposed an absolute barrier to all direct communication between the upper part of the valley and its mouth. In its own way this is as remarkable as the gorge of Sottoguda (mentioned in Rte. A), with the difference that the rock here sustains a far more vigorous vegetation. This is not nearly so narrow a cleft, but it is on a greater scale, and the fact of its being traversed by a carriage-road increases the effect. A short tunnel is driven through an angle of the porphyry wall of the defile in one place, and there are many picturesque bridges over the torrent. The defile terminates abruptly under the walls of the castle of Karneid that stands on a rocky promontory above the point where the Karneidbach issues into the valley of the Eisack, about 2 m. above Botzen.

2. *By Deutschenofen.* This way involves a considerable detour for a traveller whose object is to reach Botzen; but if his aim be merely the nearest station on the rly., he will follow the course noticed below to Branzoll on the Adige (7 m. S. of Botzen), which is easily reached in 5 hrs. from Welschenofen.

Deutschenofen (4,447′) is a large and thriving village with an inn (beim Rösslwirth), standing on the ridge that divides the Karneidthal from the valley of the Adige. Having reached Welschenofen by the Caressa Pass, the traveller follows the new road for fully 3 m. to the Birchbrücke, and then mounts by a track that bears at first SW., then nearly due W., and without any considerable ascent reaches Deutschenofen. It lies W. of the watershed, and the direct course to the valley of the Adige is along the Brantenbach, through a glen running due W., and overlooked from the village. This opens into the main valley of the Adige at *Leifers*, more than 5 m. S. of Botzen, and nearly 2 m. N. of Branzoll. A far more agreeable way to Botzen is by a path that winds among the porphyry hills between Karneid and the Adige. In 4 hrs., or less, the traveller reaches Botzen. To avoid the unpleasant walk along the hot and dusty road between Leifers and Branzoll the pedestrian bound for the latter place should cross the Brantenbach below Deutschenofen, and follow a path over a low ridge to *Petersberg*, leaving on his l. hand the mountain monastery of *Weissenstein* (4,983′). A path descends rapidly in 1½ hr. from Petersberg to Branzoll (§ 57, Rte. A).

Deutschenofen was originally a colony of German, probably Suabian, settlers, who have preserved in their speech many words of the early dialect of that part of Germany, familiar to students of the Nibelunge Noth and the early Minnesängers. Welschenofen, on the contrary, as the name denotes, was originally inhabited by Italian settlers, though they have long since adopted the language of their German neighbours.

From Deutschenofen, or from a country inn in the hamlet adjoining the monastery of Weissenstein, the traveller may ascend *Joch Grimm*, a mountain producing many rare plants, commanding a fine view, and immediately overlooking a singular crater-like hollow on its W. side. By the E. slope of that mountain he may reach the *Schwarzenbach*, which is the SE. branch of the Karneidbach, and with a local guide, may follow the torrent to the Birchbrücke. There is a decent-looking country inn at that place, where a belated traveller may seek night-quarters. Another way from Joch Grimm is to go southward to Cavalese, only a few miles distant, either over the summit of the *Schwarzhorn* (7,986'), or by either side of that mountain.

3. *By Tiers.* Though rarely visited by strangers, *Tiers* (3,323') is very well situated for mountain excursions, and a mountaineer may well make it his headquarters for two or three days. As mentioned above, there is a track leading to it from the summit of the Caressa Pass. It traverses open undulating country, covered with mountain pastures; and, as it passes near the W. base of the range of the Rosengarten, must command very fine views. At its upper end the *Tierserthal* divides into two branches. One of these, called *Purgametsch*, descends about due W. from the W. base of the Rosengarten. The northern branch, the *Tschaminbach*, flows SW. from the savage hollow between the Rosszähne and the Rosengarten, mentioned in Rte. C. The track from the Caressa Pass descends into the Purgametsch glen, about 1 hr. above the village of *Tiers*. This stands rather more than 1 m. below the fork of the valley. The inn (beim Rosenwirth) is said to afford fair accommodation, and Georg Villgrattner is recommended as a good guide. It is a short walk of 2 hrs. from Tiers to *Blumau*, the rly. station, 5 m. above Botzen.

As mentioned in Rte. C., the Schleren may be easily ascended from Tiers, so that an active traveller, starting early from Völs or Ratzes, might reach Vigo on the same day by the Caressa Pass; but if not pressed for time he should give a day to the exploration of one or other of the upper branches of the Tiers valley. On this side of the Rosengarten the German population has preserved some vague recollection of the mythic origin of the name of that mountain, and often call it the 'Rosengarten of King Laurin.'

Route E.

PREDAZZO TO CENCENIGHE, BY PANEVEGGIO, OR SAN PELEGRINO.

In the last Rte. the more frequented paths leading westward from the upper part of the Avisio valley to that of the Adige have been described. We now give a brief notice of the only frequented passes leading to Cencenighe, the chief place in the upper part of the valley of the Cordevole. These passages are rarely traversed by strangers. The writer is but partially acquainted with either of them, and none but the briefest allusions are found in any published work. Yet both passes, or at least that first noticed, offer very grand scenery, and, in good weather, they are quite free from difficulty.

1. *By Paneveggio*. In § 59, Rte. F,

the way from Primiero to Predazzo by San Martino di Castrozza is described. The valley descending to Predazzo is rightly called *Val Travignolo*, but is more commonly known in Fiemme as *Paneveggio*, that name properly belonging only to the mountain-inn, or hospice, at the upper end of the valley, now accessible by a good road. This mounts from Predazzo along the slopes on the N. side of the valley, which are covered with forest, save where occasional clearings leave space for Alpine pasture. Rather more than 3 hrs. are required in ascending the valley to reach *Paneveggio* (5,160'), noticed in § 59, Rte. B. This is a tempting spot for a mountaineer, as, though more distant than S. Martino di Castrozza, it is better placed for several fine excursions. It was from this starting-point that Mr. Whitwell, with Christian Lauener, and Santo Siorpaes made the first ascent of the Cimon della Pala in 1870, to be repeated only by such first-rate climbers as the three above named. A much easier expedition—though not advisable for novices—is the ascent of the Cima di Vezzana, the second in height of the Primiero peaks. It was reached in 1872 by Messrs. D. W. Freshfield and Tucker, without guides, by way of the short and steep glacier lying between this and the Cimon della Pala. 2 hrs. climb up steep ice-slopes, requiring much step-cutting, lead to the col between the two peaks, whence the former is easily attained. From the col—which they named *Passo di Travignolo*—there seems to be no difficulty in descending to Gares, or by bearing to the rt. the plateau near the Passo delle Cornelle (§ 59, Rte. L) may be reached, and the descent made to S. Martino and Primiero.

The ordinary way from Paneveggio to Cencenighe mouuts gently for some distance by a broad wood-cutter's track, passing below the alp of *Guiribello*, a beautiful pasture with a model *casera*, belonging to one of the members of the Austrian Imperial family.

The way to Cencenighe soon begins to mount to NE., above the rt. bank of the Travignolo, and before long the wild hollow through which that torrent descends from the base of the Cimon della Pala is seen to ESE., on the rt. hand. The view of that wonderful peak—the Matterhorn of the Dolomites—is nearly equal to that from the Monte Castellazzo. The highest alp is called *Guiribrutt*, contrasting in its stony barrenness, as in name, with Guiribello. The *Passo di Valles* (6,877') is traversed by a well-traced, though not much frequented path. It is sometimes called *Forcella di Venigia*, but that name properly belongs to a hunter's pass lying somewhat farther south, and rather higher than the ordinary way. In less than an hour from the summit the traveller reaches *Falcade* (4,287'), where Indian corn is grown at a very unusual height. The head of the valley of the *Biois* lies amidst rocks of red porphyry and other igneous rocks which are conveyed by that torrent to the valley of the Cordevole. The most direct track from Falcade to Cencenighe keeps to the l. bank of the Biois, leaving on the opposite side the village of *Forno di Canale* (3,204'), standing at the opening of the glen of Gares (§ 59, Rte. L), and possessing a fair country inn, probably as good as that at Cencenighe (§ 61, Rte. C). 8 hrs. ought to suffice for reaching the latter place from Predazzo.

2. *By the Passo di San Pelegrino* (6,619'). By road to Moëna, 6 m.; thence to Cencenighe, 6 hrs. on foot, exclusive of halts. This way, which is that commonly adopted by the natives, is far from rivalling that above described in scenic beauty, but is not wanting in attractions of a less wild and fantastic character. The Val di San Pelegrino is parallel in its course to Val Travignolo, but shorter and more open. The forests leave wider gaps of mountain pasture, and the slope of the Riccobetta (Rte. A), formed of Monzoni syenite, is in great part bare of timber. On the ascent to the *Passo di San Pelegrino*, at the head of the valley, the traveller passes a chapel, and a rude mountain inn, or

refuge, where refreshments may be obtained. According to the accurate Trinker, the height of the pass is 6,619 ft.; but the new edition of Schaubach (usually very correct in this district) gives 6,269 ft. In fine weather a guide is scarcely necessary to find the way to the summit, nor to follow the somewhat beaten track that descends to Falcade.

Route F.

CAPRILE TO VIGO, BY THE FORCELLA DI OMBRETTA.

About 10 hrs.' moderate walking, exclusive of halts.

This may be considered as a mere variation on the ordinary course from Vigo to Caprile by the Fedaya Pass, but it is so little known, and so full of attractions of the highest order, that it is here described under a separate heading, in the hope of attracting to it the attention of travellers. It involves the passage of a good deal of rough ground, and is for moderate walkers a full day's work, but there is no real difficulty in the way. Taking into account the wonderful variety of grand and beautiful scenes that follow in constant succession throughout the way, the writer is inclined to reckon this amongst the very finest excursions in this region of the Alps. It will generally be best enjoyed by starting very early from Caprile, as the Marmolata is more frequently clear in the early part of the day. In clear weather a practised mountaineer does not require the aid of a local guide, and it would not be easy to find at Caprile a man acquainted with the entire route here described.

The way to the Fedaya Pass (Rte. A) is followed through the gorge of the Serai, but soon after emerging from that singular cleft the ordinary track is left to ascend through the branch of the valley called *Val Pettorina*, and a cattle-track is followed that mounts nearly due W. through Val Ombretta. As to another track, which goes SW., by the S. side of the *Sasso Vernale* (9,845'), and leads to the head of the Val di San Pelegrino, the writer has obtained no reliable information.

Val Ombretta is a hollow trough lying immediately at the base of the vast mural precipices on the S. side of the Marmolata, which rise above it to a height averaging about 3,000 ft. Passing at first along the S. base of the Saranta, it is necessary to climb a high step that separates the upper basin of Val Ombretta from the lower part, into which the traveller has entered. There is a circuitous track for cattle, but the direct way is up a rocky declivity, where progress is made less difficult at the steepest part, by some pine trunks laid diagonally against the face of the wall, at a point where the botanist may gather fine specimens of *Artemisia lanata*. Above this is the highest shepherd's hut, and then the traveller enters the upper basin or trough, over which the majestic precipices of the Marmolata rise in surpassing grandeur.

In approaching the W. end of the trough, where it is barred across by a ridge connecting the Marmolata with the Sasso Vernale that rises on the rt. hand, the traveller is struck by the contrast of the black colour of this ridge with the light grey and pink of the dolomite masses that surround him. The ridge is formed of decomposed melaphyre, or black porphyry, or perhaps (as the writer suspects), of a rock formed by the imperfect consolidation of masses of volcanic sand and scoriæ, ejected contemporaneously with that ancient lava. Be that as it may, this is one of those places where, in toiling up the rather steep slope, with the feet sinking in soft black sand, the recollection of the final cone of Etna and Vesuvius is forcibly brought back to the traveller. The *Forcella di Val Ombretta* (9,052' Grohmann) has been vaguely known by various names. Val Ombretta, and the highest part of the Contrin valley on the W. side of the pass having both been known as Val Fredda, the pass has been called 'Passo di Val Fredda'; and German travellers have also named it Contrin Joch. On quitting the volcanic formation, which extends but a short way, the traveller descends into a wild hollow filled with masses of dolomite fallen from the crags of the Marmolata, and patches of unmelted snow forming little pools of half-frozen water. The easiest way lies to the rt., close under the ridge of the Marmolata. Finally, after passing over a good deal of rough ground, the traveller reaches a point where he must choose between two different courses in order to attain his destination. He here overlooks the glen of *Contrin*, through which a torrent flows NW., to join the Avisio near the head of Val di Fassa, between Alba and Penia. That is the easiest way for reaching the main valley; but in going to Vigo it involves a considerable detour, and the walk between Campidello and that place is not very interesting. The other course is to traverse the ridge that divides Contrin from the Monzoni valley, and descend through the latter to Pozza near Vigo. By bearing to the l. as soon as the nature of the ground makes it advisable to do so, and crossing the Contrin torrent high up, the ascent to the second ridge is reduced within very moderate limits. In the ascent, a group of arollas (*Pinus cembra*) is seen at the unusual height of about 7,570 ft. In Val Ombretta, the larch reaches to 7,500 ft.; and a single stunted tree was noticed 150 ft. higher. Throughout the ascent the view looking back at the Marmolata is extremely grand. The writer thinks it not impossible that the ascent may be achieved from this side. A slight ledge indicating a crack or fault in the strata runs diagonally upwards to a notch in the ridge some way below, and W. of the highest peak. There is a path, slightly traced, that leads to the summit of the ridge over Contrin, about 6,000 ft. in height, and it there joins a broad deserted track that seems to have been made for the passage of carts with timber, cheese, &c., from the *sennhütten* of Contrin to the lower part of Val di Fassa. This zigzags down the long, steep, and uniform slope that leads to the main branch of the Monzoni valley. The pedestrian should descend these slopes in a direct line for the bottom of the valley, without attempting to cross a projecting buttress on the rt. hand. Walking steadily, the writer reached Vigo in 2 hrs. 20 min. from the summit of the pass. The Monzoni valley, full of interest to the naturalist, is further noticed in Rte. A.

[It is probably by the way noticed above that Mr. Tuckett early in the season made his third ascent of the Marmolata. He found little difficulty in following the ridge, then covered with snow. Another party going at a later season found the rocks bare of snow, decidedly difficult and somewhat unsafe.]

Route G.

BOTZEN TO BRUNECK, BY THE GRÖDNERTHAL AND GADERTHAL.

The formation of the mountains in this district makes it very difficult to describe it in an intelligible manner. Instead of being distributed in definite ridges, they form isolated peaks, or larger blocks of high land, divided by comparatively deep depressions from the adjoining masses. Hence passes, for the most part easy of access, are very numerous, and the traveller may here vary his routes to an indefinite extent. This observation holds especially as to the district north of the head of Val di Fassa, where the drainage is irregularly distributed between the Avisio and the Cordevole on the S. side, and the torrents which flow to the Eisack through the Grödnerthal, or to the Rienz through the Gaderthal. The four valleys, whose highest sources diverge from a single huge block of mountain including the Sella-Spitz, and Monte Pordoi, are connected by many passes, most of which are noticed in the following Rtes.; while in the present Rte. we give a short description of the two chief valleys that drain the northern part of this district, as they may be visited by a traveller pressed for time, who takes them on his way between Botzen and Bruneck in Pusterthal.

The Grödnerthal is a comparatively short valley, about 18 m. in length, that pours its torrent into the Eisack at *Waidbruck*, opposite Kollmann, on the Eisack, where there is now a rly. station (§ 49, Rte. B). The lower part of the valley is a narrow and hot defile, the scenery of which scarcely rises to grandeur. It is slow work to walk, and quite equally so to mount in a carriage along the new road that is carried along the N. slope of the valley to Plan at its upper end, so that most travellers prefer either of the alternative courses mentioned below. The upper part of the valley being at a great height above the Eisack, a very long ascent is required to reach St. Peter, the first village, after which a gentler ascent leads to *St. Ulrich* (4,058'), the chief place in the valley, with two inns (zum Goldenen Adler; zum Weissen Ross), both supplying very fair accommodation. By the new road, St. Ulrich is 8 m. from Waidbruck, and 6 m. from Plan, where the road comes to an end at the upper end of the valley.

The appearance of comfort and well-being in a relatively numerous population that inhabit the upper part of this valley indicates the existence of a special branch of industry. The art of carving figures of men and animals in the wood of the *Pinus cembra* (Germ. *Zirbenholz*) was introduced here early in the last century, and has maintained itself ever since. Children's toys, and the figures of saints, are objects chiefly represented; and a considerable trade, extending to the most distant parts of Europe, has held its ground amidst changes of fashion. Many natives wander abroad retailing these articles in distant places, but after gaining a competence, usually return to settle in their native valley. The fabrication of lace has also been of late years introduced here.

It has been said in the introduction to this section that the people of this valley and those of the adjoining Gaderthal speak a dialect (locally called Ladin) which has considerable affinity with the Romantsch of the E. of Switzerland, and especially the form of that language spoken in the Engadine. It is a singular fact that there are well-marked differences, both grammatical and lexicographical, between the dialects of these two adjoining valleys, indicating kinship rather than identity of stock. This fact lends colour to the belief that these valleys were colonised during the period of Roman rule. But a previously established Rhætian population must have been driven out to make way for the Southern settlers. Supposed Rhætian antiquities have been discovered at many places in S. Tyrol, and amongst others close to the village of St. Ulrich. Since 1848, a large number of ancient graves have been found scattered over a level tract, about 40 acres in extent, less than 1 m. above St. Ulrich. Those who are interested in the subject should apply to Herr Purger, an intelligent native of the valley, the largest dealer in carved wood articles, who has collected many of the objects extracted from these graves.

In the Grödnerthal, all the men, and most of the younger women, now speak some German, but it is best to use the local names for places. In the native dialect the valley is called *Gardena*, and St. Ulrich is known as *Ortiseit*. This place supplies convenient head-quarters for many excursions, and the Seisser Alp, or even the Schleren, may be visited from hence. But most travellers will prefer to take Ratzes and the Schleren on their way from Botzen to the Grödnerthal. Those who have already ascended the Schleren may take an intermediate and very agreeable course from Botzen to St. Ulrich, by Castelruth (*Castelrotto*),* a large and prosperous village, much resorted to in the *sommerfrisch* season by persons who seek more comfortable houses than are found in most of the mountain villages of this district. It has two inns (Lamm; Goldene Rössl), both above the average of country inns in this district. It is only 2 m. distant from Seiss, and being within easy reach of the plateau of the Seisser Alp, would be a pleasant place for a retreat during hot weather. The easiest way from Castelruth to St. Ulrich keeps along the base of the northern escarpment of the Seisser Alp, and by that way the distance is accomplished in less than 3 hrs. Those who are not pressed for time should make a detour by the Seisser Alp,

* In this and the following Rtes. the Ladin names, as far as known to the writer, are added within brackets.

reaching one of the prominent points that commands a magnificent view, and then descend by *Pufls*, and through a ravine that leads to the Grödner torrent, beyond which stands St. Ulrich.

Another variation on the common way to St. Ulrich is suited for those approaching the valley from the side of Brixen, who wish to explore an unfrequented valley. At Klausen (see § 49, Rte. A), in the valley of the Eisack, the traveller passing in the rly. carriage scarcely perceives the opening of the *Villnösthal*. Though rarely traversed by a stranger, this valley, once preserved as a deer-forest by the Counts of Tyrol, sustains a thriving and industrious population. There is a tolerable road from Klausen to *St. Peter*, the chief village, said to have a good inn. This way is interesting to the geologist, and those who have time may gain a remarkably fine panoramic view from the *Raschetz Alp* (7,476'), whence St. Ulrich is reached in 2½ hrs.

In visiting the upper part of the Grödnerthal, and the passes connecting it with the neighbouring valleys, the traveller will encounter even more than the usual difficulty in identifying the names of the surrounding mountains, glens, and even the well-known passes. No doubt the confusion of dialects has aggravated this inconvenience. It may be right to say here that Mayr's map of Tyrol, which is in the hands of many travellers, is generally less correct in this region than in the central range of Tyrol. In some places, and especially at the head of the valley of the Cordevole, it is hopelessly wrong, and can do nothing but mislead those who trust to it.

About 2½ m. above St. Ulrich is *St. Christina* (with a fair country inn, kept by Dossis). Here the *Langkofel* (10,392'), always a striking object from whatever side it be seen, assumes an aspect of extreme grandeur, which impressed the minds of the earliest travellers who visited this region, and who little suspected that this is but one among a large number of dolomite peaks of equal or greater height that rival it in the fantastic beauty and wildness of its aspect. The last hamlet in the valley is *Sta. Maria* (5,129'), 2 hrs. from St. Ulrich, with a small and poor inn, standing at the junction of the Langenthal with the main branch of the Grödnerthal. Sta. Maria is sometimes called Wolkenstein, and the Langenthal Wolkensteinerthal, from the neighbouring castle of Wolkenstein, further noticed below. The ordinary way to the Gaderthal follows the road ESE. through the proper head of the Grödnerthal; and this comes to an end little more than 1 m. above Sta. Maria at *Plan*, where there is a poor inn, in which the writer long ago found a hospitable reception when the present occupants were children. A short and easy ascent of little more than 1 hr. leads to the *Colfosco Pass* (7,042'), or *Grödner Joch*, the easiest pass between the Grödnerthal and Gaderthal, commanding a noble view of the peaks near the Ampezzo Pass, seen above the intermediate ranges. Hereabouts, in addition to many of the characteristic plants of this region, the botanist may find the rare *Soyeria montana* The pass lies between two remarkable mountain masses, to which the student of Richthofen's geological writings on this district will find frequent reference. The northern mass, lying in the angle between the valleys named above, is called by Richthofen the *Guerdenazza Plateau*. It is the more extensive, but being cleft by several deep glens, and very irregular in its contour, it does not exhibit such characteristic features as the so-called *Sella Plateau* on the S. side of the pass. From most points of view this shows as a vast fortress, built on a Titanic scale, with ramparts rising from 2,000 to 3,000 ft. above the curtain of pine forest that encompasses their base. But one of the higher summits seems to have been measured. The *Monte Pordoi* attains 10,333 ft. according to the Kataster. This is apparently the same peak which is called *Boè* at the head of the Gaderthal, and was ascended by Dr. Grohmann, who makes the height 10,341 ft.

The descent towards the Gaderthal is rather steeper than the western slope of the pass, but the sadly thinned pineforest is soon reached, and traversed; and the way lies between fields of barley and rye, here grown at an unusual elevation, before reaching *Colfosco* (5,421'), or Colfuschk, the highest village in this branch of the Gaderthal, about 8 hrs. from the Waidbruck station. There is no tolerable inn here, and those who seek night-quarters must go to Corfara, scarcely half an hour's walk, though lying in a separate branch of the valley. At a small group of houses called Pescosta, a short distance below Colfosco, the torrent from that place joins that from Corfara (see next Rte.), and the united stream flows NE. through the *Corfarathal*. In 1 hr., descending along the l. bank of the torrent, the traveller reaches *Stern*, where this unites with the main branch of the Gader, which henceforward, to near its junction with the Rienz, follows a course little diverging from due N. There is much confusion as to the nomenclature of the main valley and its tributaries. The names Gaderthal, Abteithal, and Enneberg are indiscriminately applied by strangers, and sometimes even by natives, to the entire valley. Correctly, however, the names *Enneberg* should be reserved for the SE. branch of the valley, also known as *Vigilthal*, or *Mareo* in the Ladin dialect. Above Zwischenwassern, where that joins the main S. branch, the latter is called *Abteithal*, though this designation is specially reserved for the upper end above St. Leonhard. The name *Gaderthal* in its restricted sense applies only to the lower valley *below* the junction of its two main branches, but we only follow common usage in applying it collectively to the entire district drained by the stream of the Gader. Less than 1 hr. below Stern the traveller, after crossing to the rt. bank of the torrent, reaches *St. Leonhard* (4,456'), where a few houses are gathered round the church and the inn. The latter supplies fair accommodation. The name of the commune, including many scattered hamlets, of which this is the centre, is *Abtei (Badia)*. This gives its name to the upper valley, and to its inhabitants, often called Badiotes. This neighbourhood has suffered much from landslips on a large scale, differing from *Bergfalls* in the more gradual nature of the process. The traces, on a small scale, of a recent event of this kind, are seen near Pescosta, and a much more considerable catastrophe, involving the destruction of many houses and more than 100 acres of land, occurred in 1821 between Stern and St. Leonhard. To the traveller descending the valley who has left behind him the striking scenery of the higher dolomite peaks, the route from St. Leonhard to St. Lorenzen will appear somewhat tame. The short lateral glens on either side offer many interesting scenes whose existence is not suspected by one who merely keeps to the regular track. As a general rule, rough country inns are found at all the villages and hamlets by the way. The best quarters, after St. Leonhard, are at Zwischenwassern and Saalen. The distance to St. Lorenzen (which is about 2 m. from Bruneck on the high-road from Brixen) is counted 6½ hrs. The remarkable church, 'zum Heiligen Kreuz,' often visited from St. Leonhard, is noticed below.

The frequented track from St. Leonhard to the lower part of the Gaderthal keeps to the E. side of the valley, often at a great height above the torrent, but at times descending close to the stream. A short way below the village begins a steep descent over a mass of black porphyry (melaphyre) that sustains the upper basin of the Abteithal, at the base of which the Pontalg torrent runs westward through a deep cleft to join the Gader. Then a short reach of level ground leads to *Pederowa*, where there are a few houses and an inn. The interesting way from thence to St. Vigil, by Wengen, is noticed in the next Rte. The next place is *Pré Romang*, nearly opposite the opening of the Campilerthal, further noticed below. Above it is seen the peak of the

Peitlerkofel (9,422'), the northernmost of the dolomite peaks of the Gaderthal. A short distance farther the traveller reaches *Picolein* (3,662'). On the opposite side of the valley is the hamlet of *St. Martin*, the chief place in this part of the valley. It stands below the ruined castle of *Thurn* (whose records are full of grim memories of mediæval ferocity), on the site of a church which, with the adjoining houses, was destroyed by a landslip. The track keeps to the rt. bank, passing opposite the opening of the lateral glen of *Untermoi*.

[From the little village of Untermoi, about 1 hr. above the opening of this glen, a path mounts over the ridge of the *Cartazerberg* (7,208') to the upper end of the *Lüsenthal*. Through that secluded valley, which descends westward with a curve convex to the N., the Lasankabach flows to join the Rienz in the remarkable cleft near Brixen, noticed in § 52, Rte. A. On the way from Untermoi to Brixen, a walk of 7 or 8 hrs., is the village of *Lüsen* (3,040'), with an inn, and a fine church containing a curious ancient chapel. Below the village the valley is narrowed to a deep impassable cleft between rocks of mica-schist, and the best way to Brixen is by the heights on the S. side. Easy passes connect the head of the Lüsenthal with that of the Vilnösthal, mentioned above, and by that way Klausen may be reached from Untermoi in about the same time as Brixen. There are paths leading to Lüsen from Welschellen and Onach; but they are said to be more laborious than that from Untermoi.] After passing opposite Untermoi the track from Picolein, practicable for country vehicles, keeps along the slopes at a great height above the Gader, which has cut a deep cleft in the bottom of the valley. At one point the torrent, forming a loop, has almost isolated a steep rock on which stands a solitary house, called Klein-Venedig. On a terrace of the mountain above the l. bank, opposite to the road, stands *Welschellen* (4,559'), surrounded with cornfields. The road now approaches the junction of the two main branches of the valley, and descends rather steeply to *Zwischenwassern* (*Lunghiega*), a hamlet where there is annually a large cattle-fair and a tolerable inn. It is often called *Plaiken* (*Früschia*), but that is the name of the chief place of the commune, standing high above the valley, on the slope of the mountain dividing the Enneberg from the Abteithal. Below the junction the main branch of the Gaderthal preserves the character of a cleft; and the road again ascends, after traversing the Vigilbach, and runs along the slopes E. of the valley. At *Saalen* is an inn praised by German writers, either for its intrinsic qualities, or because this is the first hamlet where the native idiom gives place to German. The latter prevails in the lower part of the valley. On the opposite slope is *Onach* (3,795′), whence runs the path, already noticed, by the Lüsenthal to Brixen. On approaching the junction of the Gaderthal with the Pusterthal, the road keeps high up on the slope above the rt. bank of the stream. On the opposite side a transverse ridge, parallel to the *Pusterthal*, seems to bar the course of the valley, forcing the Gader to turn abruptly to the rt. at *Monthal* (2,851′), and to follow a course little N. of E., till it reaches the Rienz a short way from *St. Lorenzen* (§ 52, Rte. A), whither the road descends in about 6½ hrs. from St. Leonhard.

A traveller bound for Untervintl should follow the l. bank of the Gader, and take an agreeable path from Monthal by the castle of *Ehrenburg*, one of the most famous in this district. The foundations are believed to be Roman, and the masonry shows the work of many succeeding centuries.

There are at least two passes besides that described above, by which the Gaderthal may be reached from Gröden, without much lengthening the way. The most interesting of these is that called *Crespena Joch* by Messrs. Gilbert and Churchill. The way to it is by the *Langenthal*, which joins the main branch of the Grödnerthal at Sta. Maria.

This is an extremely picturesque glen, wherein smooth slopes of Alpine pasture are enclosed between walls and towers of rock, forming a sort of giant street leading to the interior recesses of the dolomite region. The castle of *Wolkenstein*, the cradle of a still existing noble family, whose name was made famous in mediæval literature as well as in arms by the minnesänger, Oswald v. Wolkenstein, is built up against the face of a vertical cliff, and was accessible only by steps hewn in the rock. Beyond the castle is a chapel, but the glen appears to be uninhabited. At its head it is gradually contracted to a ravine, or couloir, through which a faintly marked path mounts over white debris of splintered dolomite. At the summit the traveller reaches a narrow ridge whence another ravine of the same character descends on the opposite side, but, by bearing to the l., he presently reaches the high table-land of bare rock to which Richthofen has given the name *Guerdenazza Plateau*. The dolomite of this and the upper part of the Sella plateau belongs to the lias formation, and is of much later origin than that prevailing in the Fassa valley. The bare rock of the plateau retains no indications of a path, and the assistance of a guide is indispensable in order to hit the spots whence it is possible to descend. By bearing a little N. of due E., a very steep way down broken crags takes the traveller to St. Leonhard, where he joins the main track through the Gaderthal.

A rather more varied and interesting way lies across the plateau towards NE., whereby the traveller reaches the head of the *Campilerthal*, one of the finest lateral glens of that valley. It contains the rather considerable village of *Campil* (*Lungiarù*)—4,587 ft. above the sea—with a country inn. NW. of the village rises the *Peitlerkofel* (9,422′), the summit of which is reached in 5 hrs. from the inn. The last climb is said to be difficult, and fit only for practised mountaineers. There is a direct and easy way from Campil to Klausen, on the Eisack, by the Vilnösthal, and also a pass to the Lüsenthal. From the lower part of the Langenthal there is a way to Colfosco by the Puetz Alp, scarcely longer than that of Colfosco Pass already described.

There are numerous mineral springs in the main branch of the Gaderthal and its tributary glens. The utter want of decent accommodation makes most of them impracticable for foreigners. The most frequented is that of Ramwald, near the opening of the valley, and not far from Onach.

Route H.

BRUNECK TO CORTINA D' AMPEZZO, BY PASSES AT THE HEAD OF THE GADERTHAL.

Although it involves some trespass over the limits of the district described in the next section, it seems convenient to bring together under one heading several passes that lead from Bruneck to Cortina, which is the natural headquarters of that district. Besides their intrinsic interest they are convenient for travellers who after descending from the High Tauern Alps to Bruneck, would commence from that place a tour of the Dolomite Alps.

1. *By Corfara, and the Tre Sassi.* 12 hrs. to Pieve di Andraz, 5½ hrs. thence, to Cortina. This is a two days' journey, which is best divided at Corfara; but the accommodation is better at Pieve di Andraz, and that place is easily reached in one day by a traveller who takes a light vehicle from Bruneck as far as Saalen or Picolein. The way lies through the main branch of the Gaderthal as far as Stern, and thence by the western branch, called Corfarathal, following exactly the line described in the last Rte. Leaving to the rt. the path to Colfosco, a track mounts from Pescosta to *Corfara* (5,095'), standing in a green basin a little above the junction of the stream from the Colfosco Pass. The inn contains one or two tolerable bedrooms, but it is often ill supplied with provisions. At Corfara we reach the N. base of the block of high land that separates the head of the Gaderthal from the two uppermost branches of the Cordevole. A few words on the topography of this neighbourhood are the more requisite as it has been much confused, partly through errors in maps, partly through the want of fixed usage as to the names of places.

From its junction with the Piave to the village of Caprile, the valley of the Cordevole (described in the next section) belongs to Italy, and forms part of the province of Belluno. Above Caprile, the boundary between Venetia and Tyrol runs for a short distance along the stream of the Cordevole, giving the rt. bank to Italy, and the opposite side to Tyrol; but before reaching a point where the valley forks, the boundary line turns first westward, then SW. and S., following pretty closely the watershed between the Cordevole on the one side, and the Avisio and Cismone on the other. The Tyrolese district, at the head of the Cordevole, is called *Livinallongo*, and includes two branches. The longer branch originates at the base of Monte Pordoi (see next Rte.), and descends eastward, passing Araba and Pieve di Andraz. In the bottom of the deep trench which the torrent has excavated below the latter village it is joined by the stream from the other much shorter branch of the valley. This originates at the Valparola Alp, and descends by the castle of Buchenstein, and the hamlet of the same name, in a direction little W. of S., to the junction with the main branch of Livinallongo. By the German-speaking inhabitants, the name Buchenstein is given not only to the castle and the hamlet below it, but often also to Pieve di Andraz in the other branch of the valley. In the same way the name Andraz is given to all these places, by the people who retain the Ladin or Italian idioms. Since strangers have attempted to fix the nomenclature, the name *Buchenstein* is commonly given to the NNE. branch of the valley, and to the castle and hamlet. The longer (western) branch is called Livinallongo, and its chief village Pieve di Andraz, and sometimes Pieve di Livinallongo. The mountain mass over which the traveller passes from the Gaderthal to Livinallongo rises into several summits, of which the most prominent are the *Set Sass* (8,396′), also called *Monte Zissa*, and the *Col di Lana* (8,176′), the latter rising in the angle between the valleys of Livinallongo and Buchenstein. The greater part of the mass in question is, however, a rolling plateau of green Alpine pasture furrowed in places by ravines. Lying in a central position, surrounded by many of the highest summits of the Dolomite Alps, this plateau commands exquisite views.

In a waking or sleeping dream of peaks of wonder and beauty, the mountaineer can scarcely surpass the circle that includes the Tofana, Malcora, Antelao, Pelmo, and Civetta, which rise on the E. side of the Cordevole valley. Above the nearer range the snow-clad Marmolata asserts its pre-eminence, while, nearer at hand, the Pordoi, and many others, complete the panorama. The shortest way from Corfara to Livinallongo is by a pass called *Campolungo*(6,200′),leading in 2½ hrs. to Araba. This is the most direct for a traveller going to Campidello in Fassa, as he joins at Araba the path over the

Pordoi Pass (Rte. I); but it is a circuitous way for one going to Pieve di Andraz, and the views are inferior to those gained by the more direct path which leads to that place in 3 hrs. by the *Anzisa Alp*. When time is an object, it is well to take a guide over this and the other passes here referred to, as it is easy to miss the shortest way. Corte, Cherz, and other small groups of houses are passed in descending to

Pieve di *Andraz* (4,842′), the chief place in Livinallongo, and the only one above Caprile where a traveller finds tolerable accommodation. Two, if not three, country inns are all kept by one of the name Finazzer. The best (very tolerable) is that of Luigi F. with a sign (bunch of grapes) in the little piazza. The situation of the little village is singular. The available space being very limited, many of the houses, including the inn, are built on the very verge of the precipitous slope overlooking the bed of the torrent. Being near the fork of the valley, the village overlooks the deep cleft through which the Cordevole flows to the Italian frontier at Caprile.

The traveller who may halt at this place should ascend the *Col di Lana* (8,176′), rising NNE. of the village. It must command a very remarkable view. Not less interesting would be the ascent of the *Padon* (8,878′). the highest summit of the range dividing Livinallongo from Fedaya. It is the best spot for viewing the Marmolata, but many travellers will be satisfied with the view from the Forcella di Padon, noticed in Rte. I.

A new char-road, very rough on this side, has been opened from Pieve to Cortina. At first it winds round the slope above the junction of the torrent from Buchenstein with the main source of the Cordevole. The poor hamlet of Buchenstein, or Andraz, with an unpromising inn kept by G. Finazzer, is nearly 3 m. from La Pieve. Here the road crosses to the l. bank of the stream and ascends for 1½ m. to the ruined *Castle of Buchenstein* (5,892′). The building is ugly, but the position wild and striking. Soon after passing the castle, the road to Cortina turns aside to ascend eastward over the pass known as the *Tre Sassi* (7,073'). There are, however, many paths, made by wood-cutters or herdsmen, which shorten the way, and the solitary traveller should beware of short-cuts except by local advice. If he begin the ascent too soon, he will lose much time. The way lies by the S. side of Monte Tofana (see § 61, Rte. C), and conducts the traveller near to the base of some of the grand crags of that mountain, but its higher peaks are not seen from the path. The ascent to the Tre Sassi from the castle of Buchenstein is short and easy; but the descent on the opposite side, though still easier, is rather long. When clouds do not cover the surrounding peaks, beautiful views are gained by the way, and though 4 hrs. from Buchenstein are more than sufficient, most travellers will linger by the way. The route is, however, more interesting when the traveller goes this way from Cortina to La Pieve. On a fine evening the views of the Pelmo, Civetta, and Marmolata are not likely ever to be forgotten.

The commune of Cortina has undertaken to build an inn near the summit of the pass, which is to be opened in 1873.

2. *By St. Cassian and the Valparola Alp.* 8½ hrs. to St. Cassian; about 6½ hrs. thence to Cortina. This way is considerably shorter than that by Pieve di Andraz, and the scenery decidedly less interesting; but for the geologist St. Cassian is a place of extreme interest, and it is easy to take it on the way to La Pieve by a course noticed below, no longer than that by Corfara.

As mentioned in the last Rte., the Abteithal, or main branch of the Gaderthal, forks at Stern about 1 hr. above St. Leonhard. The two branches are about equal, but the SE. branch is considered to be the continuation of the main valley, and the torrent preserves the name Gader.

St. Cassian (5,087') stands about ½ hr. above the fork of the valley. Though a small place, the massive houses are well built, and have a stately air unusual in a remote Alpine village. The inn, however, is a poor place, and travellers find, or formerly did find, accommodation at the priest's house. St. Cassian is celebrated for the variety and beauty of the marine fossils which occur abundantly in the marly deposit forming the slopes surrounding the village. This appears to be a portion of those beds of marine origin in which volcanic ashes enter as a large component, and which are extensively developed in this district. The fossils are apparently the remains of animals inhabiting a shallow sea which were destroyed during periods of violent eruption, and partially buried in the deposits of ashes that fell at the same time. The fossils are found most abundantly on the slopes towards the head of the valley after a heavy fall of rain, when the lighter parts of the superficial stratum are washed away, leaving the fossils on the surface. Specimens are usually to be purchased at a reasonable rate from people in or near the village.

There is a very agreeable way from St. Cassian to Pieve di Andraz by the pass of *Stuore,* or *Prelungei* (7,061'), about 3½ hrs. The path joins that from Corfara, noticed above, in the descent to La Pieve. In the ascent from St. Cassian, the traveller passes over some of the best ground for fossil-hunting.

The direct way to Cortina follows the torrent to the head of the valley, and ascends gently to the ridge of the Valparola Alp overlooking the head of the Buchenstein valley. Descending but little, the path passes round the upper end of that glen, and joins the Tre Sassi track not far from the summit.

There is a track, as to which the writer has no details, which turns eastward from the valley above St. Cassian, and reaches Peutelstein by the N. side of the *Sas de Lagatschö*, a rugged peak rising W. of the Tofana. Another way from Buchenstein to Peutelstein, by Val Travernanze, is noticed among the excursions from Cortina (§ 61, Rte. A).

3. *By St. Vigil and Peutelstein.* About 11½ hrs. to Peutelstein—5½ m. thence to Cortina. In Rte. G, reference was made to the SE. branch of the Gaderthal, whose torrent joins the Gader at Zwischenwassern, and to which the name *Enneberg* is properly restricted. Being the least frequented division of the valley, the Ladin dialect is better preserved here than in the main branch. Besides the name Enneberg, the valley is known to the German neighbours as *Vigilthal*, while the natives call it *Marèo* or *Marebbe*. In addition to these names, the upper part above St. Vigil is known as *Rauhthal* or *Vallon di Rudo*. The way from Bruneck does not cross the Vigilbach to Zwischenwassern, but keeps along the rt. bank of that torrent to *Pfarre* (Pieve da Maro), with a fine old church. Several hamlets, of which the chief are Hof (La Court), and Mannthan (Manteria), are passed on the way to *St. Vigil*, or *Plang da Maro*, the chief place in the valley, 3,968 ft. above the sea, about 4 hrs. from Bruneck. It has a very fair country inn, without a sign, and may afford head-quarters for some interesting excursions. Three brothers, named Willert, Jakob Karneider, and Antonio Trebo, are named as competent guides. There is a mineral spring at a place called *Cortina*, near the village, which might become a place of much resort, if tolerable accommodation for strangers were provided.

The most interesting of the shorter excursions to be made here is that to *Wengen* (4,985'), a comparatively large and thriving village, lying in a short glen, or hollow, in the mountains, on the E. side of the Abteithal. The way from St. Vigil lies by the Pfannes Alp. From Wengen the traveller may visit the pilgrimage church of *Heiligen Kreuz* (6,695'), standing in a very commanding situation. and overlooking a great part of the Gaderthal.

The way from St. Vigil to the Ampezzo valley follows the upper part of the valley (Vallon di Rudo), nearly to its head, and passes by the Fodara Vedla Alp.

The only information respecting this pass that has reached the editor is contained in a note kindly communicated by the Rev. T. G. Bonney, who made the excursion from Cortina to Bruneck. He employed about 6½ hrs. from Peutelstein to St. Vigil, but moderate walkers may allow nearly 1 hr. more, excluding halts. 'A little above Peutelstein, a rough cart-road turns aside to the l. from the post-road. This ascends through an upland valley [Val Antruilles?—Ed.], commanding fine views of the northern peak of the Tofana. After crossing to the rt. bank of the stream, the track, henceforward a roughly paved bridle-path, twists and winds up the hill-side, and over sinuous depressions in the dreary and desolate limestone mountains between the Tofana and Seekofel. The actual summit is not marked, probably it is near a hut which stands in a small grassy basin; but commands little view—parts of the Cristallo and Goiselstein being seen. A few minutes' more winding and slight descent bring you to a group of châlets, called Rudo di Sotto, 3 hrs. 35 min. from Peutelstein, at the head of the Enneberg valley, and looking right down it across the Pusterthal to the Stubayerferner [?—Ed.]. Hence follows a good path on the l. bank of the stream, which in a few minutes plunges into a deep gorge in the dolomite rock. The scenery is now very fine; the path winds down a very steep descent into the Vigilthal, with a magnificent cliff rising on the l., and the deep gorge on the rt. The head of the valley, of which glimpses are now gained, is barren and dreary, the floor very level, and covered with forest. The bottom of the descent was reached in 1 hr. 15 min. There I found a fair charroad, which runs along the level bed of the valley through woods, in which, first *legföhren*, then Scotch fir, predominate, with magnificent cliffs of fawn-coloured dolomite on the rt. A clearing, with châlets is reached in 35 min. more, after which the valley begins to open. As the mountains become less precipitous, cornfields, meadows, and little villages, are seen on their sides. After 1 hr. 20 min. more, I reached the white houses and church of Enneberg or St. Vigil (Auberge near church to SW., no sign). Hence a short cut across meadows leads to the char-road by rt. bank of the stream; after 20 min. it comes to l. bank, and then soon returns. (N.B. Recross on first occasion, and take the unpromising road up the hill on the rt. bank. I took the promising one by the stream on l. bank, and had to cross lower down, and climb a steep path to regain it).'

4. *By the Gaiselbergerthal.* The way here noticed would be circuitous for a traveller starting from Bruneck, but it is inserted here in order to remind those who may approach that place from the E. side that there is an easy and agreeable way for entering the Gaderthal from the high-road between Bruneck and Welsberg. On the S. side of the Rienz are three villages, all belonging to the commune of Olang. That called *Mittel-Olang* (3,418')—said to have a good country inn—stands exactly at the opening of the *Gaiselbergerthal*, a short lateral glen of the valley of the Rienz, approached by a bridge over that river. In this glen, about 2 hrs. from the bridge, is a place called *Schartl*, with a mineral spring, resorted to for baths, and for fresh air in summer. From Schartl it is an easy walk of 3 hrs. to St. Vigil, passing below the summit of the *Plang de Corones* (7,535'), also called Spitzhörnl, said to command a fine view. From St. Vigil, taking the way by Wengen, mentioned above, the traveller may reach *St. Leonhard*, in the Abteithal, by a course much more interesting than the common way from Bruneck, described in the last Rte.

ROUTE I.

ST. ULRICH IN GRÖDEN TO PIEVE DI ANDRAZ.

Reference has already been made to a lofty mass of mountain, often designated the *Sella Plateau*, which sends its drainage in opposite directions through the four principal streams of this district—the Avisio, Cordevole, Gader, and Grödnerbach. Although very steep on all sides, there are several clefts in the great ramparts of the Sella through which it is possible to reach the summit of the plateau, but the writer is not aware that any passes—in the ordinary sense of the term—have been effected across the central part of the mass. Failing such passes, it becomes necessary to make a circuit by two sides of the mountain when a traveller seeks to pass from the head of one of the above-named valleys to that lying on the opposite side of the mountain. In going from the Grödnerthal to Livinallongo, the easiest way is to follow the Colfosco Pass (Rte. G), from Plau to Colfosco, and go thence to Pieve di Andraz by either of the paths mentioned in the last Rte. Another way, equally interesting and agreeable, passes by the W. and S. sides of the same mountain mass, traversing two low ridges. From Sta. Maria or Plau (Rte. G), the path to the Colfosco Pass is followed for a short way, when the traveller turns due S., and mounts to the

Sella Joch (7,406'), reached in 2 hrs. from Plau. A rapid descent leads to-

§ 61. CADORE DISTRICT. 501

wards the head of the Fassathal, which is reached in about 1¼ hr. from the pass at the hamlet of *Gries*, little more than 1 m. from Campidello. If bound for Livinallongo by the shortest path, the traveller does not descend far towards Gries. He will perceive that on his l. hand there is a wide opening in the mountains S. of the *Monte Pordoi*, (10,333′), the southernmost, and probably the highest part of the Sella mass. Through that opening an easy path ascends to the *Pordoi Pass* (7,396′). This is frequented by travellers going from Fassa to Livinallongo and thence to Ampezzo. The path to it from Gries turns off to the rt. from the way to the Sella Joch, but the traveller, coming from the Grödnerthal with a competent guide, may go from one pass to the other without any long descent. The gigantic ramparts of *Monte Pordoi* (10,333′) produce a fine effect when seen from the neighbourhood of the pass, but the descent thence to *Araba* is rather uninteresting. The inn at that place is very poor, but supplies tolerable refreshments. It is a walk of fully 2 hrs. thence to Pieve di Andraz.

A far more interesting but longer way is to descend from the Sella Joch to Canazei (Rte. A), and follow the head of the Fassathal to Fedaya. The basin of Fedaya is divided from Livinallongo by a ridge that culminates in the Mte. Padon (8,878′). A track passing on one side of that summit goes from Fedaya to Livinallongo over the *Forcella di Padon* (7,805′). This commands an admirable view of the Marmolata, and also of many of the Ampezzo peaks. On the N. side the path descends to *Ornella*, a hamlet some way above Pieve di Andraz, which place is reached in about 4 hrs. from Fedaya, or 6¾ hrs. from Canazei, excluding halts.

SECTION 61.

CADORE DISTRICT.

In undertaking to give some account of one of the most beautiful portions of the Alps, the writer is struck with the singularity of the fact that it should have so long remained almost unknown, even by name, to English travellers. Unusually easy of access, for its three principal valleys are traversed by good roads, better supplied with inns than many favourite haunts of tourists, containing scenery of the most fantastic wildness and beauty, and offering as prizes many peaks difficult enough to be exciting to the climber, it may fairly be said to have been unknown to all but a very few Englishmen, until the appearance of Messrs. Gilbert and Churchill's volume, so often referred to in the preceding sections. Only about the same time did German travellers systematically undertake the exploration of the district, and to one of them in particular—Dr. P. Grohmann—we owe a very accurate acquaintance with most of the highest peaks, several of which he has been the first to ascend. The writer's acquaintance with this district precedes that of the writers here named, but his visits have been brief, and, with one exception, accompanied by heavy and almost constant rain. The facts are not numerous enough to warrant a broad inference; but there is some reason to think that in rainy seasons the quantity which falls here much surpasses that of the adjoining region to the west.

The district here described may be briefly defined as including the basin of the Piave, with its two principal tributaries the Boita and the Cordevole, along with the range dividing the sources of those streams from the Pusterthal, and the less lofty, but rather extensive, tract dividing the Piave from the plain of Venetia. Although the mean height of the mountains considerably surpasses that of most of the exterior ranges of the Alps, it may be safely said that except on the NW. side, where it touches the backbone of the Carnic Alps, there is not in this district any appearance of the existence of definite mountain ranges. The general level of the central part of the district is high, and from that level the peaks rise very abruptly, without any appearance of mutual connection. That fact, together with the near approach to equality in the heights of the loftier summits, tends to confirm Richthofen's views as to the dolomite mountains of this region. Although his hypothesis as to the coral-reef origin of the masses that rear themselves so abruptly above the surrounding country is not free from difficulties of its own, it is one which presents itself naturally to the mind in endeavouring to account for the singular aspect of the mountains of this district. Until lately, there were no trustworthy measurements of the heights of any of the principal peaks, and of those named below three are undoubtedly under-estimated. The Antelao is almost certainly the highest, and reaches about 10,850 ft. The Pelmo is probably between 10,500 and 10,600 ft., and the Civetta can differ only by a few ft. The chief peaks of this district —all except the last, overlooking the upper valley of the Boita—are the Sorapis (10,798'), Tofana (10,724'), Antelao (10,679'?), Monte Cristallo (10,644'), Pelmo (10,377'?) and Civetta (10,440'?).

If the geologists who were led by the structure of the mountains of Fassa to suppose that the conversion of carbonate of lime into dolomite was due to action of igneous rocks in a state of fusion, had studied this district at the same time, their views would probably have been modified. Nowhere are dolomite rocks developed on a larger scale than here, yet, with a trifling exception near Caprile, no trace of igneous rocks has been found in the district lying E. of the Cordevole and the Gaderthal.

The natural centre of this district is Cortina d' Ampezzo, where the traveller finds good quarters and the convenience of a high-road. From that centre the active mountaineer may accomplish the ascent of most of the highest peaks enumerated below, while the moderate walker may devise a great variety of interesting and easy excursions. It is not equally well suited for those who prefer short walks, and wish to have the more striking scenes brought nearer to hand. There are, however, many other places that combine fairly good accommodation with beautiful scenery. Foremost among these must be reckoned Schluderbach; but the lover of nature will find attractions in almost every one of the secondary valleys of this district that may induce him to tarry on his way, and an entire season may be spent here with profit and satisfaction. It is right to say that there are persons, not insensible to the beauty of great mountain countries, upon whom the utter sternness and savageness of some of the wilder scenery of this district produces an almost painful effect. It would be difficult to find elsewhere in the Alps scenes so awe-inspiring as those surrounding the Dürren See, or the cirque of the Croda Malcora.

ROUTE A.

BRUNECK TO CONEGLIANO, BY CORTINA D'AMPEZZO.

	Austrian miles	Eng. miles
Niederndorf . . .	3	14
Landro	2	9½
Cortina d'Ampezzo .	2½	11¾
Venas	3	14
Perarollo . . .	2	9½
Longarone . . .	2½	11¾
Santa Croce . . .	3¼	15¼
Ceneda	2	9½
Conegliano . . .	2	9½
	22¼	104¾

Post-road. No public conveyance between Cortina and Conegliano since the separation of Venetia from Austria. A stellwagen plies between Niederndorf and Cortina.

The way from Bruneck to the point where the high-road to Venice turns southward from the Pusterthal is described in § 51, Rte. A. That point is very near the summit-level parting the waters of the Drave from those of the Rienz, but it lies a short way W. of the watershed, and the stream issuing from the short valley followed by the road to Cortina is the chief source of the Rienz. A pedestrian taking this way from Niederndorf should follow a foot-path that turns to the rt. from the road by the second bridge above that village, and after passing a brewery, rejoins the road near the *Toblacher See* (4,165′). This stands in the opening of the narrow glen (sometimes called Höllensteinerthal) that serves as a portal between the German Pusterthal and the Italian population of Ampezzo. As the traveller advances the defile becomes narrower, and the menacing-looking crags of the *Drei Zinnen* (9,833′) rise to a vast height in a glen that opens to SE., as he reaches the post-house of *Landro*, or *Höllenstein*, 4,749 ft. above the sea. Very fair accommodation is found here, but those who halt for more than a single night should prefer Schluderbach. There is no village at Landro, but merely three or four buildings that seem to be connected with the post-house. Close at hand, though not seen from the house, is the *Dürren See*. This sheet of shallow pale-green water is surrounded by a flat tract of white barren dolomitic gravel, which supports only stunted fir-trees. In the background is a group of inaccessible-looking rocks, broken into massive towers, whose highest peak, the Monte Cristallo, is one of the giants of this region. Below the vertical walls that sustain its summit a glacier hangs suspended from the rifts of the mountain, and extends on one side up to a deep cleft that divides the Cristallo from a solitary tower, quite 10,000 ft. in height —the Monte Popena. A sombre band of *Krummholz* (Pinus mughus) surrounds the base of these peaks. Even the traveller who loves Nature in her wilder moods feels the chilling influence of this savagely gloomy spot, whose ghastly grandeur seems the fitting accompaniment for some unheard-of crime. The aspect of the scene might lead the traveller to suppose himself utterly shut in by impassable rocks, and in truth none but active mountaineers can follow the southward direction to which the road has adhered since leaving the Pusterthal. But a deep cleft opens westward, through which the road is carried nearly at a level for a distance of about 6 m. About 2 m. from Landro, near the opening of Val Popena and Val Cristallo (Rte. B), is the solitary house of

Schluderbach (4,822′), where the traveller, to his surprise, finds in the midst of the most savage scenery a capital country inn, kept by Giorgio Ploner, an obliging host, and (when disengaged) an efficient guide. Anton Molins, sometimes sent in his place, is incompetent. Though less central than Cortina, this is an excellent centre for many excursions, most of which are noticed in Rte. B. At Schluderbach the Monte Cristallo is concealed by the projecting mass of the Rauhkofel, and the much lower mass of the *Cristallin* (9,238′) is the only considerable summit in view on that side. But the loss of view on the S. side is compensated by the apparition of the very singular peak of the

Croda Rossa (10,262′), or *Hohe Gaisl*, formed of massive rock, showing large patches of a bright red on its impending precipices, 'streaked as with the red drip of a mighty sacrifice.' [G. and C.] The ascent has been effected three or four times, and is steep, and fit only for practised cragsmen. Ploner and Santo Siorpaes know the way. From the base of this tutelary *numen* of the spot a slender streamlet flows by the road towards the Rienz; but it requires close attention to detect the point where the ground begins to subside in the opposite direction towards the valley of Ampezzo. The exact height of the summit level is not known to the writer, but it is certainly not much above or below 5,000 ft. The inconsiderable stream of the *Ruffredo* begins to flow westward, and another solitary house, called *O pedale*, originally built as a refuge for poor travellers, at the opening of a glen called Val Grande (Rte. B), is left behind. The Ruffredo, on the l. of the high-road, soon begins to cut a deeper channel, through which it descends to meet the more considerable torrent, in which is united the drainage of three valleys— Val Travernanze, Val Fanis, and Val Antruilles—through the latter of which lies a pathway to Enneberg (§ 60, Rte. H)—and form the Boita. In the angle between them stands the castle of *Peutelstein*, which, after surviving centuries of border warfare until 1867, was levelled with a view to the erection of a modern fort to guard this entrance into Tyrol. According to the latest information, it is no longer possible to pass by an interesting path above the l. bank of the Ruffredo, through the defile below the castle, which was frequently traversed by passing tourists who left their carriages to follow the road on the opposite side of the torrent.

Immediately after passing *Peutelstein* (Ital. *Podestagno*) the road turns sharply to the l., and begins to descend towards the valley of the Boita which stretches far away to the SSE. The noble peaks of the Tofana, Pelmo, Antelao, and Sorapis come successively into view. The road descends rather rapidly along the slopes above the l. bank of the Boita, and in about 5½ m. from Peutelstein reaches

Cortina d'Ampezzo (4,048′), the chief village of the large and wealthy commune of Ampezzo, which includes the portion of the valley of the Boita, lying N. of the frontier of Italy. Of the numerous inns three deserve favourable mention (Stella d' Oro, managed by the Sisters Barbaria, remarkably clean, quiet, and comfortable; Aquila Nera, kept by Ghedina, father of a distinguished Venetian painter, who is often here in summer; Kreuz, also well spoken of). The Aquila Nera is much improved by the addition of a separate house for tourists; the writer has hitherto found the Stella preferable.

The appearance of the buildings and the people in the village of Cortina and the neighbouring hamlets announce general prosperity, which partly arises from the vast extent of valuable forests and pastures belonging to the commune in its corporate capacity. The greatly increased price of timber has, however, tempted the natives to cut down forest to an extent that may affect their future prosperity. In the pride of momentary wealth they have erected a *campanile* 250 ft. high, on a scale befitting a great city. Near the village is an establishment for mineral baths, standing near the banks of the Boita. The waters are said to be similar to those of Prags in the Pusterthal (Rte. I).

ROUTE A.—EXCURSIONS FROM CORTINA D'AMPEZZO. 505

The establishment belongs to G. Ghedina, landlord of the Aquila Nera. Cortina is better supplied with guides than most places in the Italian Tyrol. Santo Siorpaes is first-rate, and knows most parts of this region. Alessandro Lacedelli is a bold climber, but has little judgment. Angelo Dimaj is also good, and his brother, Fulgenzio, less efficient. A tariff of charges has been established. Ghedina has two or three side-saddles for ladies.

Most of the excursions from Cortina are described in the following Rtes., but it may be convenient to enumerate them here, adding a brief notice of some which do not conveniently fall under other headings.

The paths to Schluderbach by Val Grande and the Lake of Misurina, and the ascent of Mte. Cristallo, are given in Rte. B. The tour of the Croda Malcora by the Tre Croci and Forcella Grande, and the ascent of the Sorapis, are noticed in Rte. E. For the ascent of the Antelao see Rte. F, and for that of the Pelmo, Rte. G.

Among short excursions deserving notice is that through a short glen (Val Ambriciola?) that mounts somewhat W. of S. from Cortina, and leads to a depression on the NW. side of the *Becco di Mezzodi*, a remarkable projecting 'carious tooth' of dolomite rock, accessible from the S. side by a stiff scramble. It is possible to scramble round the base of the Becco, enjoying on the way some noble views of the Civetta, Pelmo, and Antelao. Returning by a slightly different course to Cortina, this makes a very interesting excursion of 5 or 6 hrs.

To the botanist the ascent of *Monte Gusella* and a visit to the crags of the *Monte Nuvolau* may be recommended. The former is the only Italian station for *Crepis hyoseridifolia*.

The ascent of *Monte Tofana* (10,724') is for the practised mountaineer one of the most attractive expeditions to be made in this district. Starting in good time, an active walker will easily return to Cortina in time for dinner, and with favourable weather will have enjoyed one of the finest views in Tyrol. The mountain has 3 summits, all visible from Cortina, of which the central one is certainly the highest. The SW. peak —seen on the l. from Cortina—is said to have been several times reached by natives of the valley; the middle peak was attained in 1863 by Dr. Grohmann with the elder Lacedelli; and the N. peak was climbed by Mr. Bonney in 1867, with Angelo Dimaj as guide. Dr. Grohmann, having gained the crest of the ridge connecting the SW. summit with the highest, turned to the rt. and followed the ridge chiefly by the side overlooking Val Travernanze, finally attaining the summit by a rather steep ice-slope. Mr. Bonney took a course that seems to be full of interest even irrespective of the special object in view. Mounting rapidly and nearly straight from Cortina, he attained in 1 hr. 50 min. a gap, called Forcella della Cesta, overlooking the head of a small upland glen, or hollow, that descends in precipices towards Peutelstein. Passing above the head of this glen another gap, reached in 10 min. from the first, enables the traveller to overlook a much vaster hollow, once filled by glacier, above which rise the central and northern peaks of the mountain, in crags which are in most places impracticably steep. Without descending low, Mr. Bonney circled round this hollow, passing on the way below a small glacier. Having gone some way beyond the base of the northern peak, he found a cleft through which water trickles, and which afforded a practicable way to the ridge of the mountain. Turning to the l. along the ridge, the N. peak was attained in 5¼ hrs. from Cortina. The return, being hurried by bad weather, was effected in 3 hrs. 25 min. Mr. Bonney rates this view as among the finest in this part of the Alps.

The mountain mass that culminates in the three peaks of the Tofana nearly fills an equilateral triangle, one side of which is the road from Cortina to Peutelstein, another, the path over the Tre Sassi from Cortina to Buchenstein, while the third, or NW. side, is marked by *Val Travernanze*. This divides the Tofana from a more westerly and lower mass which is crowned by the peak of Lagazoi. A very interesting day's walk is the tour of Monte Tofana by Val Travernanze, returning by the Tre Sassi. Leaving the high road at the toll-bar about 1 hr. N. of Cortina, a cart-track nr. the l. bank of the Boita leads under the castle rock of Peutelstein to a bridge, and by choosing always the road most to the l. the way cannot be missed. On the N. side of the Tofana, the torrent of Val Travernanze, after passing through a very singular gorge, meets that of *Val Fanis*, which flows westward from the mountains near St. Cassian. As the united stream approaches the main valley, it receives the waters of a third torrent, named *Val Antruilles*, doubtless the same mentioned in § 60, Rte. H, through which the path runs to Enneberg. A beaten cattle-track leads amid very grand rock scenery to the upper part of Val Travernanze, and a faintly marked path goes from the highest huts to the ridge overlooking the road over the Tre Sassi. The name *Lagazoi* is given only to the southern and highest part of the ridge on the rt., dividing Travernanze from Fanis. Instead of descending towards the Tre Sassi, the traveller may keep close under the precipices of the Tofana, and on his way visit a cavern which is easy of access when snow is plentiful, otherwise hard to get at.

No moderate walker should miss the excursion to the Lago Sorapis in the great hollow, or *cirque*, of the *Croda Malcora*, that being the collective name here given to the vast range of crags whose highest summit is the Sorapis. (See Rte. E.)

The frontier between Italy and Tyrol crosses the valley of the Boita about 5 m. below Cortina. Before long the road passes the hamlet of *Chiapuzzo*, whence a path mounts to the Forcella Grande (Rte. E), and soon after reaches

San Vito (3,417′), the Italian customs-station. Neither the writer nor his friends can confirm the sweeping, condemnatory statement applied to the lower part of the Boita valley, and the adjoining district of Cadore—'inns grow nasty, and postmasters begin to cheat.' The village inn of San Vito was fairly clean, the landlord attentive, and charges reasonable, but in 1867 the Italian douaniers had taken possession of the best rooms, and the house was not a pleasant stopping-place. Gio. Batt. Giacin is recommended as a guide.

For some time before reaching San Vito two giants of this region, hitherto imperfectly seen, have come fully into view—the Pelmo and Antelao. The first cannot fail to fix the traveller's attention. An isolated, massive, bastioned tower of bare rock, rising abruptly to a height of 5,000 ft. above its base, its form is unique in the Alps. For a notice of the ascent see Rte. G. San Vito may serve as starting-point for the ascent of both peaks.

The general character of the valley of the Boita remains unchanged. Even where the stream has excavated for itself a deep bed, the road keeps along the broad gently-sloping shelf that extends to the very base of the great mountain wall that encloses the valley on the E. side. As it approaches its confluence with the Piave, the Boita gradually deepens the trench which it has cut in the superficial strata, and the road avoids this altogether by turning aside in a direction somewhat N. of E., so as to approach the Piave some way above the junction. Passing *Borca* (3,200′), and *Vodo* (3,120′), where a great bergfall from a projecting buttress of the Antelao overwhelmed two villages in 1816, the road reaches *Venas* (2,898′), a post station with a decent inn. Here a torrent from the Antelao descends through a ravine to join the Boita, and the road takes leave of that stream, which is lost to view at the bottom of an impassable cleft. Before rejoining that stream at its junction with the Piave, the road makes the circuit of the *Monte Zucco* (3,985′), which on this side shows as a mere rocky hill, but in the opposite direction towards the Piave, appears a high and steep ridge. At *Tai di Cadore*, where there is a very fair country inn, the road, which mounts to the head of the valley of the Piave (Rte. D), turns aside from the post-road. This here begins a steep and long descent of the slopes above the rt. bank of the Piave, and along the E. side of Monte Zucco, which terminates only at the post-station of Perarollo.

[*Pieve di Cadore*, the birth-place of Titian, scarcely 1 m. from Tai, on the road to Comelico, is noticed in Rte. D. The name *Cadore* belongs not to any particular village, but to the district surrounding the junction of the valleys of the Piave and Boita. In an extended sense the mountains enclosing both valleys are often styled Cadore Alps, and the name being widely known, has been chosen by the writer as the most convenient for this entire district.]

Perarollo (1,741'), fully 1,200 ft. below Tai, stands at the junction of the Piave with the Boita. There is a good inn at the post, and a large number of men are employed in the neighbourhood in connection with the timber trade, vast quantities of wood being floated hither from the valleys of the neighbouring Alps, and forwarded to Venice by the Piave. About 2 m. below Perarollo is the opening of *Val Montina*, above which are the steep crags of Monte Duranno. Mr. Holzmann effected a pass —*Forcella di Duranno* (about 6,650')— by the N. side of that peak by which Cimolais may be reached in 7 hrs.

Longarone (1,473'), a rather large village, with two pretty good inns (Post; Leone d' Oro), standing at the confluence of the Mae, issuing from Val di Zoldo (Rte. G), with the Piave. On the opposite side of the main valley the short glen of Vajont runs up to a pass leading to the upper valley of the Zelline (§ 62, Rte. I). The post-road keeps to the rt. bank of the Piave until it reaches *Capo di Ponte* (Inn: Stella Bianca), whence the road to Belluno and Feltre (Rte. D) extends SW. along the Piave, while the direct way to Conegliano and Venice turns southwards through a broad and deep opening in the mountains. Within sight of the towers of Belluno, scarcely 5 m. distant, the latter road crosses the Piave by a massive wooden bridge, 82 ft. above the stream, and 1,270 ft. above the sea-level. The road from Capo di Ponte to Ceneda is interesting to the geologist as exhibiting the scene of a comparatively recent geological event. It is considered certain that the course of the Piave once lay through the valley that extends from Capo di Ponte to Sta. Croce, and thence to Serravalle. A berg-fall, which occurred at some uncertain period, perhaps previous to the historic epoch, barred the course of the stream below Sta. Croce, whereupon a lake was formed above that village, and the river found a new channel through the broad valley, extending from Capo di Ponte to Lentiai near Feltre. The change in the channel of so considerable a stream might have been expected to effect considerable modifications in the valleys which it has passed, but these are not apparent. The *Lago di Sta. Croce* has an average height of 28 ft. above the surface of the Piave at Capo di Ponte, and the sluggish stream of the *Rai* now flows from the lake exactly in the opposite direction to the former course of the Piave through the same valley. The lake is a pretty sheet of water, and the traveller might be tempted to halt, if there were a decent inn, at

Sta. Croce (1,336'), a poor place, more than 100 ft. above the level of the lake. A short way beyond the village commences the ascent of the barrier formed by the great bergfall mentioned above. The summit of this great dam is marked by a police-barrack, 1,610 ft. above the sea-level. The descent on the S. side is much steeper than the ascent, and the village of *Fadalto* lies fully 600 ft. below the top of the ridge. It is surrounded by rugged walls of limestone with scrubby beeches in the hollows. Below the village is the Lago Morto (893'). The rocky defile extends hence to Serravalle, singular and picturesque, but so hot in summer that few travellers are tempted to traverse it on foot. The *Meschio*, a mere rivulet draining the Lago Morto, descends over two steep steps in the floor of the valley, where the vine and chestnut are the prevailing plants. After passing another very small lake, the traveller reaches

Serravalle (512′), a small town in a very singular position, standing in a gap in the line of hills that up to this point have enclosed the valley of the Meschio. The first houses are in the defile, and for a moment the rocks close together and there is barely space for the road and the torrent. This turns abruptly to SSE., and the view opens out suddenly over the low country towards Ceneda and Conegliano, while the full wealth of southern vegetation, wide-spreading fig-trees, pomegranates all ablaze with their scarlet blossoms, trellised vines creeping up walls and trees, and the contrast of sombre cypresses, assure the traveller that he has left the precincts of the Alps. In spring or autumn, when the heat is bearable, some pleasant excursions may be made from Serravalle into the range separating the present valley of the Piave from what is believed to have been its ancient course. These are chiefly formed of cretaceous rocks, partly overlaid by eocene strata. The highest summit is apparently the *Col Vicentino* (5,789′), due N. of Serravalle. It might be taken on the way from that place to Belluno. The orographer should also visit a short valley that originates a few m. W. of Serravalle, from which it is separated by a low ridge. It contains a lake—merely called Lago (775′), whence the *Soligo* torrent flows SW. for about 5 m., and then turns abruptly to SSE. to descend into the plain. The upper valley lies exactly in the prolongation of that of the Meschio, and seems to repeat exactly the peculiarities observed in the course of that stream. Some further examination may perhaps be usefully given to the supposed change

in the channel of the Piave, which has been described above in accordance with the views prevalent among geologists. The main evidence is derived from the nature of the gravel and detritus found in the valley of the Meschio; but this admits of much discussion before it can be held to be conclusive. Reference is made by Schaubach to early Roman authors whose text seems to indicate that the Piave, as known to them, followed the supposed ancient channel; but the writer has never learned what writers are referred to, and what texts are forthcoming. It is certain that Venantius Fortunatus, who died early in the 7th century, and who, though a French bishop, was a native of this region, knew the river as it flows in the existing channel.

It is a distance of little more than 2 m. from Serravalle to *Ceneda* (468′), an ancient town believed to be of Roman origin. This is overlooked by a castle on a rock, one of the last outlying spurs from the neighbouring Alps. There are here several inns (Post; Rosa; Aquila Nera). The low hills on either side of the road subside towards the plain as the traveller reaches

Conegliano (196′), a well-built and thriving town on the railway between Venice and Trieste. It has several fairly good hotels (Post; and another, at least equally good, the name of which has been mislaid), frequented in summer and autumn by persons seeking air a little cooler than that of the cities of the plain. A traveller having a few hours to spare should take a carriage to *San Salvatore*, the ancient castle of the Colalto family, and one of the finest in this part of Italy. It commands a noble view over the plain, extending in clear weather to the towers of the City of the Lagoons.

Route B.

CORTINA D' AMPEZZO TO SCHLUDERBACH, BY THE MONTE CRISTALLO.

The post-road between Schluderbach and Cortina, described in the last Rte., passes along the N. and W. sides of a small mountain mass culminating in the Monte Cristallo. It is characteristic of the structure of this region of the Alps, where the masonry of the mountains is as full of variety and richness of detail as a gothic cathedral, that there should be scope for four or five quite distinct and very interesting expeditions within so small an area. Unfortunately, the want of any accurate map of this part of the present district makes it impossible to render descriptions intelligible without entering into great detail. The writer is forced to refer those who would explore this neighbourhood thoroughly to a paper by Dr. Grohmann, in the Jahrbuch of the Austrian Alpine Club for 1866, wherein that active and persevering mountaineer describes the mass here spoken of in some detail, yet scarcely so as to dispense with the need of a map. On the S. side, towards the head of the Auronzo valley, and the Tre Croci Pass, the main mass of the Cristallo shows a rather uniform front, without those projecting towers and buttresses that are characteristic of most of the peaks of this district. On the N. side the case is very different, and not less than 6 short valleys or glens radiate from the central peaks. We shall here briefly notice the more interesting excursions which may all be taken on the way between Cortina and Schluderbach.

1. *By the Lake of Mesurina.*—4½ hrs. moderate walking. A little N. of E. from Cortina every traveller notices the deep and broad opening that separates two of the chief rock masses of this district—those of the Croda Malcora and the Cristallo. This is the pass connecting Cortina with Auronzo and the upper valley of the Piave (Rte. E). A rough cart-track goes as far as the top, and in places the way may be shortened by striking across the pastures. 1½ hr of moderate walking suffices to reach the summit of the *Tre Croci Pass* (5.970'), marked, as the name implies, by three wooden crosses. However often the traveller may pass here on his way to excursions from Cortina, he must rejoice in the noble view that opens westward over the green basin of Ampezzo, guarded on the N. by the savage crags of the Tofana. Near at hand to the N. rise the Monte Cristallo and Piz Popena. The Croda Malcora is, however, not seen in full grandeur. SE. the view extends down Val Buona, which name is given to the upper end of the Auronzo valley, and in the background rises the grand range of the Marmarolo, with small glaciers lying in the clefts between its giant towers. To ENE., nearly in the direction followed during the ascent from Cortina, is an opening similar in character to that of the Tre Croci, and about the same height, between the Monte Cristallo mass and the summits called *Cadine* or *Cadinspitzen.* In the hollow between them lies the Mesurina Alp. After descending a very short way from the Tre Croci, a track on the l. leads nearly at a level along the slope chiefly amid forest, but after some 2 m. it divides, and is gradually lost. It is perfectly easy to pursue the same direction, rising very little, and so reach the extensive pastures of the Mesurina Alp surrounding a charming little lake, *Lago di Mesurina,* famed for its delicious trout. [The regular track from Val Buona mounts from near the forester's hut (Rte. E) along the streamlet from the lake.] The way henceforward, after passing the low ridge beyond the lake, only 5,930 ft. in height, lies through *Val Popena,* the easternmost of the valleys lying on the N. side of the Cristallo mass. The summit of Piz Popena is not seen from the valley, and

the dominant mountain is the *Drei Zinnen* (9,833′), whose triple peak is seen from the post-house at Landro. Passing between the ridge extending N. from Monte Popena and the Monte Pian, the traveller descends to the level of the barren plain S. of the Dürren See, and reaches Schluderbach in 1 hr. from the Mesurina Alp. This is the more interesting and agreeable way for a traveller going from Cortina to Schluderbach. That next described is to be preferred by one travelling in the opposite direction.

2. *Schluderbach to Cortina by Val Grande.*—About 4¼ hrs. The high-road is followed as far as Ospedale. There, as mentioned in Rte. A, the glen called *Val Grande* opens somewhat E. of due S. This almost divides the higher part of the Cristallo group from the lower western portion. This shows above the high-road between Peutel-stein and Cortina as a steep and rugged, but not very high, ridge, called *Pomagognon*. Adjoining this, at the head of Val Grande, is the somewhat higher *Croda Cerdellis*. An easy ascent of 2 hrs. from Ospedale leads to the summit of the pass—locally called *La Forca*—between the latter summit and the main mass of the Cristallo. To enjoy the view it is necessary to ascend a slight eminence beside the pass. A rather steep, but not difficult, descent, leads in ½ hr., or less, from La Forca to the summit of the Tre Croci Pass, whence Cortina is reached in another hr. There is another pass, called *Zummelles*, lying farther W. than La Forca (between the Croda Cerdellis and Pomagognon?), which is a rather more direct way to Cortina; but it is a little higher, and the descent rather steeper.

A traveller starting from Schluderbach, and having no occasion to descend to Cortina, may traverse the Forca, then bear to the l. below the great cliffs of Monte Cristallo, and return by the Lake of Mesurina and Val Popena, in little more than 6 hrs., exclusive of halts—an easy and charming expedition.

3. *By the Cristall-Pass.*—About 6 hrs. Unlike those above described, this must be counted a rather difficult pass, very attractive to practised mountaineers, but requiring rope and ice-axe, and a steady head. The pass had been very rarely traversed by chamois-hunters, until Dr. Grohmann first crossed it in 1864. He has named it, and determined its height by careful barometrical measurement. The *Cristall-Pass* (9,282′) is a deep cleft between the two highest peaks of this mass, the *Monte Cristallo* (10,644′), and *Piz Popena* (10,389′), resembling in many respects the Bocca di Brenta, described in § 40, Rte. H. On the N. side a rather considerable glacier descends towards Val Fonda, one of the recesses of the Cristallo, the opening of which is reached in ½ hr. from Schluderbach. *Val Fonda* is a hollow floored over by dolomite debris, and enclosed between walls of the same rock. It terminates, about 1½ hr. from Schluderbach, in a ravine through which the water from the Cristallo glacier descends between steep rocks. There are two passages, known to a few of the Ampezzo guides, and to Ploner, the landlord at Schluderbach, by which the rocks are surmounted. On attaining the rock terrace above the ravine, the glacier, with a small terminal moraine, is seen near at hand. In order to avoid the steepest part of the glacier, it is best to ascend for nearly ½ hr. by the rt. lateral moraine (on the traveller's l. hand ascending), till he reaches a point where the slope of the glacier is gentle, and the crevasses few. Only at one point, near the middle of the glacier, Dr. Grohmann found any difficulty from the crevassed condition of the ice. In approaching the summit, which is reached in 3½ hrs. from Schluderbach, the slope is very gentle. But little distant view is gained from the pass, and the interest of the excursion lies in the grand rock scenery. There is scarcely another spot in the Alps so wild and so strange that can be approached with so slight an outlay of time and labour. The descent, though steep, is easy and not fatiguing. It lies through a cleft, or furrow, the

channel of which is full of fine debris, which is here called *grava* (gravel). In the descent the views of Sorapis, Pelmo, Civetta, and other peaks of this region are very fine. The ground being favourable for a rapid descent, an active mountaineer may easily reach Cortina in 2 hrs. from the summit. In the early summer, the cleft through which the descent lies would probably be the channel for water from the melting snow of the upper part of the pass, and might be found difficult and disagreeable.

The ascent of Monte Cristallo was accomplished for the first time from the Cristall-Pass, in September, 1865, by Dr. Grohmann with two local guides. Mounting a short ice-slope, they accomplished the greater part of the ascent by ledges that run along the face of the mountain overlooking the Tre Croci Pass. Though looking very slender from below, these ledges generally afford fair footing. At a height of about 10,000 ft., Dr. Grohmann attained a little shelf on the verge of the precipice, whence a rather deep cleft leads up to the topmost part of the mountain. The summit is reached in 2½ hrs. from the pass, not reckoning halts, and the greater part of the way is sheer climbing; but it would appear that there are only one or two 'bad places.' The view is naturally very extensive, but it must be owned that the chief inducement to the ascent of the peaks of this region is in the climb itself. When the cragsman has acquired a little familiarity with the rock, so as not to feel uneasy in places where the surface is rotten, and pieces are detached by the hand, he gets to prefer dolomite climbing to all other rock-work, finding it afford far more of excitement and variety than the crystalline slates, or even granite. Mr. Tuckett has reached the summit with Santo Siorpaes in 5 hrs. from Cortina, and descended to Schludernbach in 3¼ hrs., not counting halts.

The *Cristallino* (9,238′), one of the secondary ridges of the Cristallo, rising between Val Popena and Val Banche,

was ascended by Dr. Grohmann. Mr. Sowerby, who attempted to go that way to the Lake of Mesurina, was led into many difficulties by the guide above named—A. Molins—and forced to descend Val Popena and so return to Schludernbach.

Route C.

CORTINA D' AMPEZZO TO BELLUNO, BY AGORDO.

Various bridle-paths and foot-paths lead from Cortina to Caprile in from 5 to 7 hrs. Rough track thence to Cencenighe 8 m. Road from Cencenighe to Agordo, 6 m.; thence to Belluno, by Mas, about 18 m.—in all about 46 m.

Reference has frequently been made in preceding sections to the valley of the Cordevole, the longest affluent of the Piave, though the Boita has probably a more abundant stream. The former, flowing from the valleys conterminous with the Fassathal and Gaderthal, joins the Piave midway between Belluno and Feltre. An active traveller may easily reach Belluno in one day from Cortina; but it is a far better plan to give one or two extra days to the journey, and to see something of the fine scenery of the lateral valleys of the Cordevole. There is good accommodation at Agordo, the chief place in the main valley.

As mentioned in § 60, Rte. H, the upper end of the Cordevole valley, N. of the Tyrolese frontier, is collectively called Livinallongo. This is divided from the district of Ampezzo, at the head of the Boita valley, by a ridge rather higher and more continuous than most of those in this district that lie between the main peaks. The most conspicuous summits in the ridge in question, which serves to connect the Monte Tofana with the Pelmo, are the *Nuvolau, Monte Gusella, Monte Car-*

nera, Punta di Formin (8,858'), and *Becco di Mezzodi* (8,789'). This range is traversed by many cattle-tracks, and the way to Caprile may be much varied; but it suffices here to mention those most convenient to travellers.

1. *Cortina to Caprile by Monte Giau.* This is sometimes called Pass of Monte Gusella, but *Monte Gusella* (8,499') is the name of a projecting summit between the pass and the Nuvolau. There are several possible tracks, of which two are frequented, both commonly called Monte Giau, but that described first is also known as Passo di Falzarego. Excepting over a portion of the descent to Caprile, ladies may ride without inconvenience; but it is not easy to find suitable animals in this district. The way from Cortina, after crossing the Boita, and passing the hamlet of Meleres, ascends gently through the wooded glen of the Rio Torto, till it reaches the extensive pastures of the Monte Giau, which extend some way on either side of the summit. Before reaching it the track divides, as there are two points of about equal height, separated by a craggy knoll, where it is usual to pass the ridge. Either is reached from Cortina in from 2½ to 3 hrs. From the summit the Marmolata is conspicuous; but the Pelmo is best seen lower down from Col di Sta. Lucia. The two passes mentioned above correspond to two short green glens locally called Val Zonia and Val Piezza, which unite lower down in Val Fiorentina. The height of the pass leading to Val Zonia is 7,511 ft. The torrent of this valley, which flows to join the Cordevole at Caprile, forms for some distance the frontier between Tyrol and Venetia, leaving to the former the village of *Col di Sta. Lucia* (4,858'), (often called *Colle*) above the rt. bank, while *Selva* (4,482'), at a lower level on the opposite side, belongs to Italy. There are many tracks; and it is possible to avoid both villages. The ground is very uneven, and in one place it is necessary to reascend along the slope above the rt. bank before the final descent to Caprile is reached. The traveller is, however, well rewarded for the extra labour by an exquisite view, in which the Pelmo and Civetta rival each other in grandeur. The writer, although he has passed this way twice, can throw no light on the current story which, in varied forms, affirms the existence of a picture by Titian in the village of Sta. Lucia. According to Schaubach, it was painted in fresco on the outer wall of the Vidum, or parsonage. Covered with whitewash by some subsequent occupant, it was, he says, uncovered with difficulty. A steep and rough descent leads in about 2½ hrs. from the top to

Caprile (3,376'). The Lion of St. Mark, on a marble tablet at the upper end of the village, shows that this has long been a frontier village of Venetia. The inn kept by Madame Pezzé is praised by all travellers, and a favourite place of resort. By a delicate attention to English feeling, the *Pall Mall Gazette* is supplied in summer by the Agordo branch of the Italian Alpine Club. The statutes of the Cadore republic, dating before 1600, are preserved in the house. This village is so near the base of the Marmolata, Pelmo, and Civetta, that although most travellers making the ascent of those peaks will prefer to start from some spot nearer to the summit, they can easily return to dinner at Caprile. Very many short excursions of great interest are available for less ambitious travellers, and the good inn attracts frequent visitors. The guide for excursions of any difficulty is Pellegrini, of the neighbouring hamlet of Rocca. He is a fairly good mountaineer, and a pleasant companion.

2. *Cortina to Caprile by the Tre Sassi.* The road of the Tre Sassi has been noticed in § 60, Rte. H, as being in the direct line from the Gaderthal to Cortina. It may be taken on the way to Caprile, being only a little longer than the pass of Monte Giau, and much easier for ladies, as they may go in a light carriage as far as the bridge over the Cordevole below Buchenstein, whence it is a walk of little more than 1 hr. to Caprile. The road from Cortina keeps

to the N. side of *Val Falzarego*, which runs eastward from the pass along the southern base of the Tofana. The summit (7,073 ft. in height) lies between the Tofana and a group of ruinous-looking columns and towers of dolomite belonging to the range of Monte Nuvolau. Descending by the castle of Buchenstein to the hamlet of Buchenstein, or Andraz, the traveller bound for Caprile must quit the new road which follows the rt. side of the valley to Pieve di Andraz (§ 60, Rte. H), and take the rougher road by the l. bank. This passes in part through pine-forest, gaining at intervals a noble view of the Civetta, rising behind the lake of Alleghe. The descent to Caprile is steep, but the track has been made passable for light vehicles. 3 hrs. should be allowed for reaching the Tre Sassi from Cortina, and about 3 hrs. for the descent to Caprile. On the whole, the scenery of this route is superior to that first described, but there is no single object so grand as the Pelmo seen from rear Col di Sta. Lucia.

3. *By Monte Val.* In Rte. A, reference is made among the excursions from Cortina to a glen (named by Dr. Grohmann Val Ambriciola) that mounts from near that village in the direction of the Becco di Mezzodi. By that way the traveller may reach one of the upper branches of Val Fiorentina, whose extensive pastures are known by the name *Monte Val.* A good path descends thence to *Selva* (4,482') the chief village of Val Fiorentina, and so to Caprile. The writer has no acquaintance with this route beyond the head of Val Ambriciola. It appears to be rather intricate, and it would not be wise to undertake it without a guide.

Caprile to Belluno. A rough cart-track runs along the valley of the Cordevole below Caprile. At first the scenery is not very interesting, but within little more than two miles from Caprile, the traveller reaches the charming little *Lake of Alleghe* (3,220'), the gem of this valley. The one defect of the Dolomite Alps is the absence of lakes—for the tarns lying here and there in mountain-hollows do not deserve that name—and the accident that produced this sheet of blue water gives to the Civetta, whose form is mirrored in its surface, a charm not possessed by any of its rivals. The lake originated in a great bergfall from the Monte Pizzo, on the W. side of the valley, that fell in January 1772, crushing three hamlets and drowning a fourth in the lake, which rapidly rose behind the barrier so formed. A second fall, four months after the first, caused even greater destruction by driving the water of the lake in formidable waves that utterly destroyed the greater part of the houses in the valley. The track, which on leaving Caprile kept the l. bank of the stream, crosses to the opposite side, and passes along the slopes above the W. shore of the lake. Most travellers will prefer to traverse the lake in a boat, which may be ordered overnight by those who sleep at Caprile. The village of *Alleghe*, with a pretty spire to its church, lies some way from the E. shore at the opening of a glen, or recess, that seems to penetrate to the very base of the Civetta. This shows as a cleft mass of not very bold outline, but with a vast face of precipice, adorned with the most delicate fretted work of spire and crag. For a notice of the ascent see Rte. G.

At the S. end of the lake the track makes a steep descent over the great pile of rocks and debris that serves to dam up the waters. Though partly overgrown with trees, this mound still shows the appearance of its origin. The valley bears to SSW., and is contracted almost to a defile in passing round the W. base of the Civetta. The cart-track keeps the rt. bank of the Cordevole, and about 4 m. below the end of the lake, or 8 m. from Caprile, reaches

Cencenighe (2,544'), a village standing at the junction of the Biois with the Cordevole. The former torrent issues from Val di Canale, through which lie the routes to Val di Fiemme described in § 60, and the remarkable way to San Martino di Castrozza by Gares (§ 59, Rte. L). There is a humble but decent inn at Cencenighe, and thence the traveller may ascend the *Cima di Pape* (8,239'), a peak SW. of the village, mainly formed of consolidated volcanic ashes and scoriæ. The ascent is said not to be difficult. The view is probably finer from *Mte. Pelsa* (7,943'), on the opposite side of the main valley. This may be considered as a SW. outlier from the dolomitic mass of the Civetta. It is best reached from Listolade (see below), but is more difficult of access than the Cima di Pape.

[A traveller wishing to see something of the grand dolomite peaks that rise between the Cordevole and San Martino di Castrozza should start from Cencenighe, or the rather better inn at Forno di Canale, and ascend thence to Gares (§ 59, Rte. L). From that place a cattle-track leads by the Malgonera Alp to the summit of the ridge dividing Gares from the Valle di San Lucano. From the pass called *Caos la Forcella* (6,355'), a beaten path leads down the last-named glen to its junction with the Cordevole valley.] At Cencenighe begins the carriage-road that extends to Belluno. At the hamlet of Faë the road crosses to the l. bank, and soon after reaches *Listolade*, a hamlet standing at the opening of *Val Corpassa*, an extremely wild and savage glen by which the ascent of Monte Pelsa is sometimes effected. The writer believes that it is possible to cross the ridge connecting that summit with the Civetta; descending to the Cordevole above Cencenighe. This must be a very fine excursion.

On the opposite side of the Cordevole, about 1 m. below Listolade, is *Taibon*, at the opening of *Val di San Lucano*, through which lies the interesting way to Primiero, noticed in § 59, Rte. K. Little more than 1 m. farther is

Agordo (2,060'), the chief place in the valley of the Cordevole. It is a small town of nearly 3,000 inhabitants, with a large piazza, one side of which is occupied by the *palazzo* of Count Manzoni, a resident proprietor. The best inn, of which recent accounts are very favourable, is in the piazza. Nothing can be finer than the position of Agordo. It stands near the opening of several lateral valleys, in the midst of a small tract of level or gently sloping ground, but encompassed by rock-scenery of the grandest character. Especially striking is the *Palle di San Lucano*, rising in a sheer precipice in the fork between the main stream and the Valle di San Lucano. Many mountain paths converge at Agordo. The most frequented are those leading to Primiero, either by the quicksilver mine in Val Imperina, or the shorter way by Gosaldo (§ 59, Rte. K). In the opposite direction, or ENE., two passes (noticed in Rte. G) lead to Forno di Zoldo. Through the Val di San Lucano is the way to Gares mentioned above, and the circuitous but highly interesting way to Primiero by Val di Canale (§ 59, Rte. K). The vegetation of the valley about Agordo is very singular. Under the shade of the surrounding crags many Alpine species descend into the valley, and flourish on the same level with the peach-tree, chestnut, and even the vine. The drawback on the attractions of Agordo is the neighbourhood of the mines in the adjoining Val Imperina. The copper-mine, a government establishment, has been long in operation, and a few years ago produced about 200 tons of copper yearly. Farther from Agordo, in the same valley, is the more important quicksilver-mine worked by a private company. The process adopted to obtain the mercury in the metallic state is said to be effective, and to spare the health of the workmen. The fumes felt at Agordo when the wind blows from the S. are sulphureous exhalations from the copper-mine, and have no relation to the quicksilver-mine.

An omnibus plies between Belluno and Agordo, starting from the former city early in the morning, and returning in the afternoon. After passing close to the copper-mine, and below a rock which retains the name Castello di Agordo, although the castle has utterly disappeared, the road enters a defile of the grandest character. It is narrower, wilder, and more savage than the defile of the Brenta, described in § 59, Rte. A, but wanting in the contrasts that make that so imposing an entrance into Italy. As that is called Canal di Brenta, so this retains the Venetian denomination, *Canal di Agordo*. Near a roadside inn, called La Stanga, the traveller passes a lateral cleft, which is all that is seen of the opening of *Val di Piero*. As far back as local memory went, the torrent that descends through the cleft had left no room for human foot, and it was not till 1862 that the accidental fall of large quantities of sand and gravel, during a fit of wet weather, opened a way into it. It was found to be possible to penetrate a considerable distance through the cleft, so narrow that in places the sky is completely lost to view, and finally to reach a fine waterfall, in an extremely picturesque spot—an Oread's bath, never before profaned by human presence. Floods in the stream interrupted the access to this singular spot, but it is believed that by means of planks it is now made permanently accessible. Inquiry should be made at the inn at La Stanga, or from the official authorities in Agordo. The defile comes abruptly to an end in a very wild spot, near a large road-side inn called *El Peron* (1,311'). The road now passes close to the site of one of the most formidable bergfalls of which the traces are preserved in the Alps. At some period, not extremely remote, the Cordevole flowed SW. from the opening of the defile to join the *Mis* torrent, which descends from NNW., until an enormous mass of mountain was detached from the Spizzo di Vedana that rises between the two streams. The ruins cover a space nearly 4 m. long by 3 m. wide. The Cordevole was driven to make a circuit to the E., and the Mis towards the W., and they now meet at the S. end of the ruins. A town called *Cornia*, spoken of in early documents relating to this region, but no longer known to exist, is supposed to lie beneath the hills of debris on which has arisen the hamlet of *Vedana*. A small lake is formed near at hand, in a depression of the surface. On reaching *Mas* (1,215'), a short way below Peron, the ranges that have hitherto confined the channel of the Cordevole subside towards the broad open valley of the Piave. The road to Belluno quits the Cordevole, which joins the Piave half-way between that town and Feltre, and goes over a tract of undulating tertiary hills, till it joins the road from Feltre close to

Belluno (1,256'), a picturesque city, with nearly 12,000 inhabitants. It has numerous inns, of which the best are Due Torri (very fair), and Leone d' Oro. The cathedral by Palladio has a *campanile*, which commands a very fine view of the surrounding country. The broad trough of the Piave valley is overlaid by a tertiary sandstone, through which the Piave and its tributaries have cut deep channels. The height given above is that of the floor of the cathedral, but at its ordinary level the river is lower by 179 ft. The valley of the Piave is further noticed in the next Rte.

A *succursale*, or district branch, of the Italian Alpine Club has been opened at Agordo; and mountaineers planning excursions in the neighbourhood may count on a courteous reception, and on receiving any available information.

Route D.

FELTRE TO FORNO AVOLTRI IN FRIULI.

	Italian geog. miles	Eng. miles
Belluno . . .	16¼	18¾
Longarone . . .	8½	9¾
Pieve di Cadore . .	16	18½
San Stefano . . .	14	16¼
Forno Avoltri . .	11½	13¼
	66¼	76½

Within the last few years the road through the valley of the Piave, which was not practicable for carriages over the pass connecting the head of that valley with Friuli, has been completed to Forno Avoltri, the highest village on the northern branch of the Tagliamento. This is in itself a very interesting route, and it affords an easy way of connecting a tour in the Cadore Alps with a visit to the upper valleys of the Tagliamento. Very fair accommodation is found at San Stefano, and at Sappada.

The lower part of the valley of the Piave was noticed in § 59, Rte. C, in describing the road from Bassano to Feltre. The latter town stands on a terrace some 300 ft. above the Piave, and 2 or 3 m. distance from the river. Thence to Capo di Ponte, above Belluno, the valley is a broad trough gently sloping between mountains, whose undulating floor is covered by sandy deposits of tertiary age. Without pretensions to grandeur, for only at intervals are the higher peaks of the Cadore Alps in view, the scenery is extremely pleasing. Many of the large villas belonging to the proprietors are surrounded by meadow land, with scattered plantations, more resembling English parks than anything commonly seen in the S. of Europe. There is a road by the l. bank of the Piave, by Lentiai and *Mel*, which probably commands fine views of the high mountains NW. of the valley; but the post-road keeps near the base of the hills, usually at a considerable distance from the rt. bank of the river. Rather more than half-way from Feltre a long bridge at *Bribano* crosses the wide bed of the Cordevole, in which are seen rolled blocks of porphyry and other igneous rocks, brought down from the mountains that surround the sources of the stream. The valley loses something of its breadth in approaching *Belluno*. (See last Rte.)

In the space between that city and Capo di Ponte, the most conspicuous object is the *Monte Serva* (6,968′). The summit, rising WNW. of the latter village, commands an extremely interesting view, as, in addition to most of the higher peaks of the Cadore Alps, it overlooks the finest part of the valley of the Piave, as well as the ancient channel of that river between Capo di Ponte and Serravalle. The blue lake of Sante Croce, and in the far distance the lagoons of Venice and the Adriatic, complete the panorama. The view from Monte Cavallo (§ 62, Rte. I) includes a larger portion of the coast and of the low country; but the mountain view is inferior to this. The ascent of Monte Serva is best made from the glen of the *Ardo*, which torrent joins the Piave at Belluno. An active walker may take the summit on the way to Longarone, descending to rejoin the road about 2 m. N. of Capo di Ponte; but the ascent is more laborious than might be expected by a mountaineer who forgets that his starting-point is a low and hot valley. The road from Capo di Ponte to Tai di Cadore is described in Rte. A. Above Longarone the botanist will observe *Spiræa decumbens*, frequently occurring on rocks by the roadside. It is confined to the upper valley of the Piave, and the adjacent valleys of Friuli. At Tai di Cadore the high-road to Cortina turns sharply to the l., while a short piece of road to the rt. leads to

Pieve di Cadore (2,907′), a picturesque little town with a fair country inn (kept by Toscani ?), cheaper and quieter than that at Tai. It stands on a sort of saddle connecting the W. side of the valley with a bold projecting rock that stands out as a promontory above the deep gorge of the Piave. This was crowned by an ancient castle, long held by the Venetians to protect this entrance into their territory till it was blown up by the French in 1796.

The name of the little town has been made known afar as the birthplace of Titian—Tiziano Vecellio. One (the last?) of the great painter's collateral descendants—Alessandro Vecellio, died here within the last few years. The paternal home of the painter (an ordinary village house) is marked by an inscription; and a large figure of him, some 14 ft. in height, is painted on a campanile adjacent to the *pretura*, or court-house. The great man did not leave much evidence of his genius in his native place. There are two pictures here attributed to him. That formerly in Casa Jacobi, now in the church, was probably in part executed by the master. The other, known as the 'Genova' picture, has been so much retouched or repainted, that it is hard to decide on its claims.

The traveller who may halt here should not lose the view from the castle rock, and should make a somewhat longer stroll along the ridge of Monte Zucco (Rte. A). From the farther end of the ridge there is a striking view into the gorge of the Boita, and the Pelmo is seen in full grandeur a little N. of W. A rather longer walk, recommended by Messrs. Gilbert and Churchill, is the ascent of a point NW. of Tai, marked by a little chapel of San Dionigi. 3 hrs. are required for the ascent. The Forcella Piccola, leading to San Vito, is described in Rte. F.

Horses and vehicles are more often to be had at Pieve di Cadore than at Tai, but it is sometimes necessary to send to Venas.

The scenery of the upper valley of the Piave is extremely fine, and as the traveller passes the opening of successive lateral glens, he usually receives the promise of scenes still more wild and striking. The first considerable village, towards which the road descends from La Pieve, is *Domegge*, between 3 and 4 m. distant. There are here pictures of doubtful authenticity, attributed to Titian, in the chapels of San Barnaba and San Rocco. The road now passes along the E. end of the range of the Marmarolo, which deserves to rank among the dolomite giants. The summits of some of the extraordinary towers of rock that form the range are seen from Pieve di Cadore, and from other spots on the road, but to appreciate the grandeur of the group, the traveller must visit the Auronzo valley (Rte. E). After passing *Lozzo* (2,482'), with an inn kept by an apothecary, the road begins to ascend more steadily towards the opening of that beautiful valley, wherein the dome of the new church of Auronzo is seen for a moment. The skill of the engineer is shown at the *Tre Ponti* (2,401'), erected at the junction of the Piave of the Anziei from the Auronzo valley. Arches thrown 90 ft. above the three streams are made to abut upon a single central pier, thus allowing communication with either bank of either stream. Above the junction the *Monte Cornon*, towering over the l. bank of the Piave, becomes the dominant object in the valley. The scenery is as wild as the mountaineer can desire, but the defile opens out before reaching

San Stefano (3,127'), the chief place in the uppermost branch of the valley, which forms the district of *Comelico*. The inn (Aquila d' Oro?) is very good for so remote a place. A good guide, by name Felice Pomarè, formerly lived near the village. He knows the country well, and could tell many curious tales of bears, who appear to be more common here than in any other part of the Alps. On the Alpine pastures the traveller may often hear a boy sounding a horn, intended to warn off these mischievous visitors.

At San Stefano the valley forks. Hitherto the prevailing direction has varied between NNE. and NE. Henceforward the traveller mounts about due E. towards the head of the main valley; while the *Padola* torrent descends from NNW. through an equally considerable branch. That way runs the road to Innichen, noticed in Rte. II.

Above San Stefano the valley has a pastoral air, and the eye, almost fatigued by the stern grandeur of grey precipices, rests with pleasure on the green meadows and deciduous trees of Comelico. Passing the opening of *Val Visdende*, a beautiful glen that in one direction runs up to the peak of Monte Paralba (§ 62, Rte. D), and leads northward by another branch to the upper end of the Gailthal, the new road ascends to *Sappada*, known to its German inhabitants as *Plon*, and also called *Grandvilla*. It includes two principal groups of houses, of which the farther, on a level with the top of the pass, is locally known as *Cima*. The commune is inhabited by a German colony that appears at some remote period to have migrated from the Pusterthal. There is a fair country inn, and the position is agreeable, and may serve as centre for several excursions. A little below the largest hamlet (4,026 ft. above the sea), a glen opens to SW. that runs up towards the *Terza Grande* (8,474'). On the opposite or N. side of the valley is the *Monte Rinaldo*, but at Cima (about 1½ m. above the chief village) a short glen opens to the N. and leads straight up to the noble peak of Monte Paralba, further noticed in § 62, Rte. D. It is not directly accessible from the S. side. A short but rather steep descent leads from Cima to *Forno Avoltri* (3,492'), the highest village on the Degano, or N. branch of the Tagliamento. Standing in the immediate neighbourhood of magnificent scenery, this place might be much resorted to by travellers if provided with a good inn. That found by the writer in 1857 was dirty and disagreeable, but subsequent travellers have given a rather more favourable report of the Cavallo Bianco. Maize grows luxuriantly about Forno Avoltri, while no grain but oats seems to grow round Sappada. The valley of the Degano, or Canal di Gorto, is described in the next §.

Route E.

San Stefano to Cortina d' Ampezzo, by Auronzo. The Croda Malcora.

The exquisitely beautiful valley of Auronzo lies in the direct way for a traveller approaching Cortina from the head of the valley of the Piave; but it has such powerful attractions, and is so easy of access, that no traveller will regret making the slight detour necessary to reach Cortina this way from the high-road at Tai di Cadore, the excursion being easily completed in a single day. Many travellers, besides the present writer, have experienced the difficulty of avoiding the use of superlatives in describing this region; but it is not too much to say, with the images of many other glorious scenes present to his memory, that he seeks in vain for any valley offering more exquisite combinations of the grand, the beautiful, and the fantastic, than are here found in favourable weather. A good road for light vehicles is carried up the valley for a distance of 9 m. above the village of Auronzo; and though rough is practicable all the way to Cortina. The traveller who would become thoroughly acquainted with the valley will also cross the Forcella Grande, even if he be not tempted to undertake the difficult ascent of the Sorapis.

ROUTE E.—VALLEY OF AURONZO.   519

Starting from San Stefano in a carriage, it is necessary to descend the valley of the Piave for a distance of 5 or 6 m. to reach the opening of the Auronzo valley, and then to ascend to the village, nearly 4 m. from the Tre Ponti, mentioned in the last Rte. The pedestrian with a local guide, crossing a low hill, may in 2 hrs. from San Stefano reach

Auronzo. It includes two separate villages, of which the lower, called *Villa Piccola* (2,911'), has a large new church. Farther on is *Villa Grande.* The accounts of the accommodation here are discordant, but there are now at least two very fair inns. The best is that of Pampanini, half-way between the two villages. Another, kept by Beppe Bombasei, at the Villa Grande, is clean, and gives tolerable food. Piero Orsolina, a famous chamois-hunter, is the best guide here; he knows well most of the Cortina country. The great variety of scenery enjoyed by a traveller passing through the valley of Auronzo arises in great part from the sinuous course pursued by the stream. The head of the main valley is bounded by the low Tre Croci Pass, noticed in Rte. B, lying between the masses of the Croda Malcora and the Cristallo. On the S. side of the valley, divided from the Malcora by the Forcella Grande, and extending to the slopes above Auronzo, is the range of the *Marmarolo.* This probably exceeds the limit of 10,000ft., but falls short of the height of the chief peaks of this district. In Oct. 1867 the Cav. Somano, with Giuseppe Toffoli of Calalzo as guide, reached one of the higher summits, but the highest was not attained until 1872, by Messrs. Utterson, Kelso, and Trueman, with Santo Siorpaes and Luigi Orsolina of Auronzo. The mountain shows, from whatever side it is viewed, a group of high towers and pinnacles, and many small patches of glacier hang from the rifts that separate them. The western end of the Marmarolo range, nearest to the Forcella Grande, is locally called Meduze. The mass of mountains lying N. and W. of Auronzo is still imperfectly known and very ill laid down on maps; but much information as to the passes leading that way to Sexten will be found in Rte. H, in which it will be seen that the mountaineer has a choice among several very grand routes to Landro as well as to Sexten. Besides those there mentioned should be noted a pass which Mr. Holzmann has named *Forcella di Marson* leading from the head of Val Marson to that of Val Rimbianco by the S. side of the peaks of the Drei Zinnen.

A very fine view of all the mountains enclosing the valley, besides several of the more western peaks, is gained from a rather steep grassy ridge (Monte Melone?) rising W. of the village, which may be considered a NE. spur of the Marmarolo. The scenery of the lower part of the valley of Auronzo is far less striking than at the upper end, but beautiful throughout. The peculiarity of the valley is the contrast of charming park scenery—open spaces of green smooth sward, and masses of noble pine-trees—with the shattered pale grey peaks that rise on every side. The general direction, in ascending the valley, is at first about NW.; it then bends to SW., winding back to NW., after rounding the base of a projecting summit called Campoduro. Only two or three small clusters of houses are seen on the way. The road keeps to the l. bank of the Anziei, but at a bridge about half-way up the valley the pedestrian seeking shade may with advantage cross to the rt. bank, and follow a pleasant path through the forest. In fully 4 hrs. from the Villa Grande the traveller reaches the lonely forester's house in *Val Buona*, as the upper end of the Auronzo valley is locally called. From an open green space of meagre sheep-pasture the traveller obtains a view which, under moderately favourable conditions, leaves an ineffaceable impression. Nearly due S., through dense pine-forest, lies the way to the Forcella Grande (see below), while to SW. the eye penetrates through Val Sorapis into the innermost recesses of the Croda Malcora, culminating in the peaks of the Sorapis and Foppa di Mathia. Above a first high barrier, down which hangs a slender waterfall, the rocks rise, seamed with transverse bands of ice, till they become one vast mass of shattered wall. Even an experienced mountaineer may doubt whether there be any other outlet to this rock-prison. It is a *cirque*, less complete and regular in form than that of Gavarnie, but even surpassing the latter in the grandeur of the rock-scenery. The passes connecting the head of Val Sorapis with Ampezzo are fit only for practised cragsmen, but an excursion to the lake, which lies concealed behind the first high step of rock, is easily made in 1½ hr. from the forester's house. The owner, named Bastian. is thoroughly acquainted with the surrounding forests, through which a stranger cannot easily find his way.

His house (4,557 ft. above the sea) is a convenient starting-point for several Alpine expeditions, and he receives strangers hospitably; but the resources of the place are very limited, often failing even in milk, and the house is at night sometimes unpleasantly crowded by country people. Soon after passing Bastian's house the view of the Val Sorapis is shut out by one of the spurs from the N. end of the Malcora mass which Dr. Grohmann has called the Cesta ridge. To the rt., however, the crags of Monte Cristallo rise very grandly, and the interest of the walk is renewed when the traveller gains the summit of the *Tre Croci Pass* (5,970'), and looks out westward over the green basin of Ampezzo, guarded by the Tofana and many another rugged peak. The distance from Bastian's house to Cortina is about 2½ hrs.' steady walking. The track though rough and steep is passable for light vehicles, but there are one or two places where a stranger might confound the woodcutters' roads through the forest with the true way to Cortina. The descent from the Tre Croci to Cortina is perfectly easy, and it is impossible to miss the way.

A traveller who has made the excursion from the forester's house to the Lago Sorapis need not return thither if bound for Cortina. There is a path by the Alpe di Malcora, and by a little stream called Potamei, that rejoins the ordinary track over the Tre Croci on the E. side, at no great distance below the summit.

The Forcella Grande. Reference has been already made to the Forcella Grande, the depression which divides the Marmarolo range from the Croda Malcora. By that way the traveller may reach the Ampezzo road at San Vito or Chiapuzzo, choosing the latter if he be bound for Cortina. The scenery is wild and strange, rather than beautiful, and there is no distant view until he has descended some way on the E. side. From the forester's hut, mentioned above, the way lies through dense forest, and then up very steep slopes, in great part covered with *krummholz*, on the rt., or Marmarolo side of the torrent. A good local guide is here necessary; there is only a faintly marked path, which quite disappears at intervals. On attaining the upper end of this long and dark ravine, locally called *Valle di San Vito*, the practised mountaineer may send back his guide. The highest point of the *Forcella Grande* (7,536') is shut in on either side between great rock-walls. A steep but not difficult couloir filled with fine debris leads rapidly down to a ridge that projects somewhat from the main mass towards the Ampezzo road. This ridge, called Col del Prato di Mason, commands an extremely fine view over the valley of the Boita, and its colossal guardian peaks. A track by the l. side of the ridge leads to San Vito (Rte. A), but those bound for Cortina keep to the rt., and reach the road at *Chiapuzzo*. On the way to Cortina is a spring of cold water, well known as Acqua Buona, which always tempts the mountaineer to an agreeable halt. This pass is best fitted for a traveller who wishes to make the circuit of the Croda Malcora from Cortina, a fine day's walk. He should start early, and endeavour to secure beforehand the assistance of Bastian the forester to guide him as far as the summit of the Forcella Grande. The distances may be reckoned—Cortina to Bastian's house, 2½ hrs.; thence to Forcella Grande, nearly 4 hrs.; descent to Col di Prato da Mason, ½ hr.; thence to Cortina, 2¼ hrs.; in all rather more than 9 hrs.

By the Croda Malcora. Ascent of the Sorapis. The writer has in this district very generally followed the authority of Dr. Grohmann, who has been its most persevering and successful explorer, but he is unable to abandon the generally-adopted name *Croda Malcora*, as the collective designation of that vast mass of crag that rises on the E. side of the valley of the Boita below Cortina. He willingly adopts the names Sorapis and Foppa di Mathia for the two highest peaks, of which the former was first reached in 1864 by Dr. Grohmann with two Ampezzo guides (F. Lacedelli and Angelo Dimaj) after two exploring excursions, and two previous unsuccessful attempts to reach the top. Those who wish for full information are referred to the Jahrbuch of the Austrian Alpine Club for 1865. In the course of his explorations, Dr. Grohmann traversed two singular passes across the ridge of the Malcora connecting Val Sorapis with the Ampezzo road. Such passages in the most hopeless-looking spots are found from time to time by chamois-hunters; but the most experienced mountaineer has little chance of hitting upon them without a guide.

The principal part of the Croda Malcora consists in the long ridge of precipice extending from the Forcella Grande towards Cortina, and culminating in the *Foppa di Mathia* (10,763'). From that peak a shorter but higher ridge diverges to NE. It includes the *Sorapis* (10,798')—the highest peak of the entire mass—and falls away in a descending series of pinnacles and towers towards the valley of Auronzo. In the angle between these two ranges lies *Val Sorapis*, and through that wild glen the traveller will approach the heart of the mountain. Starting from Cortina, the traveller reaches the *Lago Sorapis* (6.334') in about 3½ hrs., by the Alpe di Malcora (see above), or fully 4 hrs. if he should make the detour by Bastian's house. Nothing can be wilder than the lake and its surroundings, and the gnarled trunks of the creeping pine (*krummholz*) scarcely relieve the sternness of the scene. Near at hand is a cave, in the local dialect *landro*, with a spring of fresh water, which gives lodging to a herdsman for a few weeks in summer. Above the lake a second step in the ascent has to be surmounted, a small glacier is passed, and the head of the glen is a hollow called I Fondi. Here the traveller has on his l. hand the walls of rock that run up to the two highest peaks and the ridge connecting them. To the rt. is the steep slope leading to the Selletta Pass, while straight forward a steep ascent leads to the pass known to a few chamois-hunters as *Sora la Cengia del Banco* (8,493'). It lies to the l. of the lowest point in the ridge connecting the Foppa di Mathia with the Cima Negra. Here the traveller stands on the crest of that formidable range of precipices that overlooks the valley of the Boita, and marvels how the descent is to be effected. He follows for some 100 yards a horizontal ledge along the face of the Foppa di Mathia, and then reaches a point where the rocks become comparatively easy, and give good hold for feet and hands. Lower down short zigzag slopes of debris render the way still easier, and the high-road is reached about 1½ m. below the Acqua Buona. An active walker will reach the summit of the pass in less than 2 hrs. from the lake, and may descend to Cortina in 3 hrs.; of course excluding halts. There is a more direct, but scarcely so interesting a way, from I Fondi at the head of Val Sorapis, to Cortina, by the *Selletta Pass* (8,697'). This is a slight depression that separates the northern end of the Malcora range (called by Dr. Grohmann, Cesta range) from the main mass. The summit is reached in about 1 hr. of steep, but not difficult, ascent from I Fondi (2¼ hrs. from Lago Sorapis). The descent lies in part through a steep ravine called Val Faloria, that falls some way towards the Boita, and then comes to an abrupt end. To the rt. are the pastures of *Monte Casadio*, whence a broad easy track leads to join the ordinary way from the Tre Croci to Cortina.

The ascent of the *Sorapis* (10,798') appears to be the most difficult of those hitherto accomplished in this district, as is shown by the fact that so practised a mountaineer as Dr. Grohmann employed 7¼ hrs. in reaching the summit from I Fondi. A stiff scramble leads thence to a sort of shelf on the face of the Foppa, called by Dr. Grohmann Pian della Foppa. Still steeper was the climb from that point to the topmost ridge. Much time was consumed in following this ridge, which seems to have been the most difficult part of the expedition. In returning, Dr. Grohmann and his guides effected, though with difficulty, the descent on the opposite side of the highest ridge through an excessively steep rocky ravine, called by him Sorapiskar. This opens on the Auronzo side of the pass of the Forcella Grande; and Dr. Grohmann draws the just conclusion that future ascents should be attempted from San Vito rather than from Cortina, which is too distant, and involves a circuitous route. The only alternative is to pass the night in the cavern near the Lago Sorapis.

Route F.

SAN VITO TO PIEVE DI CADORE. MONTE ANTELAO.

About 6 hrs.' steady walking from San Vito to La Pieve.

The Forcella Piccola, a much deeper and wider depression than the Forcella Grande, described in the last Rte., divides the range of the Marmarolo from the Antelao, which, though the fact is not yet positively ascertained, is most probably the highest of the Cadore Alps.

Like the Marmolata, this affects a form not common among the dolomite peaks, the declivity on the N. and NE. sides being that of a moderately steep houseroof. This allows of the accumulation of sufficient snow to form a rather extensive glacier, and makes the ascent, save at one point near the top, easier than that of any of its lofty neighbours. An active mountaineer may combine the ascent with the pass of the *Forcella Piccola* in one long day. This is an easy and somewhat frequented pass, as it much shortens the way from San Vito to Domegge and Calalzo, and offers to the tourist a more agreeable and interesting way than that by the high-road. A guide appears to be scarcely necessary. In 2½ hrs., or even less, the summit of the Forcella is reached from San Vito. It does not appear to have been measured, but cannot, in the writer's opinion, much surpass 6,000 ft. The most conspicuous and striking object in the view is the Pelmo, which shows grandly. The ridge of the Antelao close at hand on the rt. is also well seen. The pass is broad, and nearly level for some way, and then the track begins to slope rapidly towards *Val Oten*. It lies for a considerable distance in a couloir or channel wherein water runs in rainy weather, while in the hot season it is unpleasantly exposed to the unshaded force of the sun. When possible, it is best to pass this way in the afternoon, when the sun begins to sink behind the mass of the Antelao. In 3 hrs. from the top the traveller reaches the thriving village of *Calalzo* (2,684'), near the opening of Val Oten, but some way above the road from Pieve di Cadore to Domegge. It is necessary to descend some 300 ft. to the road, and remount at least twice that height, in order to reach the former place, for which see Rte. D.

The first ascent of the highest peak of the Antelao was made by Dr. Grohmann in 1863, and the next by the late Lord F. Douglas and Mr. F. L. Latham in 1864. Both were accompanied by Matteo Ossi of Besinego, of whom the English travellers gave a good account.

Dr. Grohmann reports less favourably of his qualifications, and found his demands unreasonable.

On reaching the summit of the Forcella Piccola, the NW. ridge of the Antelao is seen to descend towards the pass, but is separated from it by a deep hollow that runs into the mass of the mountain, and is enclosed by steep walls of rock. To gain the ridge it is best to follow the l. hand side of this hollow for about half its length, and thus reach a point whence the rocky wall is climbed without difficulty, and the traveller sets foot on the ridge, which is long, but of moderate steepness and quite easy. Late in the summer it is not necessary to touch the snow-slopes, which, as seen from Cortina, partially cover this side of the peak. On reaching the summit of this long ascent, the traveller is confronted by a pinnacle or horn of rock, the highest summit of the mountain, which rises with formidable steepness to a height of 200 or 300 ft. This had always passed for inaccessible until one of Dr. Grohmann's companions, a man from Cortina, detected a cleft by which the ascent is effected without real difficulty, except at one point, where a traveller not used to steep rock-climbing should adopt the rope as a security. About 11 hrs., exclusive of halts, should be allowed for going and returning from San Vito, and 13 hrs., if the peak be climbed on the way from that place to Pieve di Cadore.

ROUTE G.

SAN VITO TO LONGARONE, BY VAL DI ZOLDO. MONTE PELMO. MONTE CIVETTA.

In the preceding Rtes. it has been seen that San Vito is the best starting-point for the ascent of the Antelao and the Sorapis, and also for the passes of the Forcella Grande and Forcella Piccola. From the same place it is also possible to ascend the Pelmo, or to pass round the base of that mountain in order to visit a retired but beautiful valley which remains to be noticed. This is *Val di Zoldo*, which originates between the peaks of the Pelmo and Civetta, and descends between the nearly parallel valleys of the Boita and Cordevole to join the Piave at Longarone. Another track, noticed below, goes from San Vito by the N. side of the Pelmo, and leads directly to Caprile, or, by a circuitous but beautiful way, to the head of Val di Zoldo.

It is obvious that San Vito is destined to be a favourite resort of tourists whenever this district shall be more fully known, and when adequate accommodation shall be provided there. See Rte. A.

The most direct way from San Vito to Val di Zoldo is to follow the post-road as far as Borca, and there cross the Boita, and ascend over undulating, hilly, partially wooded country to the rounded ridge that forms the E. boundary of a branch of Val di Zoldo, in which stands the village of *Zoppè* (4,850'). Admirable views of the near mass of the Pelmo and of the Antelao, here seen to the best advantage, are gained in the course of this pleasant walk. The traveller approaching Zoppè from Pieve di Cadore should leave the high-road at Vodo, instead of Borca, but it is there necessary to descend about 400 ft. to reach the bridge over the Boita.

The summit of the ridge is easily reached in less than 2 hrs. from Borca, and in rather less time from Vodo. The parish-priest of Zoppè was an active chamois-hunter, and is said to have discovered one of the possible routes for the ascent of the Pelmo. It is not, however, necessary to take Zoppè on the way; and in following the path from Vodo, which crosses the summit of the ridge at a place called *La Chiandolada* (5,237'), that village lies considerably to the rt. of the direct course. This follows the stream down the Zoppè branch of the valley, and in less than 2 hrs. from the summit reaches its junction with the *Mae*, which is the main torrent of Val di Zoldo. A few minutes' walk above the junction, in the main W. branch of the valley, is *Forno di Zoldo* (2,854'), the chief village, with comfortable quarters in Cercena's inn. As the name indicates, there are forges here, and the occupation of a large part of the population is making nails, which are sent on muleback to the high-road at Longarone. The scenery of both branches of Val di Zoldo is extremely fine. The Pelmo towers grandly over Zoppè, which lies close to its base, while the Civetta is the presiding genius of the main branch above Forno.

There is a way, shorter in distance, though not in time, than that by Vodo, from Pieve di Cadore to Forno di Zoldo. Quitting the high-road at Valle, a hamlet standing little more than a mile W. of Tai di Cadore, a track descends about 400 ft. into the deep gorge of the Boita, where a bridge is thrown across the stream at a height of 193 ft. above its bed, and 2,824 ft. above the sea. A rather steep ascent leads thence to *Cibiana* (3,408'), and then the track winds somewhat S. of W. through the hills till it reaches the summit of the dividing ridge (called *Cima Copada*?), 5,101 ft. above the sea. In the descent the most conspicuous object is the Monte Pramper, dividing the valleys of Zoldo and Agordo.

Of two passes leading from Forno to the Cordevole the writer has little information. The easier of these is approached from *Dont* (3,126'), a village where a lead-mine was formerly worked, a short distance above Forno. It stands by the junction with the Mae of a torrent from a tributary glen called *Val Duram*. Along the N. side of this glen a track mounts nearly due W. to *San Tiziano di Goima* (4,177'). At the latter village the track turns SSW., descends to cross the Duram torrent, and then mounts to the *Duram Pass* (5,365'). The descent to Agordo lies through the *Dugonthal*.

The other pass, probably more interesting to the mountaineer, lies between the *Monte Pramper* and *Cima Vescova*, and is known as *Passo Pramper* (7,558'). The valley of the Cordevole is reached about 1 m. below Agordo. From both these passes, but especially the latter, there should be very fine views of the great dolomite range of Primiero.

Below the junction of its two principal branches Val di Zoldo is contracted to a narrow gorge, and for a distance of nearly 10 m. intervening between Forno and Longarone there is no space for a village or hamlet, and none but a few scattered houses. At Longarone the traveller reaches the high-road through the valley of the Piave (Rte. A). If he has followed the direct course from San Vito, without the very slight detour to Forno, he will easily accomplish the entire distance within 8 hrs.

A longer, but, on the whole, a more interesting way from San Vito to Val di Zoldo passes round the N. side of the Pelmo, by the pass called *Forcella Forada* (6,896'), over the ridge connecting the Pelmo with the *Rocchetta* (7,793') —a minor peak laid down on all maps, while its much higher neighbours the Punta di Formin and Becco di Mezzodì are omitted. The Forcella Forada offers a direct way from San Vito to Caprile, a walk of about 5½ hrs. The descent is through Val Fiorentina, by the hamlet of *Pescul* (4,764'), where there is a rough inn, not worse than that of *Selva*, which must also be passed on the way to Caprile. (See Rte. C.) From Pescul, or from a point above that place in descending from the Forcella Forada, the traveller bound for Val di Zoldo turns off southward over the low ridge of *Monte Grotto*, which divides the head of Val Fiorentina from that of Zoldo. The first hamlet is *Pecol*, with a rough but bearable inn. The landlord's son is a good mountaineer, and would probably make a serviceable guide. The next hamlet is *Maresson* (4,485'), to which soon follows *San Nicolò*, where the traveller finds with surprise a clean and comfortable inn in a spot very rarely visited by strangers. It is an easy walk of 1¾ hr. hence to

Forno. The valley must be populous, as numerous hamlets occur at short intervals.

San Nicolò has many inducements for the mountaineer, being very finely situated, and within convenient distance for the ascent of two of the great mountains of this region—the Pelmo and the Civetta. From this side the former appears by far the more remarkable mountain, and the ascent is most conveniently made from hence. *Monte Pelmo* (10,377'?), from whatever side it be seen, but especially from the E. and S., shows as a gigantic fortress of the most massive architecture, not fretted into minarets and pinnacles, like most of its rivals, but merely defended by huge bastioned outworks, whose walls in many places fall in sheer precipices more than 2,000 ft. The likeness to masonry is much increased by the fact that, in great part, the strata lie in nearly horizontal courses, and hence it happens that many of the steepest faces of the mountain are traversed by ledges wide enough to give passage to chamois and to their pursuers. As chamois-hunting seems to be a favourite pastime in Val di Zoldo, the hunters gradually become well acquainted with the network of narrow ledges that cover the greater part of the mountain, and thus in time they have found out not merely one, but four different ways to reach the topmost plateau. As the most practised mountaineer is not likely to hit upon any of these without a guide, it suffices to say that the two best routes are commenced from the S. side of the mountain, either from above San Nicolò, or from Zoppè. The writer ascended from Borca by the E. face of the mountain, with a chamois-hunter who professed to have discovered the course which they followed. At a comparatively low level, (less than 7,000 ft.?) a ledge was gained which had to be followed horizontally along the face of the precipices that show so boldly on the side facing the Ampezzo road. Three deep recesses were rounded in succession. In two places the ledge had been broken away, but it was found possible to clear the gap thus created. The most eccentric obstacle was encountered at a place where the overhanging rock came down so low as to leave a space of only about 18 inches; far too little to make it possible to creep on hands and knees. The guide, who had hitherto gone first, declared that the breaking away of a projection of rock that overhung the precipice on the l. hand, had made the passage impossible. Unwilling to be baulked, the writer contrived to crawl along the narrow ledge in reptile fashion, and was followed by his guide. Soon after a place was reached from which the ascent to the topmost plateau is merely a long and steep, but not difficult, scramble.

In addition to the characteristic species of the Dolomite Alps, *Valeriana repens*, *Campanula Morettiana*, and *Androsace Hausmanniana* were gathered on this side of the mountain. Whatever course the traveller may take, he finds with surprise a not inconsiderable glacier lying on the broken plateau which is surrounded by the topmost ridges of the mountain. On a small rock-terrace above the upper end of the glacier, the writer was told that they had reached the top, and on his pointing to the shattered ridge above, was assured by the guide that this being all '*croda morta*'—disaggregated rock loosened by weathering—the further ascent was entirely impracticable. It required some time and some caution to loosen with the Alpenstock considerable masses of rock, still hanging together, but detached by a slight effort, before the real topmost ridge was reached by the writer, without his guide. No token of a stone-man was seen, and it is not unlikely that the barometer observation recorded by Fuchs was made some way below the true summit. The height must be about the same as that of the Civetta, and can scarcely be 200 ft. below that of the Antelao. Melchior and Luigi Zugliani of Selva, near Caprile, are recommended as guides for the Pelmo; but there must be several competent men in Val di Zoldo.

None of the giants of this region produces a more imposing effect than does the *Monte Civetta* (10,440'?) from the neighbourhood of Caprile and Alleghe. The grand wall of rock, massive in its central and loftiest section, and flanked by a serrated ridge with many pinnacles and slender teeth, that descends towards NE., is shown in the frontispiece of Messrs. Gilbert and Churchill's book. The first traveller to reach the summit was Mr. F. F. Tuckett, with Melchior and Jakob Anderegg. Serious and unavoidable risk from avalanches was incurred by making the ascent so early as the 31st May, and in the descent the party had a narrow escape from inevitable destruction. Apart from this risk, which would not be incurred later in the year, Mr. Tuckett does not seem to consider the ascent as very difficult for a moderately practised cragsman. The view from the highest point, which is on the brink of the great wall overlooking Alleghe, is probably one of the most remarkable in this remarkable region of the Alps. The son of the innkeeper at Pecol informed Mr. Tuckett that, with one or two companions, he had twice reached the summit of the Civetta; and as he satisfied that gentleman that he had attained a point above all the main difficulties of the ascent, there seems to be no reason to doubt his assertion.

The easily accessible summit NE. of the Civetta, and near to Pecol, is called *Coldai*, and by its N. side is an easy pass from Pecol to Alleghe and Caprile, locally called *Passo d'Alleghe* (6,103'), or quite as often Alleghe Cima. By that way, *Alleghe*, where there is only an 'osteria' of the poorest class, is easily reached in 3 hrs. from Pecol. Between the Coldai and the Civetta is a small tarn; and from the ridge close above it, overlooking Alleghe and its blue lake, a view is gained which is declared by those who have reached that point to be one of the very finest in this district. It is within reach of all moderate walkers, and the excursion involves no difficulty of any kind. Still easier of access is a point of view N. of the Passo d'Alleghe, and attainable in 10 minutes from the summit. In connection with the names of several places in this neighbourhood, it may be observed that English travellers get confused by forgetting that in South Tyrol and Venetia, Col does not mean a pass, but does mean a hill or mountain. Thus the village in Val Fiorentina above Caprile is called Col di Santa Lucia, because, as seen from below, it appears to crown the summit of the ridge on which it stands.

ROUTE H.

INNICHEN TO SAN STEFANO BY THE SEXTENTHAL.

In the foregoing Rtes. it has been seen that nearly all the valleys of this district are tributaries of the Piave. We have now to notice one very fine valley, a tributary of the Pusterthal, whose copious torrent, after descending WNW. to Innichen, joins the infant stream of the Drave, and flows eastward towards Carinthia, in a direction nearly exactly opposite to its previous course. This valley is the *Sextenthal*, noticed in § 51, Rte. A. A road, practicable for light country carriages, goes from Innichen through the valley, and over the low pass dividing it from the district of Comelico at the upper end of the valley of the Piave. The passes leading from Sexten to Auronzo lie through scenery of the grandest character, and one of them at least is not difficult.

1. *By the Kreuzberg, or Monte Croce Pass.* About 7 hrs. in a light carriage, and fully 8 hrs. on foot.

The opening of the Sextenthal is not seen from Innichen, being shut out by the low hill on which stood the Roman city of Aguntum; but the traveller following the road into the valley, which passes round the W. base of the hill, soon comes in sight of the noble mass of rugged summits that bound it on the

SW. side. Foremost among them is the *Dreischusterspitz* (10,368′), which rises in the fork between the main valley and a western branch called *Innerfeld*, by which lies a choice between several rough but not difficult passes leading to Landro. Another fine pass called the *Innicher Riedel* connects the head of Innerfeld with that of the W. branch of the Altlasteiner Thal. The most prominent summit on the W. side of Innerfeld is the *Bürkenkogel* (9,520′). In a wood on the rt. of the road, near the opening of the valley, is the *Innichner Wildbad* (4,330′), with a rustic establishment frequented for the sake of three mineral springs, one of which is chalybeate, the others saline. Farther on the pedestrian may slightly shorten his way by pleasant foot-paths. The lower part of the valley is finely wooded; but as the road ascends the clearings are wider; and on reaching (in 1½ hr. from Innichen) the chief village of

Sexten (4,374′), locally known as St. Veit, the valley stretches upward in an open basin backed by a magnificent group of dolomite peaks. There are two or three inns at Sexten, one of which, at least, affords very fair accommodation. Owing to frequent intercourse with Italy, most of the people here speak or understand Italian. Herr Gander, the curate (co-operator) of Sexten, is a botanist, well acquainted with the flora of the district. Above St. Veit is *Moos* or St. Josef, the second hamlet of the valley, near to which, at the opening of the Fischleinthal, is the *Sextnerbad* (4,476′), a small establishment for mineral baths, affording rough but tolerable accommodation amid scenery far superior to that of Sexten. The mineral springs are strongly impregnated with earthy salts.

The *Fischleinthal* runs deep into the mass of dolomite peaks that enclose the valley of Auronzo on the N. side, and present forms that for variety and strangeness of outline are not surpassed elsewhere in this district. The topography of this mass is yet ill understood: all the published maps are incorrect, and there is much confusion as to the names of the peaks, each having at least a German as well as Italian designation. No mountaineer who visits Sexten will fail to make some excursions into the upper branches of the Fischleinthal; but it belongs to the native members of the Austrian and Italian Alpine Clubs, rather than to strangers, to fix the nomenclature of the peaks of this Tyrolese valley.

A rough road mounts very gently from Sexten through the main (SW.) branch of the valley to the *Kreuzberg* (5,361′), the scarcely perceptible ridge between the waters of the Drave and those of the Piave, now marking the frontier between Austria and Italy. The ancient Mauthhaus, standing at the summit, had been converted into an inn, but since the separation of Venetia from Austria may probably have reverted to its original destination as a customs-station. The pass is known in Comelico as *Monte Croce*; but it is desirable to suppress that name in order to avoid confusion with the better-known pass described in § 62, Rte. E. The road descends thence into the northern branch of the Comelico valley (Rte. D), which is drained by the Padola torrent. The lower part is populous, but the upper end has a deserted air, the pastures being owned by the people of Sexten, and reserved for horses and oxen, so that no *sennhütten* enliven the scene. *San Stefano* (Rte. D) is reached in about 5½ hrs. by carriage from Sexten, or in 1 hr. more on foot, excluding halts. There is here a tolerable country inn kept by Girardis.

Mr. Tuckett was the first traveller who crossed the high range between Sexten and Auronzo, and he has been followed by several others; but it is to Mr. Holzmann that the writer is indebted for the fullest account of this group of peaks, not surpassed elsewhere for the grandeur and wildness of their forms. The passes will be best understood by supposing the traveller to approach them from the side of Auronzo. About 1 hr. above the Villa

Grande (Rte. E) is the opening of *Val Giralba*. A path mounts for about 40 m. by the l. bank, then crosses to the rt. bank, and follows that for ¾ hr. till it begins to bear to the l. or about NW., and finally after a steep but not difficult ascent, chiefly over fine débris, or *grava*, reaches the summit of the *Forcella di Giralba*, lying between the *Col Agnello* and the *Monte Popera*. The summit is formed of large slabs, with *grava* on either side, and a small tarn below. In descending it is necessary to bear to the l., between NW. and WNW., first over *grava*, then among blocks of dolomite. The way lies under the precipitous W. face of the Hohe Leisten, a great promontory from the mass of Monte Popera. The *Oberbacher Thal*, which mounts nearly due W., is passed on the l. hand, and the way lies nearly due N. through the lower part of the same glen, locally called *Unterbacher Thal*. The way is first by the l. bank, then by the opposite side for about ¼ hr., till at the junction of the Altlasteiner Thal, descending from the W., the traveller enters the head of the Fischleinthal, where a beaten track leads to the Sextnerbad. This way is the most direct and easiest, requiring less than 6 hrs. moderate walking, from Auronzo to Sexten. The scenery is unsurpassed by that of any other pass in this region.

The other passes next to be mentioned are rarely used, and known only to the smugglers who here carry on a perilous trade between Tyrol and Italy. They are approached through the Val Marson, which opens into the main valley, ¼ hr. above the junction of Val Giralba. A path mounts along the l. bank of the stream about WNW., and after passing two or three narrow glens on the rt. hand, reaches in nearly 1 hr. the opening of Val Cengia, through which a considerable torrent descends from the N. A faintly-marked track mounts along the rt. bank, and after nearly ½ hr. crosses to the l. side, and before long passes a deserted hut. Here the ascent lies for a short distance NW.,
along the W. face of a projecting rock, whose N. shoulder is climbed. Above this the path crosses the torrent where it falls in cascades through a ravine, and mounts in zigzags nearly due N., till it reaches an Alpine pasture. Thence the way lies at first E. for 25 min., passing a small tarn, and then N. for 15 min., till it attains another higher shelf of pasture. Facing E. an ascent of ¼ hr. leads to the *Oberbacher Joch*, between the Col Agnello and the craggy mass, locally known as Oberbacher Wand, that lies between the Oberbacher Thal and Altlasteiner Thal mentioned above. Amidst rock scenery of the grandest character the traveller descends eastward through the Oberbacher Thal till he meets the track from the Giralba Pass. Fully 7½ hrs., exclusive of halts, should be allowed for this way from Auronzo to Sexten.

From the uppermost pasture last mentioned an ascent of ¼ hr. to WNW. leads to the *Santebüchl*, a pass lying between the *Patern Kogel* and the Oberbacher Wand. Descending thence to a small bright blue tarn, and then bearing nearly due N., the traveller may reach the head of the Altlasteiner Thal, which runs about ENE. into the head of the Fischleinthal.

The native hunters speak of a fourth pass between Auronzo and Sexten called *Lämmerbüchl*, which seems to lie between the pinnacles of the Col Agnello, but Mr. Holzmann failed in repeated attempts to find it, and no other traveller has been more fortunate.

From the head of the Altlasteiner Thal a very fine pass to Landro may be made by the N. side of the Patern Kogel, passing two small tarns near the summit of the pass, which is called at Sexten *Toblacher Riedel*, whence, keeping to the l. at the upper part, it is easy to descend into the eastern branch of the Rienz valley that descends to Landro. A still finer course is to bear S.W. from a little way below the pass to another pass, *Drei Zinnen Joch* (M. H.), close to the wonderful peaks of the Drei Zinnen. This leads into the head of *Val Rim-*

bianco, the S. branch of the Rienz Valley. This way takes fully 8 hrs. from Sexten to Landro, or 1 hr. more than the more direct course.

The *Drei Zinnen*, or *Cima di Lavaredo*, is one of the most singular of the dolomite peaks, the highest tower actually overhanging its base. It is counted by Siorpaes as the most difficult of ascent of all the peaks of this district. The height must be considerably greater than that commonly quoted—9,833 ft. On the other hand, the height of the passes above enumerated has apparently been exaggerated. There is no wide difference between them, and none of them much exceeds 8,000 ft.

From the blue tarn on the NW. side of the Santebüchl, bearing about due W., it is easy to join the path over the Toblacher Riedel near the summit, and in that way a very fine route may be taken from Auronzo to Landro. Perhaps a still finer way is to quit the path to the Oberbacher Joch at the lower shelf of Alpine pasture mentioned above, and to ascend thence in a WNW. direction to the *Forcella di Lavaredo*, a pass between the Drei Zinnen and the Patern Kogel, whence the path from the Toblacher Riedel is joined near the head of the Rienz Valley.

[The Val Rimbianco mentioned above is connected by low and easy passes with the head of Val Popena, and the lake of Misurina, see Rte. B.]

ROUTE I.
WELSBERG TO CORTINA D'AMPEZZO, BY PRAGS.

The mass of mountains lying in the rt. angle formed by the high-road to Cortina, between the Toblacherfeld and Peutelstein, are in great part drained by a torrent that joins the Rienz about half-way between Welsberg and Niederndorf (§ 51, Rte. A). Those approaching the valley from the eastward will take a vehicle from the latter place, but travellers coming from the N. and W. will make Welsberg their starting-point. The valley in question is collectively called *Prags* (sometimes written *Brags*), but includes two diverging branches that join at Saag, about 1½ m. above its opening into the Pusterthal. The S. branch of the valley, which is the shorter, is called *Inner Prags*, while the SW. branch, called *Ausser Prags*, extends more deeply into the mountain range that encloses the head of Enneberg. In Inner Prags, little more than a mile above Saag, stands the mountain bath-house of *Alt-Prags* (4,624'). The name is appropriate, as a part of the building is very ancient. A modern wooden house has been added. The accommodation is rude but tolerable, and the charges very cheap. It may be reached in a light carriage from the main valley of the Rienz. From the head of Inner Prags a path leads southward to the Ampezzo road, which is reached not far from Schluderbach, over a pass between the Croda Rossa and the Dürrenstein. If the former peak—10,262 ft. in height—can be ascended, the attempt may be best made from the side of Inner Prags.

Ausser Prags, the SW. branch of the valley, extends for some way above Saag nearly at a level. It includes two small villages—Schmieden and St. Veit. Near the former place are the baths of *Neu-Prags* (4,313'), intended apparently for guests of the humbler class.

At the upper end of Ausser Prags is a picturesque little lake called *Wildsee* (5,563'). Here an uppermost branch of the valley, locally called Innerste Alp, leads to a pass connecting this with the Enneberg. St. Vigil (§ 60, Rte. G) is said to be 5 hrs. distant. Another path leads southward to Cortina by the E. side of the Seekofel (9,214')—a mountain whose outline, as seen from the S. side, resembles that of an elephant. The summit of the pass to Cortina is called *Welscher Boden* (6,499').

A traveller may well approach Cortina from the side of Bruneck by this route, but not unless he be already acquainted with the more striking scenery of the ordinary route by the Dürren See, and the road thence to Peutelstein.

www.ingramcontent.com/pod-product-compliance
Lightning Source LLC
Chambersburg PA
CBHW022133160426
43197CB00009B/1272